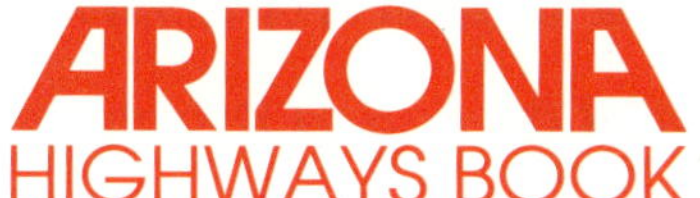

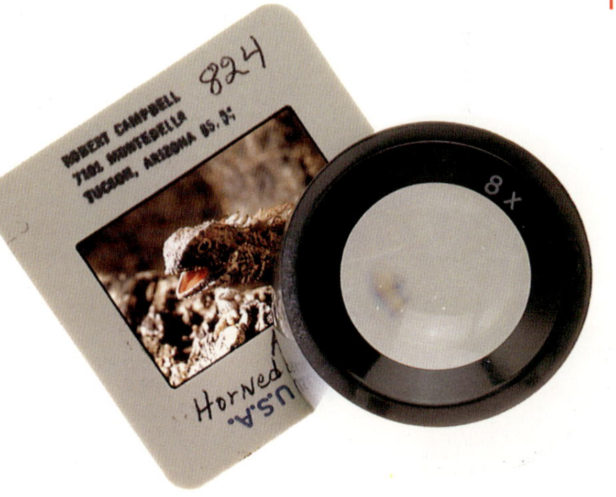

PHOTOGRAPHING ARIZONA

PRACTICAL TECHNIQUES TO IMPROVE YOUR PICTURES

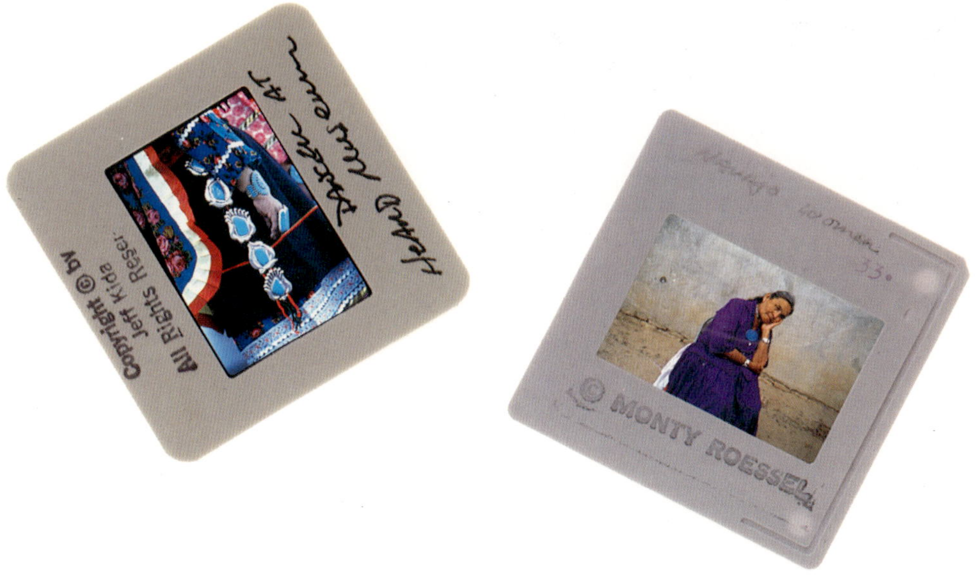

TEXT BY LAWRENCE W. CHEEK

PHOTOGRAPHS BY *ARIZONA HIGHWAYS* CONTRIBUTORS

Prepared by the Book Division of *Arizona Highways* magazine,

a monthly publication of the Arizona Department of Transportation.

Hugh Harelson—Publisher / Wesley Holden—Managing Editor / Robert J. Farrell—Associate Editor

Peter Ensenberger—Picture Editor / Gary Bennett—Design & Production / Cindy Mackey—Production Manager

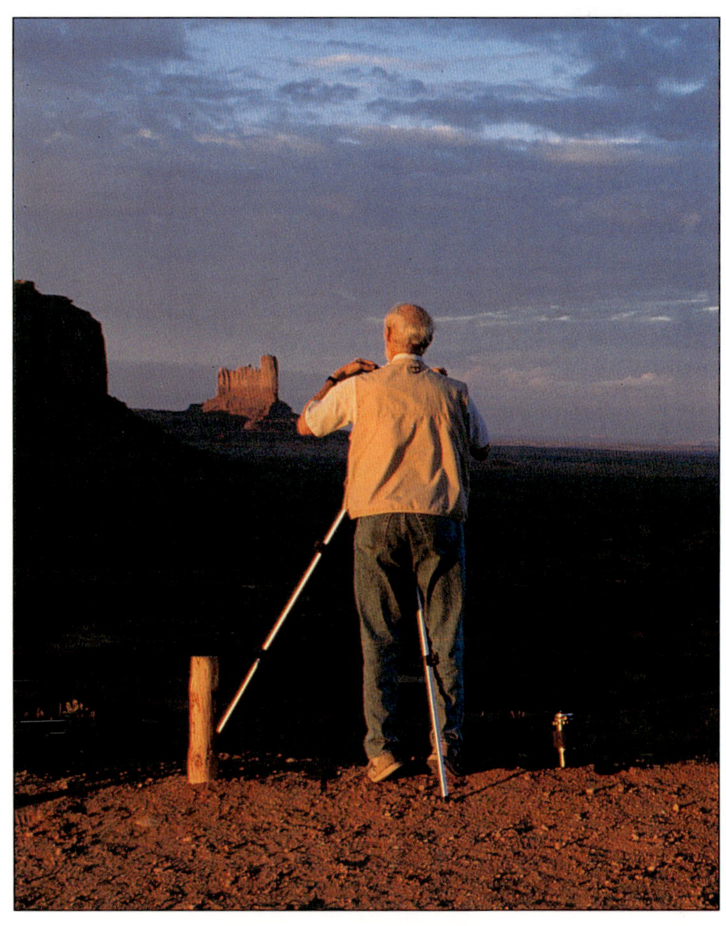

Attracting amateurs and professionals alike, Monument Valley reigns as one of Arizona's most photographed locations. MONTY ROESSEL

Library of Congress Catalog Number 92-81969 ISBN 0-916179-36-2

CONTENTS

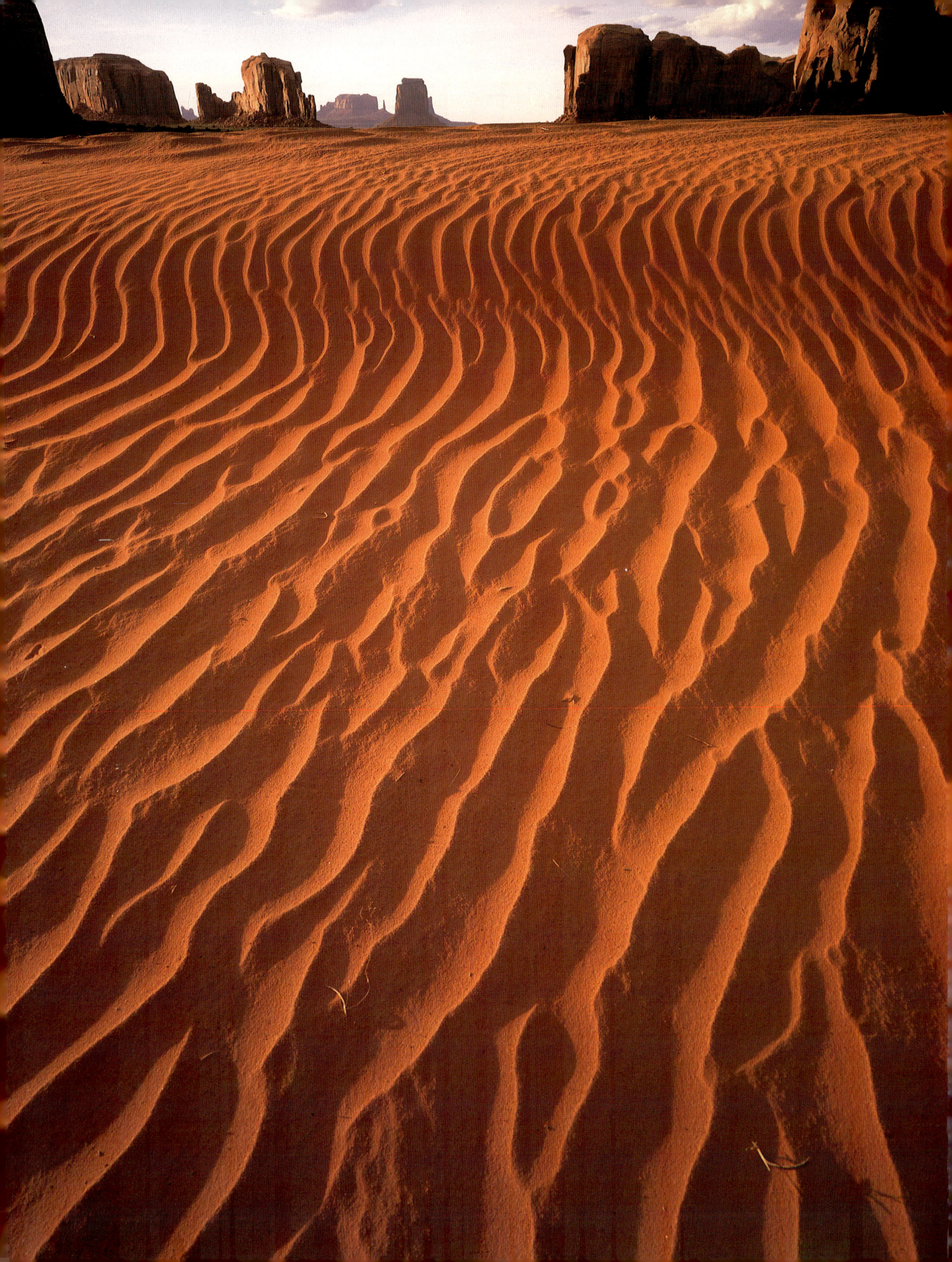

FOREWORD

The key to raising your success rate in photography is training yourself to recognize the potential in a scene, and then utilizing your awareness of lighting, equipment, technique, and composition to record it in the best way possible.

Here, in very readable style, are the working techniques you need to improve your photography, plus insightful commentary from some of the professionals whose photographs have helped to make *Arizona Highways* the premier showcase for photography in the world.

Author Lawrence W. Cheek, himself a published photographer, is right on target with his "how to" discussions aimed at advancing your photography of landscape, nature, and people.

In addition, beautiful color photographs by some of the magazine's top contributors illustrate the practical application of techniques discussed throughout the book.

And finally, there are portfolios of images that will both inspire and motivate you to load your gear and, armed with your new knowledge, venture out in quest of some great photographs of your own.

You'll learn to see things in new ways, have some fun doing it, and perhaps even discover something new about yourself and the world around you.

Peter Ensenberger

Peter Ensenberger
Picture Editor
Arizona Highways

(LEFT) *Most photographs of Monument Valley focus on the permanent monuments—the big rocks—and finding fresh images takes a practiced eye. Here the seductive geometry of light, shadow, and rippled sand make the picture, and the monuments appear only for context.*
DAVID MUENCH

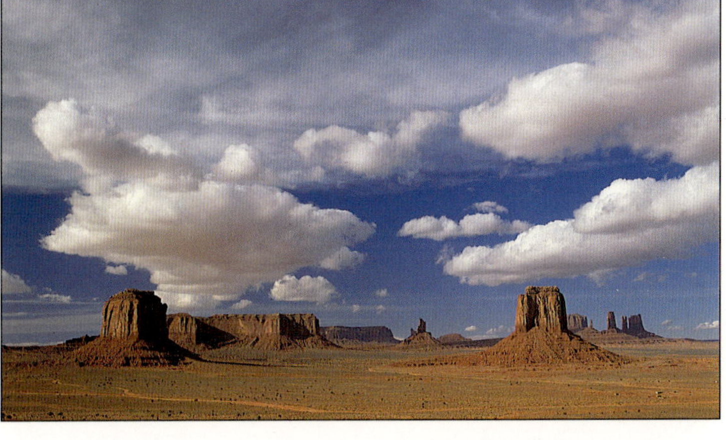

(ABOVE) *By contrast, in this image midday light renders the monuments rather dull, so the camera turns to the sky for color and action.*
PETER ENSENBERGER
In each photo, the lines formed by sand or clouds lead the eye to the distant monuments.

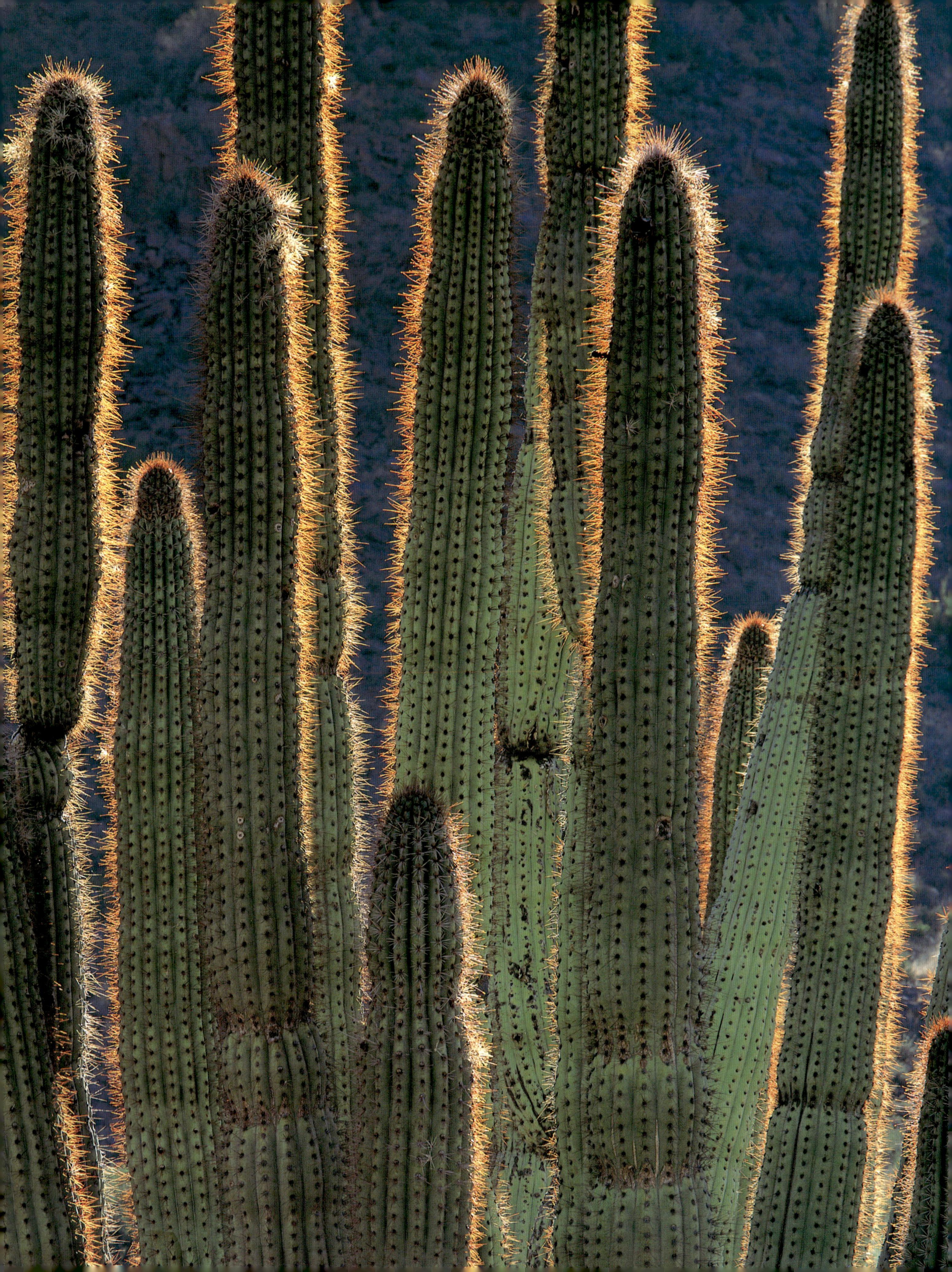

PHOTOGRAPHING ARIZONA

To a photographer arriving from anywhere else, Arizona presents itself as the Promised Land. The bravura land forms, the drama of fierce light and cryptic shadow, the choreography of gunmetal thunderclouds rumbling over a mountain or canyon wall all suggest endless opportunity. So do the life forms staking out their living here: thorn forests of Joshua trees and saguaro cactus, fauna as diverse and colorful as cardinals and coyotes, and three layers of human cultures: Native American, Hispanic, and Caucasian. A photographer setting out to document all this would have a life's work ahead.

Maybe more. Initially there is the problem of *learning* to photograph Arizona. There are unique difficulties here along with the opportunities, and they dog both professional and amateur.

Among those difficulties is that many accessible locations in Arizona have already been photographed so thoroughly and so well that the state's natural beauty forms a minefield of repetition and cliché. Fresh images are not impossible, but they can be elusive. I was setting up my camera at Monument Valley one sunrise, planning to position a softly rounded sandstone outcropping in the foreground, when another photographer walked by, tripod over shoulder. "That's the Ansel Adams Rock, isn't it?" he commented. A splendid shot, spoiled by a ghost.

Arizona light is both friend and enemy. It cannot be taken for granted. "It's a force here, like weather," says Terence Pitts, director of the University of Arizona's Center for Creative Photography. Arizona light can paint a landscape with astonishing yellow, amber, orange, or crimson light at sunrise or sunset, but it also can render much outdoor photography worthless for the hours in between. Understanding the qualities of this light and putting it to work is the foundation of successfully photographing Arizona.

Arizona's Native Americans have fascinated photographers since the late 19th century and the groundbreaking work of such photographers as Edward S. Curtis and Kate Cory. This subject is now laced more with problems than opportunities.

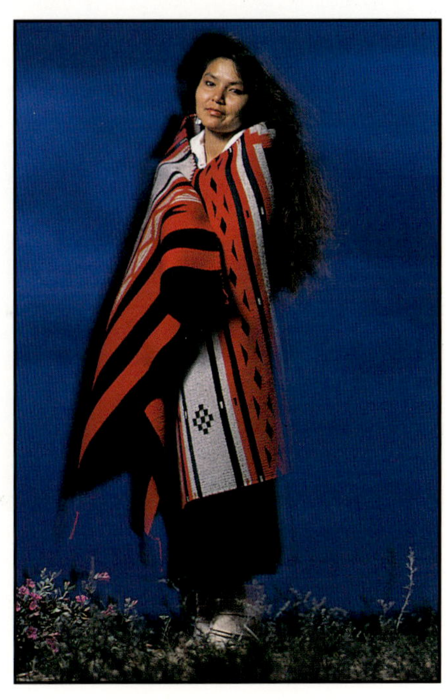

(ABOVE) *Fill flash highlights Jennifer Jackson, Miss Navajo, 1990-91, before a dark, stormy sky.* MONTY ROESSEL

(LEFT) *Isolated against a dark background, spines of an organ pipe cactus, backlit by a sunrise, exhibit a fierce but lovely golden glow.* JACK DYKINGA

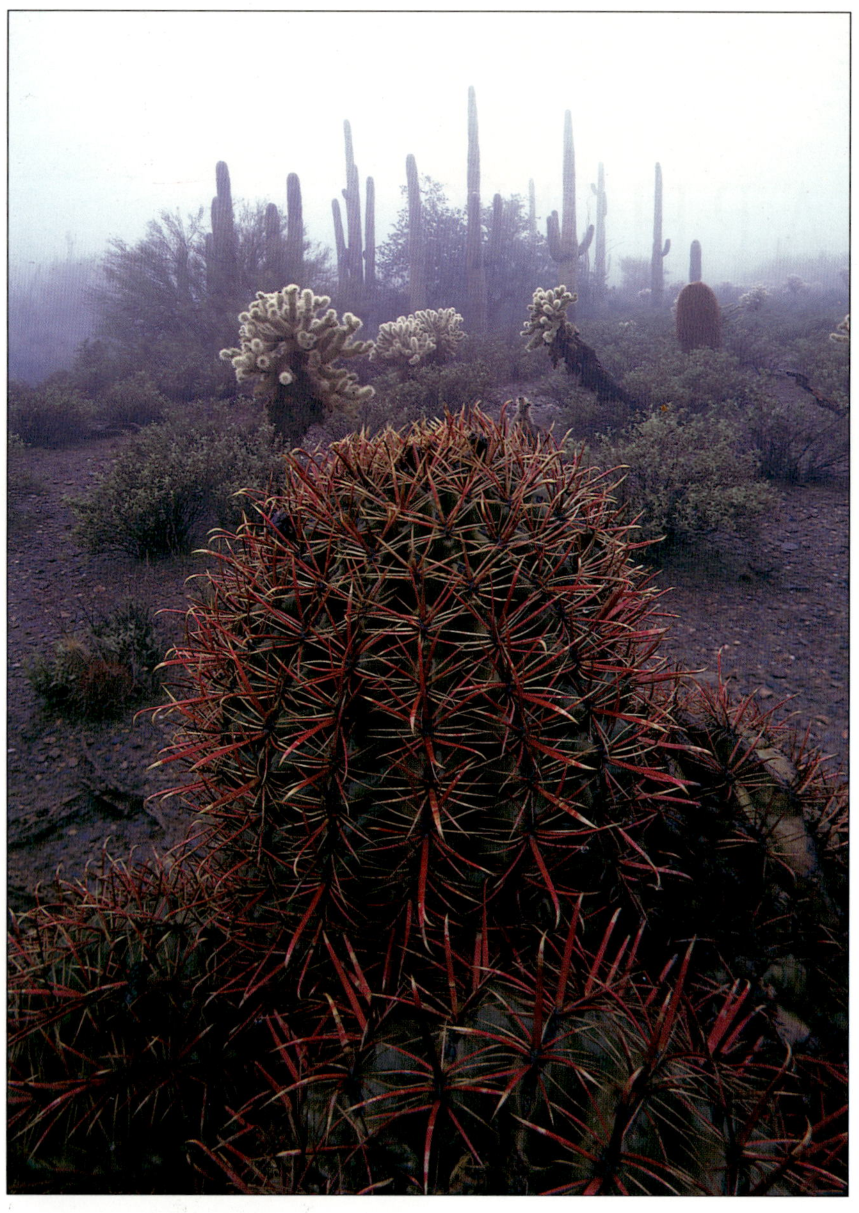

Fog is rare in the Sonoran Desert, which makes a compelling argument for venturing out with a camera. It drapes the landscape in mystery, creating unexpected opportunities. An improbable display of color — the red spines of barrel cactus — forms a dramatic contrast to the teddy bear cholla and the ghostly saguaros in the distance.
JERRY SIEVE

Photography is all but forbidden today on the Hopi reservation, and other tribes have become increasingly testy about what they see as outsiders' exploitation and crass insensitivity to their cultures. In a sadly ironic replay of the 19th century, broken promises form part of the problem. "People come onto the reservation, take pictures, and promise to send copies," says Monty Roessel, a Navajo photographer. "Then they hardly ever do." Still, there are ways to break through the barriers of distrust.

Good photography is demanding work, and in Arizona it can seem more demanding than elsewhere — ask the person who's just lugged camera bag and tripod several miles up a mountainside trail whose edges bristle with desert cutlery. But great pictures are worth some discomfort.

I am fortunate enough to live a 10-minute walk away from one of the most spectacular canyons in southern Arizona. Photographic opportunities abound: There are heroic landscapes, seasonal waterfalls and river rapids, autumn color pageants staged by the sycamores on the canyon floor, 211 Audubon-confirmed species of birds, and herds of deer and javelina. I hike in the canyon almost every morning, but take my camera only in bad weather — which translates into photographic opportunities. The canyon's natural drama is multiplied when a storm lumbers in, or when fog turns the saguaros into ghost sentinels guarding the slopes. If there is fog or rain, I will be in the canyon with an umbrella, which of course is used to keep the camera dry, not me. Invariably someone will splash by and say something like, "Boy, you wouldn't find me out here taking pictures on a day like this." And I'll think — but never say — right, which is why my pictures are going to be more interesting than yours.

Photographing Arizona is worth the trouble. No other place in North America is so compelling. Former Governor Bruce Babbitt tells a story about standing on the South Rim of the Grand Canyon one evening while a world-class sunset unfolded in the western sky. Someone snapped a Polaroid, and a gaggle of tourists huddled to watch it develop, ignoring the real-life spectacle over their backs. In Arizona, the landscapes and skyscapes can sometimes

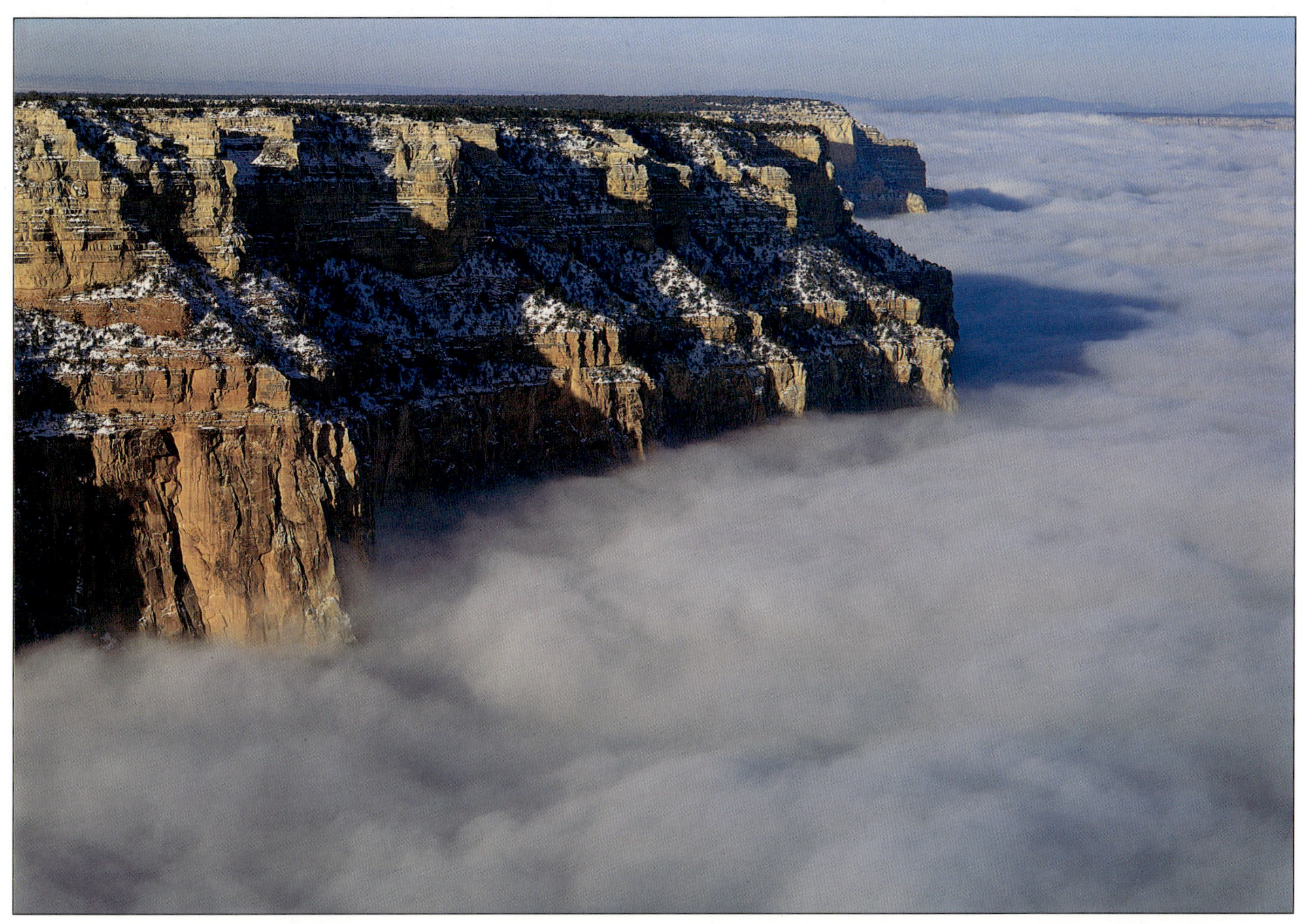

be too powerful for contemplation, and so the photograph becomes our intermediary — as well as our way of preserving a priceless moment.

This book is intended for the amateur photographer visiting or living in Arizona. "Amateur" here is intended in the graceful sense of its Latin root, *amator*, which means "lover." This is for people who love taking pictures. And who would love to do it as well as professionals.

A little basic knowledge of photography is presupposed. I have kept the techno-babble to a minimum, but the reader will benefit from already understanding the basic relationships of shutter speed, aperture, and depth of field. However, for those bearing pocket cameras (which relieve the photographer of all technical concerns except composition), there is still much to follow about capturing the unique character of Arizona. And, maybe, some inspiration to move up to a more versatile camera system and begin capturing *Arizona Highways*-quality pictures.

I have been photographing Arizona for 20 years, mostly as a sideline to writing about Arizona. I have made every stupid mistake an amateur or professional can make. I have learned from all of them, but that alone is not enough to make a book. The advice to follow is also the product of many long conversations and photographic outings with expert Arizona photographers, some of them very familiar names to *Arizona Highways* readers. For these superb artists, Arizona has indeed fulfilled its promise. ■

A cloudy day at the Grand Canyon can be a photographer's godsend if the clouds do something odd or dramatic, such as descending into the chasm. Because it often accentuates Arizona's already spectacular landscapes, snow or bad weather is often no photographic curse, but a blessing.
GARY LADD

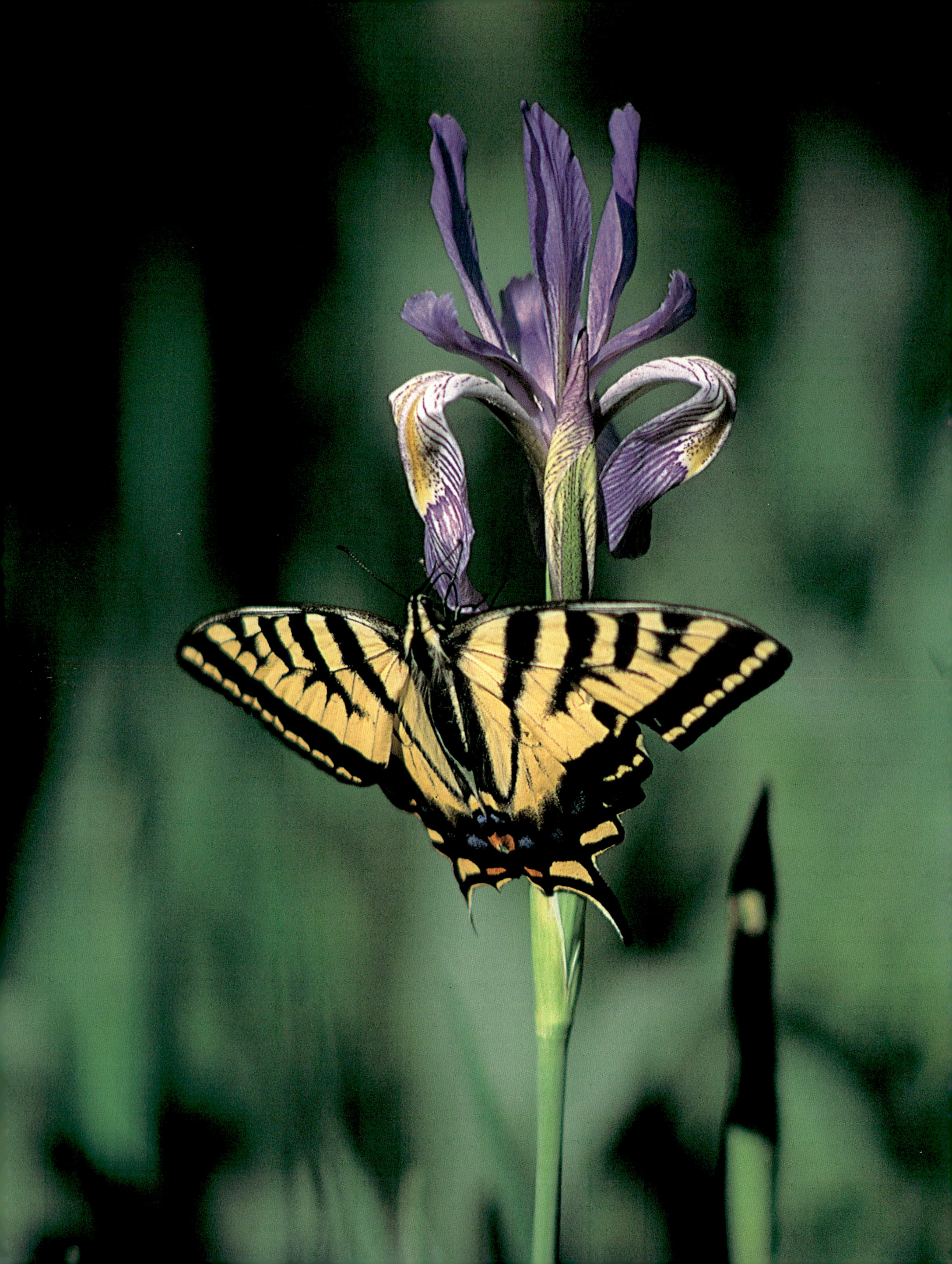

Chapter 1

EQUIPMENT

Most photographers are gadget freaks. Sometimes we tend to pack more equipment than we need, which in mountainous Arizona is more of a liability than other places. Consider the trek to photograph Bridalveil Falls in the Santa Catalina Mountains northeast of Tucson: three hours and six miles (each way) and a 2,500-foot elevation gain. This gossamer waterfall yields lovely pictures, but the hiker who lugs 20 pounds of camera gear, plus food and water, may not survive to take them.

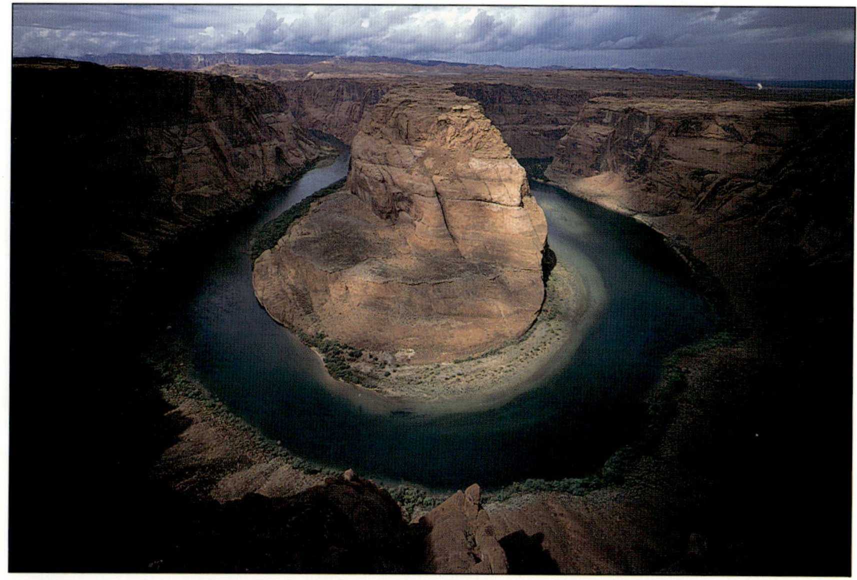

Light weight, quality, and economy are three critical touchstones in photography. Together they dictate a 35mm system: With the quality of today's lenses and films, there is little reason for the amateur to bother with the much more expensive medium- and large-format equipment. If taken with care, a 35mm image on slow, fine-grained film can be enlarged to a print as large as 20x24 inches with acceptable sharpness.

How much equipment you buy, and what type, depends on your goals and expectations. If you want only packets of vacation photos for personal memorabilia, a point-and-shoot camera with a zoom lens may be all you need. If you crave to hang your own *Arizona Highways*-quality images on the wall, expect to pay the price of more equipment, more complexity, and more weight.

Most serious photographers pack two camera bodies, usually loaded with different films in order to respond to different situations. I carry a Canon T90, which has the computer power of Mission Control, and an old, clothespin-simple Canon AE-1. All seven of my lenses will fit on either camera, and the T90's brain will spill out the exposure information I need to set the older camera in

(ABOVE) *This wide-angle photo of Horseshoe Overlook in Glen Canyon was made with an 8 x 10 view camera, but a 20mm lens on a 35mm camera would offer a similar view.*
MICHAEL FATALI

(LEFT) *This portrait of a western tiger swallowtail on a wild iris required a fast (f/2.8) 200mm telephoto lens. It also demanded an afternoon's patience, waiting for the butterfly to cooperate in a perfect composition.*
EDWARD McCAIN

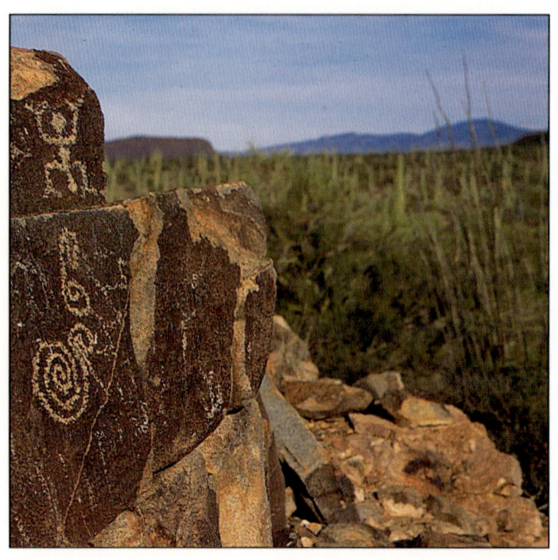

Shooting Hohokam petroglyphs, a photographer might want a wide aperture (here f/8) for its shallow depth of field, which emphasizes the ancient art as the subject.

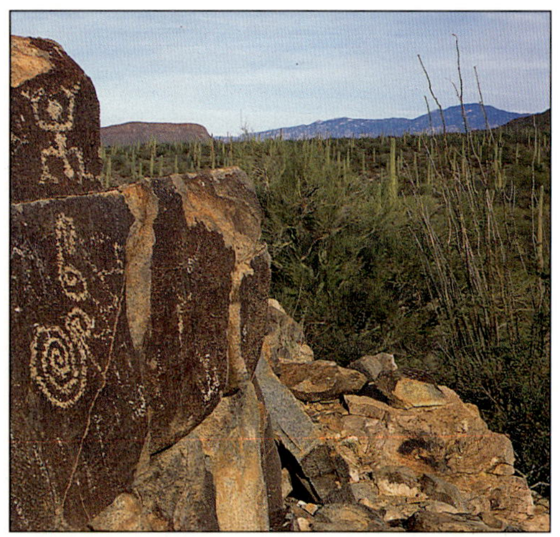

If the photographer decides the context of the landscape is equally important, stopping down to f/22 pulls everything in this frame into sharp focus. The penalty is a slower shutter speed. Packing a tripod ensures that you will have the choice.
JERRY JACKA

tricky lighting situations. On long hikes I pack only the lighter AE-1.

The choice of lenses grows more difficult all the time. Manual or autofocus? Fixed focal length or zoom? Proprietary (e.g., Canon, Nikkor) or less expensive aftermarket brands? Since these questions alone could expand into an entire handbook, we'll leave them for general photography guides. One suggestion, however: Having some specialized lenses can strengthen your photography more than anything else except years of practice.

A lens with a **macro** feature allows focusing as close as a couple of inches, which is vital for photographing insects, flowers, and the intimate patterns of nature such as tree bark and cactus spines. A medium focal-length macro (50 to 105mm) is most versatile because it is easy to hand-hold.

A **perspective control** lens has limited applications, but is essential in architectural photography because it can straighten images of tall buildings which in normal lenses will appear to taper, lean, or twist. Unfortunately, most PC lenses are on the far side of $500.

An **extreme wide-angle** 20mm lens provides interesting environmental portraits of people, drawing them close to the camera while taking in much of their surroundings (distortion can be a hazard).

Finally, although most amateurs carry **telephoto** lenses of no more than 200mm, longer ones (300 or 400mm) bring in better wildlife photos. But long focal length lenses have a very shallow depth of field, and that's a good news/bad news situation. By definition this shallow depth of field will help isolate a subject from its environment, but unless you are very careful, it will also cause many out-of-focus images.

After a good assortment of lenses, a **tripod** is the most useful accessory you can carry. It opens up low-light situations to photography, allows you to use slower film (which translates to sharper images), steadies the camera for telephoto work (a 300mm lens is very difficult to hand-hold), and enables you to be more precise in composing pictures. Most importantly, it allows you to select whatever lens aperture you want, giving you complete control over depth of field. Example: There's a petroglyph on a boulder in the foreground and a sunset-tinted mountain in the background. At a shutter speed of 1/30 of a second, the slowest most of us dare try hand-holding, the light meter dictates an aperture of f/8. That will give a shallow depth of field, so the photographer must choose between focusing on the petroglyph or the mountain. With a tripod, the shutter can be slowed to 1/4 second, allowing the aperture to shrink three stops to f/22. Now the depth of field encompasses foreground and background.

Incidentally, buy the best you can afford. A flimsy tripod is worse than no tripod at all, because it fools you into thinking camera shake has been eliminated when it hasn't. Compact table-top tripods, which extend to a height of about 15 inches, are seldom useful because nature seldom provides a table where you need it. A shoulder sling for carrying the tripod is *very* useful, especially in Arizona's craggy terrain where you need to keep both hands free.

Several **filters** are important in Arizona because of our atmospheric conditions. If the sunshine is coming from a position roughly perpendicular to the subject, a **polarizing filter** will accentuate cloud formations and enrich the color of a pale, washed-out sky—a chronic problem here in late spring and early summer. It also screens out reflected light. Petroglyphs on a wet, shiny rock (for example) will pop out from their environment in greater contrast. An **ultraviolet filter** will improve color saturation of long-vista shots taken at high elevations and will actually help penetrate haze.

An **81A filter** is sometimes a good idea when shooting color film under heavily overcast skies or deep in a shady canyon; it reduces its tendency to go excessively blue in such conditions. However, its effect is unpredictable; I always take duplicate unfiltered frames. And there are times when the bluish cast of the photo may more accurately represent the mood of the land.

The **graduated neutral density filter** sounds intimidating but actually is easy to use. It's a godsend to

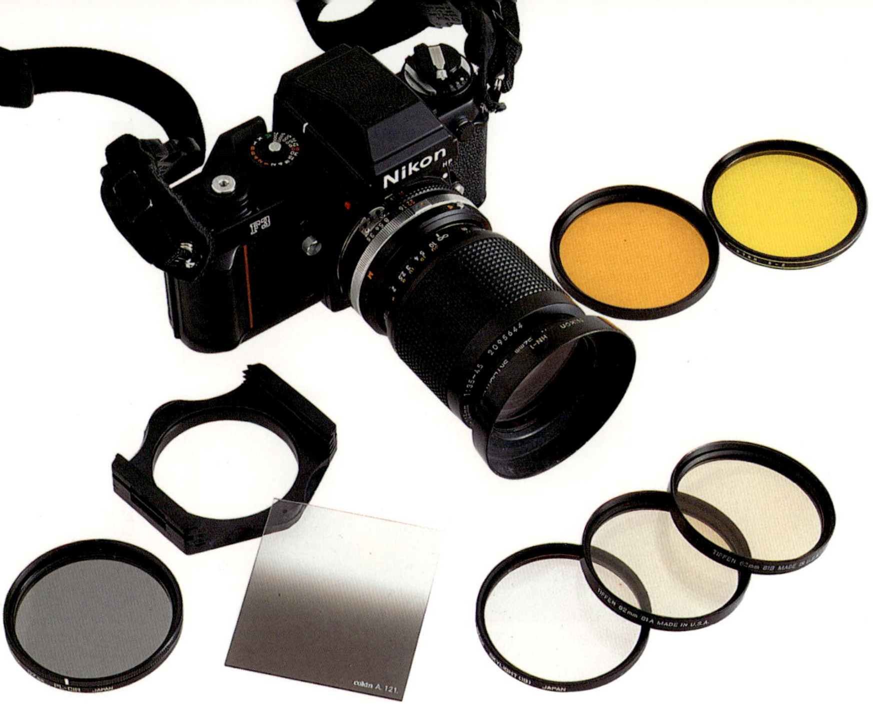

(ABOVE) *The most useful filters in a photographer's arsenal, from left: polarizing filter, graduated neutral density filter with adapter, Skylight 1B (very slight warming effect), 81A (warming), 81B (warmer still). For black-and-white photography, the orange and yellow filters increase contrast, making the sky and the dark areas of the clouds even darker, orange giving the more extreme effect.*
JERRY JACKA

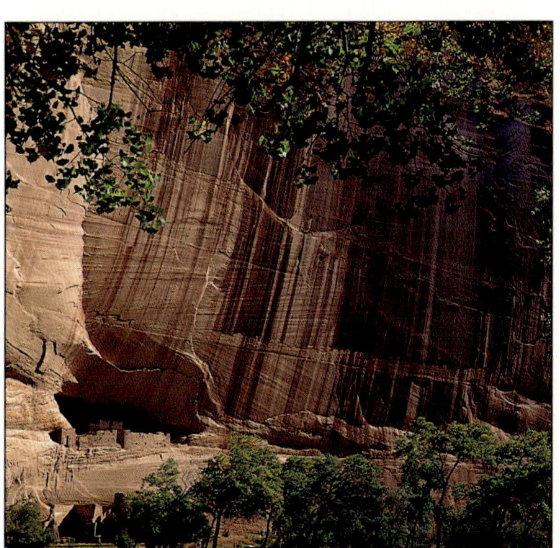

(LEFT) *A polarizing filter has rescued many a picture from Arizona's harsh, flattening sunlight. Besides darkening the sky, it may—depending on the sun angle—bring out the color of reflective surfaces, such as this water-stained canyon wall over White House Ruin at Canyon de Chelly National Monument. The filtered photo is at right.*
JERRY JACKA

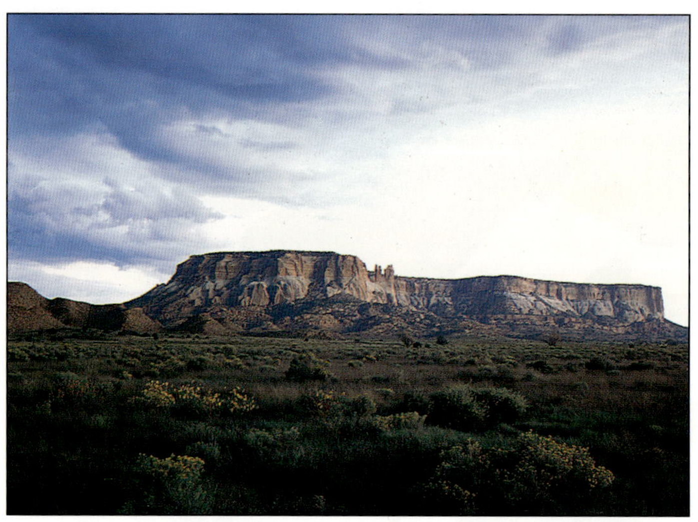

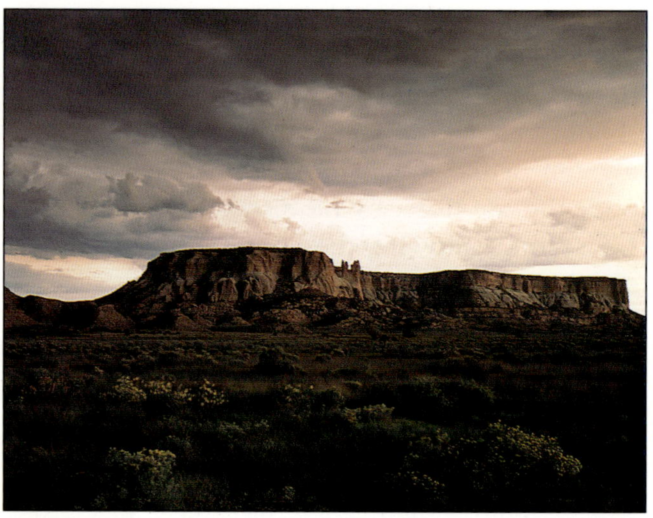

The split screen neutral density filter enhances the drama of an approaching storm. Without the filter the clouds tend to lose contrast and appear nearly white.
JERRY JACKA

the photographer struggling with Arizona's fiendishly contrasty light. Half the filter is clear, but the other half has a color-neutral density (it looks gray) that cuts the light passing through it by one or two f-stops. If your foreground is in gloomy shadow and background in brilliant sun, arranging the gray half over the sunlit part of the frame will help balance the light. (Best tip for metering: Meter the shadowed area before attaching the filter, and use that exposure. Then bracket one or more stops on either side of that reading.)

For black-and-white photography, an **orange filter** is indispensable. It darkens a pale sky, enhances white clouds and lightens green foliage, thereby dramatizing many nature scenes.

Incidentally, either a skylight or ultraviolet filter should remain on every lens worth owning. It's much less painful to replace a scratched $10 filter than a $100 or $500 lens.

One other indispensable that many of us, to our chagrin, forget: spare batteries. I also carry a spare cable release, since experience has taught that this is the accessory most likely to break or get lost.

No one film is uniquely suited for Arizona photography. Color print film can record a wider range of light-to-dark values in a given scene than slide film can. Given our high-contrast environment, this is a distinct advantage. It also is much more tolerant of incorrect exposure. Although automated "machine prints" are grossly imprecise, you can take your negatives back for custom printing. The lab can adjust the color balance and compensate for up to three stops overexposure or 1 1/2 stops underexposure.

If you want the deepest color saturation and accuracy, however, or aspire to have your photos published, you need to shoot color transparencies (slides). Prints can be made from slides through internegatives (inexpensively) or through the Cibachrome process (expensively), which prints directly from a slide. Most gallery quality photographic color prints are Cibachromes.

Black-and-white film is largely neglected by the amateur today, which is too bad. It has a richness and expressive power that sometimes surpasses color, and the images can easily be manipulated in the darkroom. Unless you have your own darkroom, however, you may have to pay custom-lab prices to get good prints.

Many amateurs routinely shoot fast film (ISO 400 or higher) because of its versatility in a wide variety of situations. This is a mistake. Fast film should be reserved for fast-moving subjects, such as rodeo events, or extremely poor light. Everything else should be shot with slow film (ISO 100 or less) because of its fine grain and enlargement capability. Most professional Arizona photographers embrace either Kodachrome *Professional* 64 or Fujichrome *Velvia* 50 (both are slide films) as their routine films.

Arizona's climate can be unfriendly to sophisticated gear if the photographer is careless. The three natural enemies of a camera are heat, dust, and water. Of the first two, at least, we have plenty.

Ernst Weegen, owner of Phoenix Camera Repair, begs photographers not to leave their cameras in a car parked in the sun on a hot day. Temperatures in the trunk or passenger compartment easily can exceed 150° F., which will melt lubricants and allow them to ooze onto components where they don't belong. For the same reason, a light-colored camera bag is preferable to a dark one. Keep it clean and closed as much as possible: sand and dust particles can jam gears and electromagnets. If moisture finds a way inside a camera body, it may cause immediate failure by shorting an electronic circuit or delayed disaster as rust and corrosion build up, unseen.

Some Arizona environments present all three hazards at once—most conspicuously the Colorado River at the bottom of the Grand Canyon. Before taking cameras river rafting, Weegen advises buying a watertight plastic case. Some Arizona photographers use Tupperware containers to keep their lenses dry and dust-free.

Some also religiously store their film in the refrigerator at home and carry it in an icebox while traveling in summer. Others don't, saying they've never had a problem with the color shift that theoretically can occur with prolonged heat exposure. A Kodak technical representative says that unless you've bought professional film (which is intended to be refrigerated until use), don't worry about keeping it cool — not even in a desert summer. Do, however, have it processed promptly after exposure.

Finally, cameras are made to be used, and overprotective photographers are going to miss opportunities. Example: You're bouncing along a dusty jeep trail in red rock country. Do you keep the camera packed away, or is it ready at hand for that shot of a javelina herd plodding across an arroyo? The professional will always choose readiness over caution. As Weegen says, "Ultimately you're going to have to pay the price if you take pictures in adverse conditions, and it's adverse conditions that produce the best pictures." ■

(BELOW) *A polarizing filter improves this north Scottsdale landscape by darkening the rather wan sky. The filter will have its greatest effect when sunlight is coming from an angle perpendicular to it.* JERRY JACKA

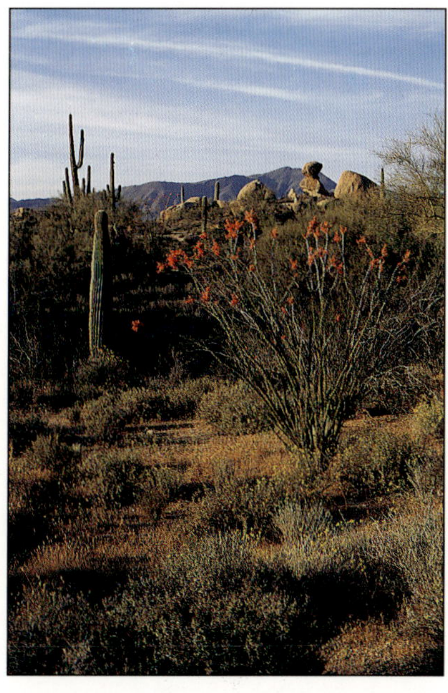

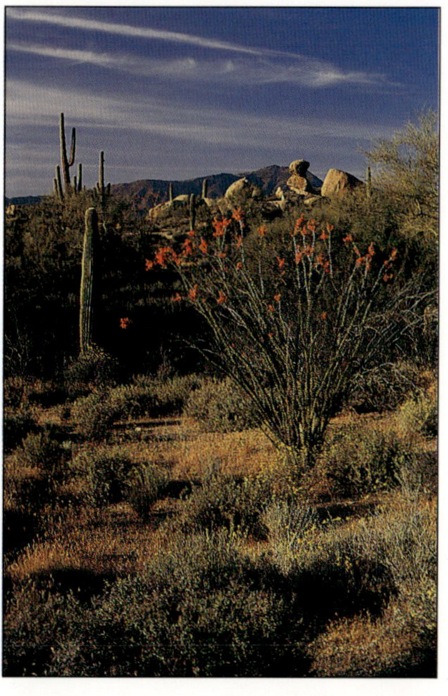

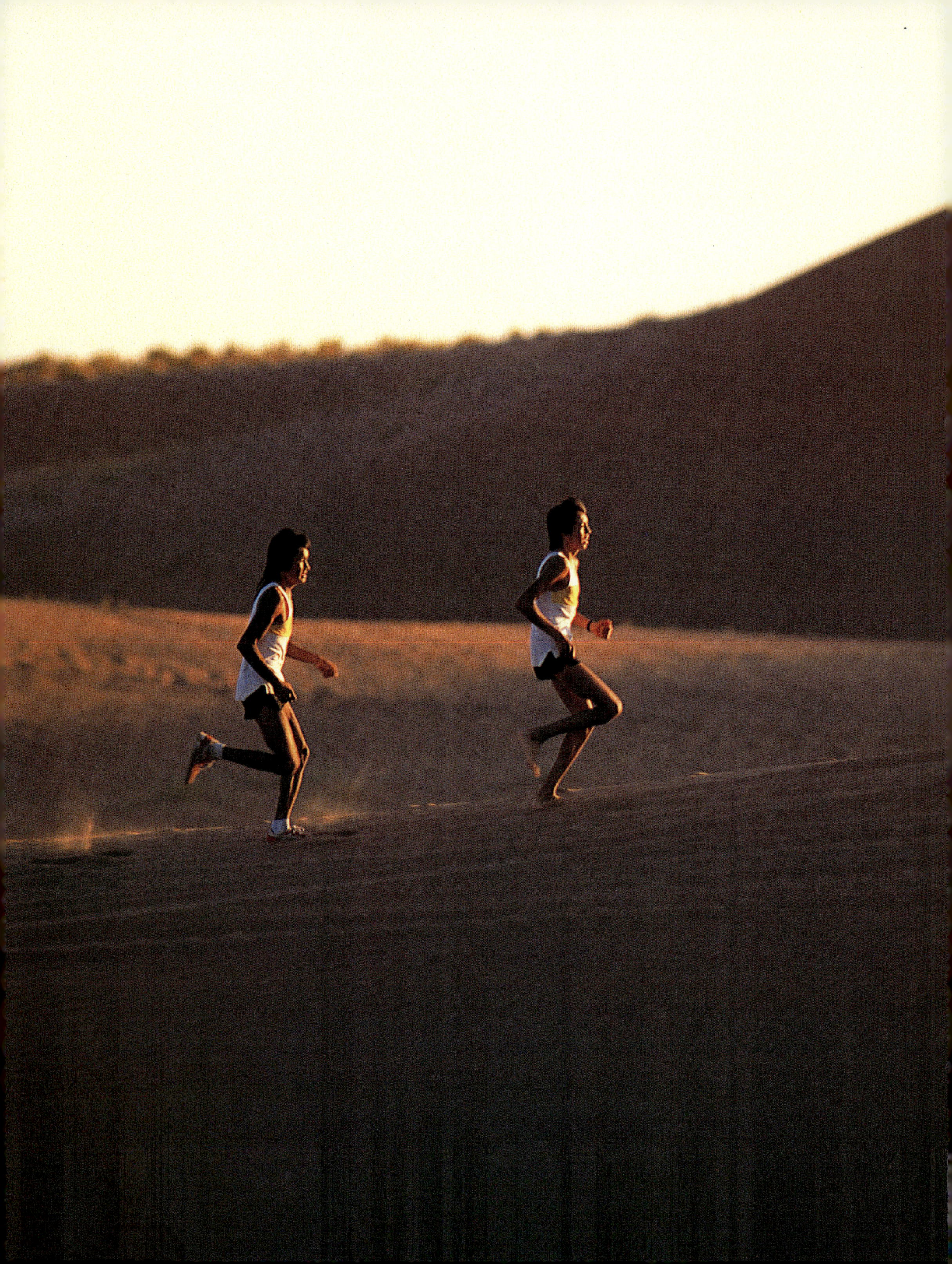

Chapter 2

PEOPLE

First, notice the picture's mood: silent, reflective, rather lonely. Then think about its design: exceedingly simple, with only the suggestion of a textured wall and a column behind the monk. Finally, its lighting: It is almost otherworldly, that gentle but transcendent blue light flowing into the face from some unseen source.

Photojournalist Jeff Kida, a regular contributor to *Arizona Highways*, took this extraordinary portrait of Brother Joseph at the Holy Trinity Monastery in St. David. It is helpful here—no, *inspirational* is the better word—because it illustrates so much at once about the art of photographing people.

Kida used a 180mm lens which, in his words, "allowed the monk to be alone." This was a conscious decision, since the monastic life is all about solitude and introspection. The entirely natural light, which was coming through a shaded open door, added to the mood — color film tends to record shaded and reflected sunlight as slightly blue, and our subconscious minds in turn interpret blue as the color of peace and solitude. The background column as the only design element in the picture, Kida says, suggests the simplicity of the monastic life. Had it been taken in a cluttered room, or even outdoors, among the lush cottonwoods and wildflowers around St. David, this portrait would have lost much of its emotional power.

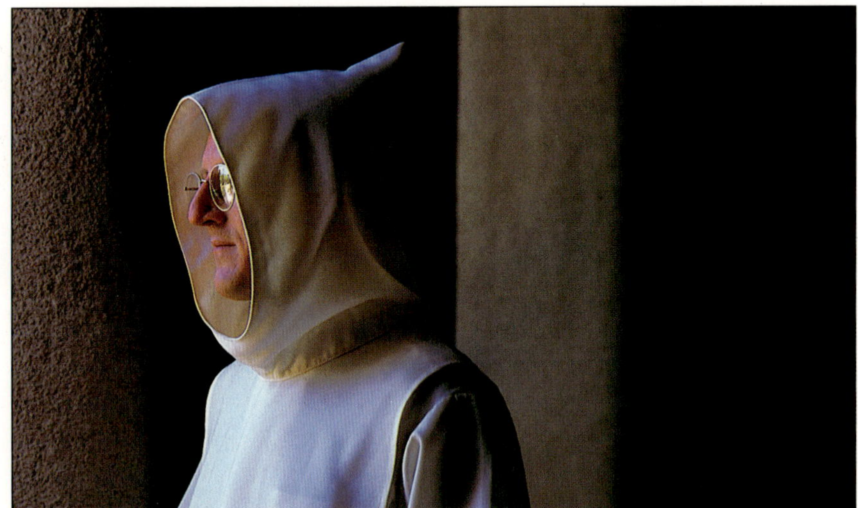

Environmental portraits often portray the subjects' lifestyles through lighting and contrast: **(LEFT)** *The starkness of the Navajo reservation, the rhythm of motion, and the direct sunlight impart a feeling of vast distances and wildness.* MONTY ROESSEL *The portrait of Brother Joseph at Holy Trinity Monastery in St. David* **(ABOVE)** *utilizes indirect lighting, a closed environment, and the reflection of the outside world in his glasses to symbolize the essences of monastic life.* JEFF KIDA

Taking powerful pictures of people is the most fascinating challenge in photography. To take pictures of people in their environment, and to make their relationship with that environment reveal something about their lives, personality, or character, may be the most rewarding opportunity in photography. Even vacation photos of family members can have this quality. The key is to portray them interacting with an unfamiliar environment in some revealing way.

Arizona presents some special

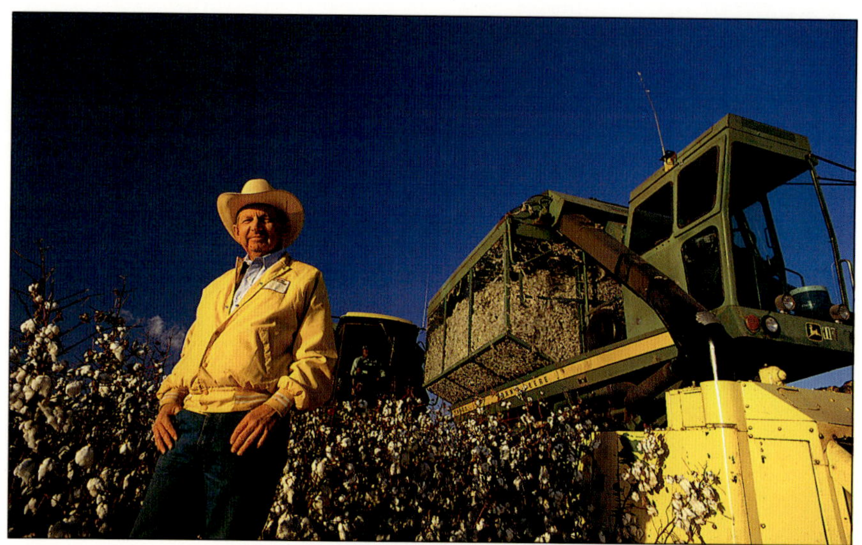

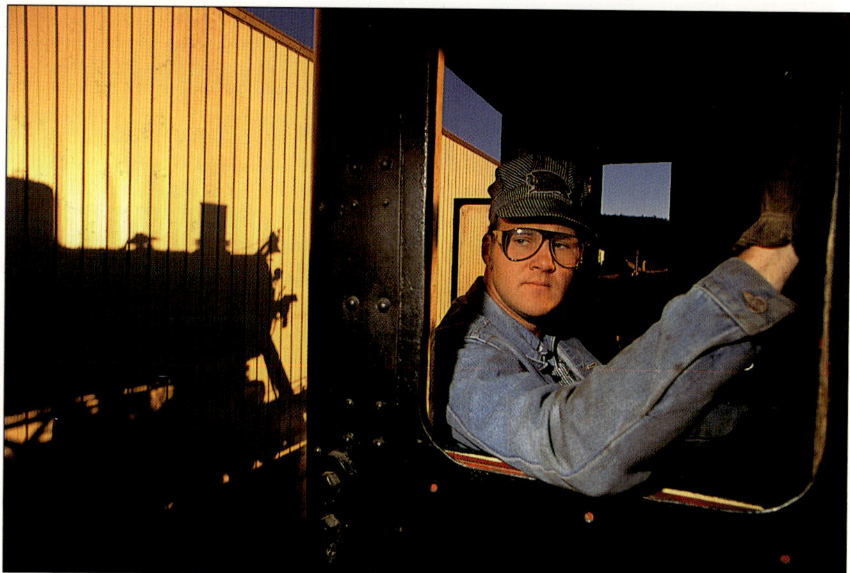

(TOP) *A low camera angle, wide-angle lens, and striking contrast between complementary colors (enhanced by a polarizing filter) make this a striking portrait of a cotton farmer.* FRED GRIFFIN **(ABOVE)** *For this photo the photographer stood on the step of the engine cab and used a 20mm wide-angle lens to draw in both the engineer's face and the engine's shadow on the wall behind. A fill flash helped highlight the face.* JEFF KIDA

problems. One is the severe light, which can wash out skin tones and cause distressed eyes to narrow into unnatural slits. Another is our amalgam of cultures, which the outsider may not understand how to approach. Some of these cultures, particularly Native Americans, are wary of being approached by anyone with camera in hand.

For most of us, the fundamental problem lies in that word "approach." How do you walk up to a stranger and ask permission to take a picture? "I think inside all of us, there's a reluctance to do this," says Kida. "In some small way, it's always an invasion, an intrusion."

The easiest way around this is to photograph people at public events, such as a marathon, parade, or demonstration. You have no legal or ethical obligation to ask a participant's permission for a photo, and a long telephoto lens can bring in revealing expressions. Says Kida, "I use a 300mm like a lot of people use a normal lens."

When the intended subject is someone working in a field, fishing in a mountain stream or engaging in any other kind of private activity, the photographer should ask permission. To shoot without it is theft — the taking of someone's privacy. The exception is a scene in which the individual would remain unrecognizable — for example, a hiker on a ridge some distance away, where the human figure would provide only a sense of scale.

When approaching someone with a request to shoot, sincerity is your first and best asset. You're obviously intrigued by this person's activity or appearance; say so. Ask questions that illustrate a genuine interest in your subject ("I'm from Minnesota, and I can't imagine what it's like to farm cotton in Arizona — how do you do it?") Phoenix photographer Fred Griffin recommends approaching people with a "childlike quality" of curiosity. When the topic finally rolls around to photography, be honest about your intentions. Explain that you want to capture Arizona with a few *good* photos, not the usual vacationer's snapshots. If you've established rapport, your subject should feel complimented.

Second asset: a minimum of equipment. Nothing intimidates the average cotton farmer more than a photographer stalking across his field with two or three cameras draped over the neck and a bulging bag of accessories at his side. Survey the situation before entering, and leave most of your paraphernalia in the car. Take *one* camera, extra film, no more than two lenses, a strobe (for fill flash), and, if you can render it inconspicuous in a shoulder sling, a tripod.

Third: imagination. If you sense that someone may be shy about having his/her face photographed, look for alternatives. Hands in action can tell as powerful a story as a face. In a calendar he produced for the Navajo Nation, photographer Monty Roessel included some wonderful photos of Navajo hands — a softly graceful woman's hand, lavished with turquoise jewelry; a pair of man's hands, sunburned and sinewy from a lifetime of shearing sheep. Another fruitful option: your subject's children. Parents' pride exists in all cultures. I have taken my cameras to 17 countries and have not yet had a request to photograph someone's child rejected.

If your quarry agrees to let you shoot, you need to work quickly. Most volunteer subjects will lose patience if the session stretches more than a few minutes. Phoenix photographer Hal Martin Fogel, who specializes in black-and-white portraits, says he rarely shoots more than two frames. Like all professionals, he surveys the environment as he approaches, deciding in advance where (or if) to ask the subject to pose and which lens to use. A photographer who seems indecisive will quickly annoy the subject.

The next issue is how to put the cotton farmer, who is not used to being photographed except stiffly at family reunions, at ease. One technique is to be unobtrusive: Let him go back to work, wait a few minutes for him to begin forgetting about you, then start shooting. If you're posing him, keep up a stream of conversation. Experiment with humor. Griffin, who occasionally takes jobs photographing powerful Phoenix executives, will tell them, "I love photographing you guys because I get to tell you what to do."

When posing someone, use a tripod and cable release for the shutter — even if you don't need them to steady the camera. The reason is that this allows you to slide out from behind the camera and relate to your subject as one personality to another, without the imposition of a machine in between. Invariably, the subject relaxes and brightens.

What to include in the composition? If the subject's face radiates character, Kida will isolate it from the details of its environment with a long telephoto — 180 to 300mm. Griffin tends toward the opposite extreme — the 20mm wide-angle, which draws in a great deal of the subject's immediate environment. "I think of it as the anthropological approach," he explains, "documenting the slice of the world that someone lives in." Either technique will work, although be wary of the wide-angle's tendency to exaggerate the size of whatever

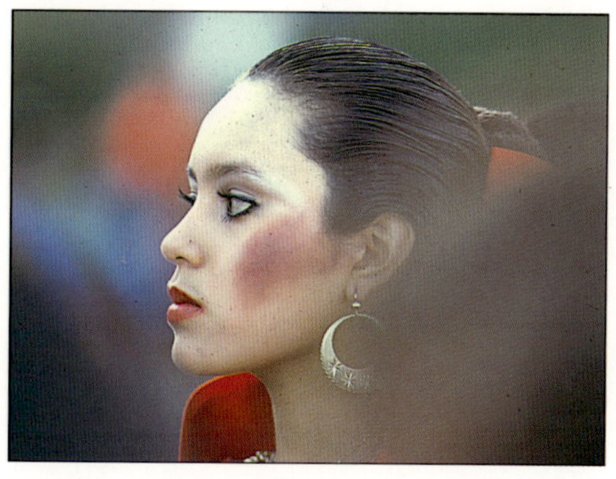

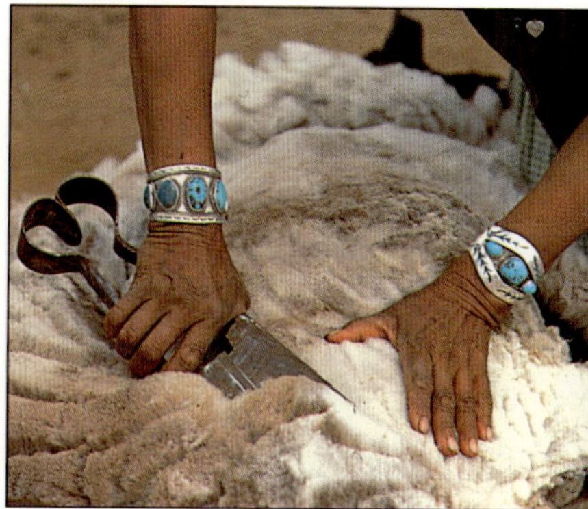

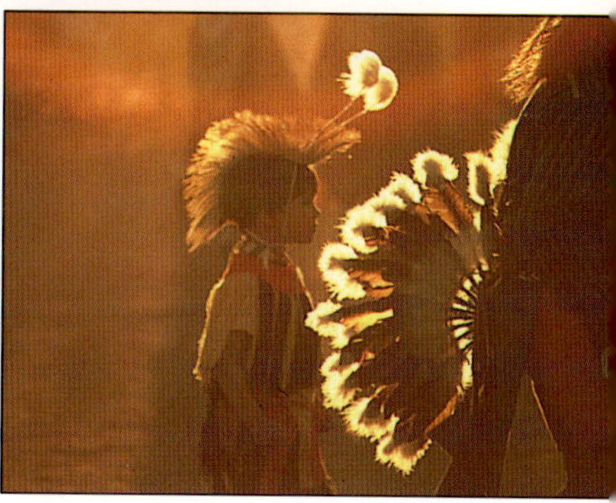

(BELOW, LEFT) *A 300mm lens is a powerful tool in portrait photography. It can isolate subjects from their environment, as in this picture of a young woman at a* cinco de mayo *celebration.*
JEFF KIDA

(BELOW) *Hands can express character and tell a story as surely as faces. These belong to a Navajo shearing sheep.*
MONTY ROESSEL

(BOTTOM) *Photographed at child's eye level, the unconventional composition and backlighting dramatize this photo of a junior grass dancer.*
KATHLEEN NORRIS COOK

feature (a nose, particularly) is closest to it. The "normal" 50mm lens may be the least useful in portraiture, because its view of the subject is so ordinary.

When and where to photograph? In Arizona, an open-sun midday portrait is as futile as a landscape photo under the same conditions. When subjects cooperate, the easiest solution is to shoot in the tawny light of early morning or late evening. Otherwise, make use of: **The soft, reflected light in open shade**. When your subject is near the shade line, bright sunlight bouncing off bare earth will tend to enhance skin tones, lending them a warm, auburn cast. Deep shade, remember, will record on most color films as slightly blue. If you wish to light a shaded face, use a sun-reflecting device (camera shops sell sun-reflecting discs, but a large piece of white cardboard will do) which throws warmer, gentler light than a strobe — the only catch is that you may need an assistant to hold it.

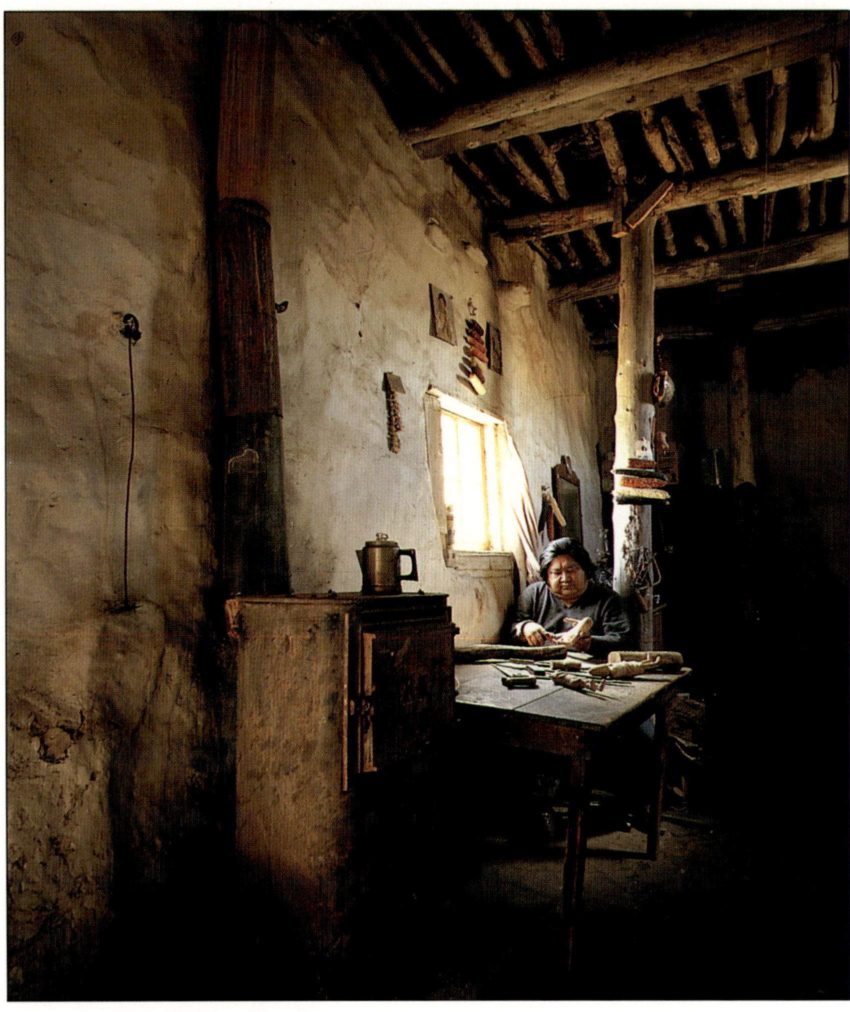

When photographing an artist at work, our usual reflex is to move in tight, to better capture the details of his work. Here, however, a wide-angle lens effectively draws in Hopi carver Jerry LaCapa's environment — his centuries-old home in Walpi village — with window light for illumination.
JERRY JACKA

The indoors. Many photographers love to take portraits indoors *without* strobes, just a single source of sunlight streaming in through a door or window. There are great beauties in this technique. The light is warm, it can be used to emphasize a single element in a picture (such as a person's cheek or the potter's wheel he's working on), and figuring the exposure is simple — just take the reading tightly from the subject's face.

Mottled light. Faces illuminated by the sunlight prying its way through the leaves of a tree can be lovely, and careful positioning of the subject may provide gentle backlighting of hair. The delicate filigree of desert trees such as mesquite and paloverde is especially effective. Usually you will want to use tight depth of field to smudge the detail in the background foliage.

How to take striking, intriguing vacation photos, worthy of hanging on the wall? They don't have to be clichés, as in the kids sprinkled around the base of a towering saguaro. Consider:

The contemplative picture. Subject (husband, wife, or daughter) is not looking at the camera, forcing a smile, but is studying or interacting with the landscape. Example: a child picking up a sun-bleached coyote skull on a desert path, or gingerly touching a teddy bear cholla to test its sharpness. Consider *not* soliciting smiles. The people in many portraits seem to intrigue partly because they are not smiling. "Smiles are fleeting," photographer Hal Fogel says. "We don't see people in that mode much of the time. To see people hanging on the wall smiling forever is a contradiction of their real character; it's contrived."

The action photo. Suppose part of your vacation involves hiking to Seven Falls in Tucson's Santa Catalina Mountains, a four-mile trek that in spring runoff season requires seven calf-deep fords across Bear Canyon Creek. Camera bearer goes first, helpfully charting the route across the creek, then sets up for shooting. The portrayal of family members *doing something* in a scenic place tells more of a story than a posed, static shot.

Whatever the type of portrait, fill flash is an extremely useful tool for coping with high-contrast environments or backlit figures. It must be used with restraint, however; an overly aggressive flash will "paleface" the subject or trick the camera into underexposing the background. Many sophisticated cameras now have a fill-flash mode that calculates the flash power needed and sets it automatically — a very desirable and useful feature, especially in contrasty Arizona. Lacking such computer power, here is how to do it manually: Meter the ambient or background light in the landscape, which will be brighter than the face you need to fill. If it is f/8 at 1/60, say, then set the camera for that exposure and the flash for 1/2 to one stop (f/5.6) less. This will reduce the flash output, illuminating the face more gently. ■

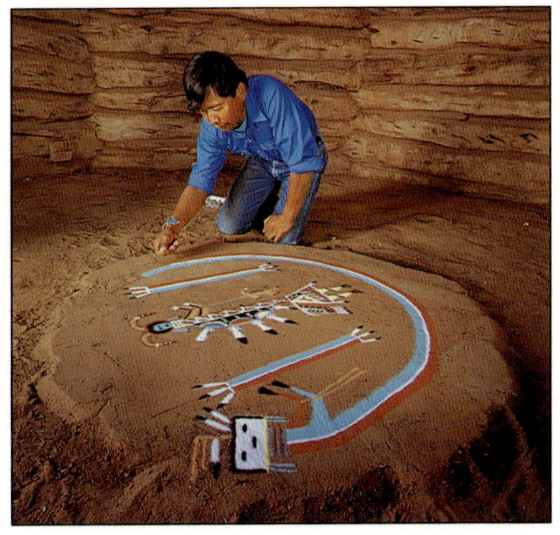

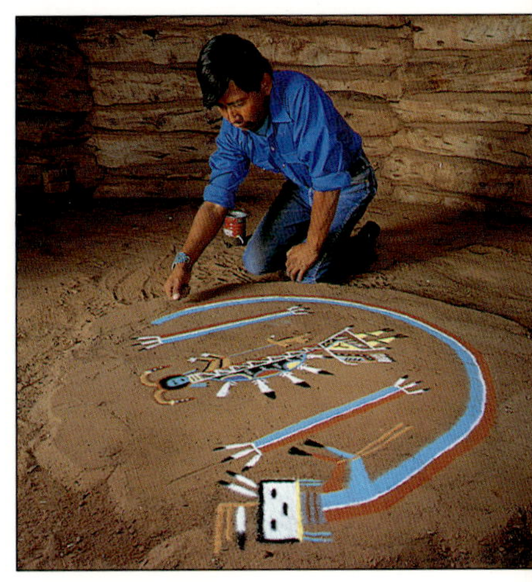

PHOTOGRAPHING OTHER CULTURES

This is such a sensitive but rewarding undertaking that it demands a thorough engagement here. Photographing Native American culture can be a diplomatic challenge. Says Jerry Jacka, Arizona's best-known photographer of Indian subjects, "You have to deal much, much more delicately with them than with people in the mainstream of Anglo society."

Let's watch a professional photographer/diplomat at work.

It's 6:00 on a cold April morning as P.K. Weis and I walk into the camp of an extended Apache family on the San Carlos Indian Reservation. Weis, the long-time photo editor of the *Tucson Citizen*, has read in the tribal newspaper that there will be a sunrise ceremony here this morning. The ceremony, a lovely and elaborate ritual of song, dance, and prayer, will bless a 13-year-old girl's emergence as a woman.

The family has a fire blazing to heat coffee, and Weis asks if we can share it for a moment. He introduces us, explains that we're here to photograph the ceremony — if we may —

The above photos of Navajo sand painter Art Etcitty illustrate two techniques, both valid, of taking the same photo. **(LEFT)** *A fill flash creates more interplay of light and dark in the hogan, while* **(RIGHT)** *sunlight bounced through the doorway with a white reflecting disk illuminates the artist and his environment more evenly. The less experienced photographer may find the reflecting disk easier to use and the light softer and more flattering than the flash.*
JERRY JACKA

and compliments Lisa, the honoree, who is having her hair braided. Lisa's mother is noncommittal, but she offers us coffee, which we accept.

After the coffee, we're not entirely sure whether we have permission, but we walk over to the ceremonial grounds to wait. In a few moments Lisa's father appears for the first time, glares at us and our equipment with remarkable intensity, and declares that he will not have us exploiting his daughter's ceremony. I assume his next words will be an order for us to get out of town, but Weis gently introduces us, explains that we're here because we appreciate the beauty and sacredness of this ceremony, and that we would feel honored if he would let us stay. His stare not wavering, the Apache says he doesn't want any pictures of his daughter showing up in any postcards or magazines. We promise they will not. Gradually, as Weis continues to talk, repeating his appreciation for Apache culture and tradition, the father begins to soften.

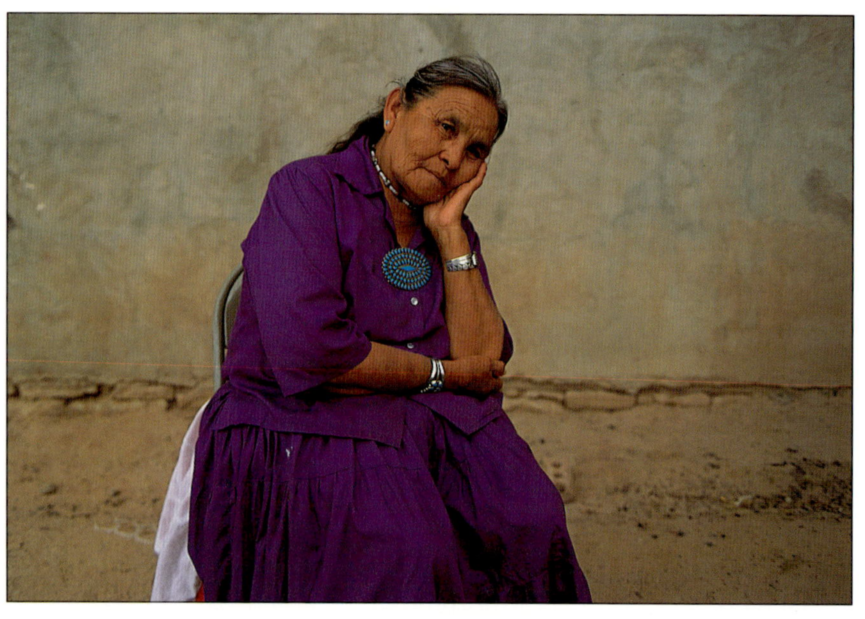

Diffuse light and a relaxed pose emphasize naturalness and softness in a contemplative portrait of this Navajo woman. MONTY ROESSEL

"I believe you," he says at last. "You may stay."

When the ceremony begins, Weis deliberately hangs well back, adopting a much less aggressive posture than his photojournalistic norm. He greets spectators, jokes with them, asks permission if he needs to stand near them for a picture. Gradually, over the course of two hours, he senses that the Apaches have grown accustomed to his presence, and are tolerating it, and he moves in for tighter and tighter shots. By the end of the ceremony, he's in intimate range with a 20mm lens, shooting photos of relatives hugging an exhausted and tearful Lisa, her head now encrusted with the ceremonial corn pollen. These may be the best shots of the day, because they transcend all cultural boundaries. They show Apaches crying, laughing, and loving each other, like human beings everywhere. Because of our promise, they remain unpublished — photographs for us and our families to savor privately.

As 300 villagers pass to pay their respects, Weis slips to the end of the line to offer his also — along with professional-quality prints that he'll mail later from Tucson, as an expression of thanks.

Other photographers have different ways of establishing rapport, but they all agree on basic principles: Express interest in and respect for the culture. Be sincere. And make no promises you won't keep. Arizona's Indians have been evaluating white people's promises since the 16th century, and they have learned to judge character very, very well.

The prime reason many are reluctant to be photographed is that they see it as exploitation. "They'll see a picture in a magazine and say, 'He's getting $1,000 for this and I'm getting nothing,'" says Navajo photographer Monty Roessel. "And this is in a context, remember, where the people being photographed are making maybe $4,000 a year." The poverty also causes sensitivity about photography, Roessel adds. In some situations, Indians feel that the camera is stealing their dignity. Here, the photographer's solution is obvious: photograph what people are proud of — their art, their land, their traditions, their children.

Jacka, who specializes in photographing Indian art and artists, says he never takes pictures of Indian people without compensating them — "and compensating them very nicely." His reasoning: "I think it's both a practical necessity and an ethical obligation. Would I ever ask a model here in Phoenix to pose for me without being paid? Of course not." What he pays, he says, depends on the situation.

This is a controversial view; many photographers feel that paying for pictures corrupts the culture being photographed — that, in time, people will come to perform for the camera rather than being themselves. In any event, for the amateur photographing on the reservations, "payment" is also possible in terms of good-quality prints or, as Roessel suggests, food brought to ceremonies.

There are many photo opportunities on the reservations that are not unwelcome or intrusive. Roessel suggests Indian rodeos, powwows, and tribal fairs. Or, he says, simply walk into a chapter house (in Navajo government, roughly equivalent to city hall) and explain that you're interested in weaving — and is there a weaver nearby whom you could photograph? Sincere interest, Roessel says, will open doors on Indian reservations, just as it will almost everywhere you want to shoot.

In any event, don't be afraid to make the approach. Explains Roessel: "You're from New York City, you're driving through the Navajo Reservation and you see someone off the side of the road herding sheep. Think about it: She's out there in the sun all day herding sheep, and it's pretty likely she's thirsty and lonely. Take a cold drink over and start by saying, 'Say, I'm from New York City and I'm interested in how you herd sheep.' Remember that Navajos are interested in what life is like in New York City, too."

Arizona's Mexican neighbor, the state of Sonora, is rich in photographic opportunities. Says Jeff Kida: "You handle it exactly the same way you would here — except in Spanish." Few Sonorans outside the tourist haunts speak English, and they are invariably appreciative of a foreigner's efforts to communicate in Spanish, even if halting and ungrammatical. Family and neighborhood networks are tight in Mexican culture, so rapport established with one person may lead to many more opportunities. Again: Photograph people in the context of what they are proud of, the environments and situations that afford them pleasure and dignity. This is no less than what we would ask for our portraits. ■

Public events provide opportunities to photograph other cultures without being obtrusive.

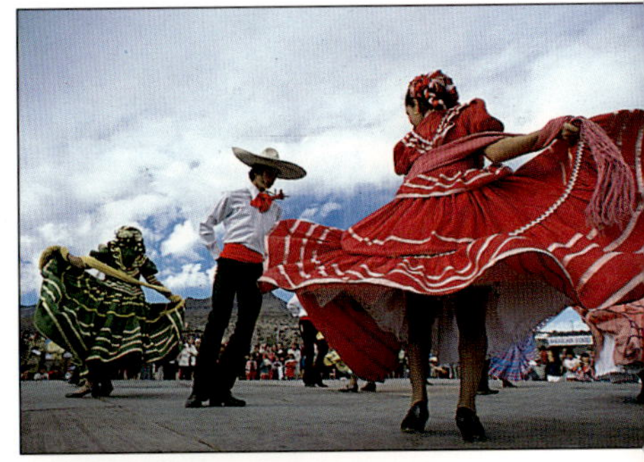

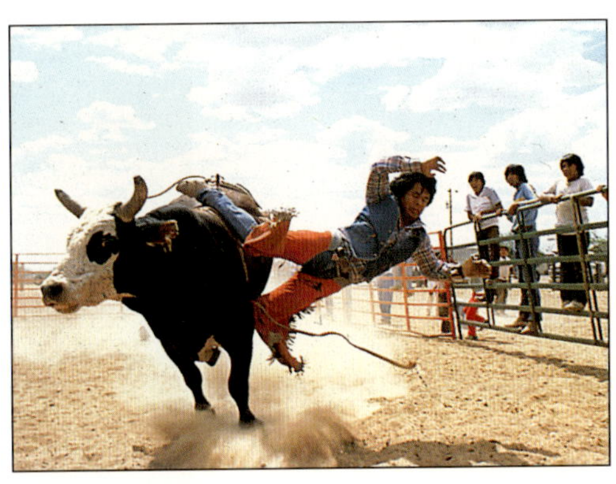

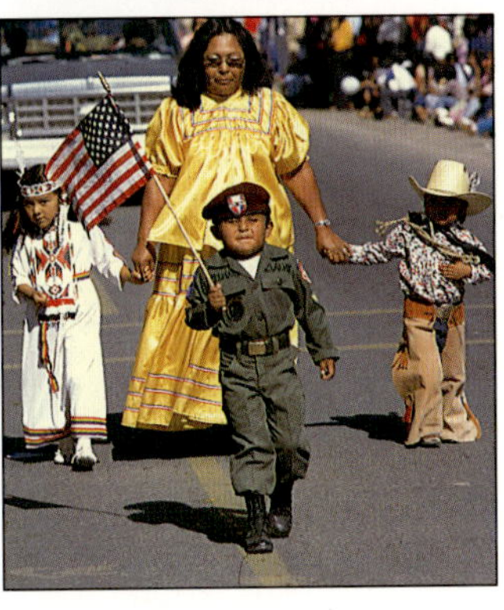

(TOP) *Mexican folk dancers perform at a fiesta at Tumacacori National Monument. The energy and color of the dance are emphasized by the swirl of the red dress.* JAMES TALLON

(ABOVE LEFT) *Rodeo action photos depend on anticipation and quick reactions. At small rodeos, such as this on the Papago reservation, you can move closer to the action.* P.K.WEIS

(ABOVE) *Patriotism and poignant irony both are beautifully expressed in this photo of Apache children marching in a San Carlos Veterans Day parade.* P.K. WEIS

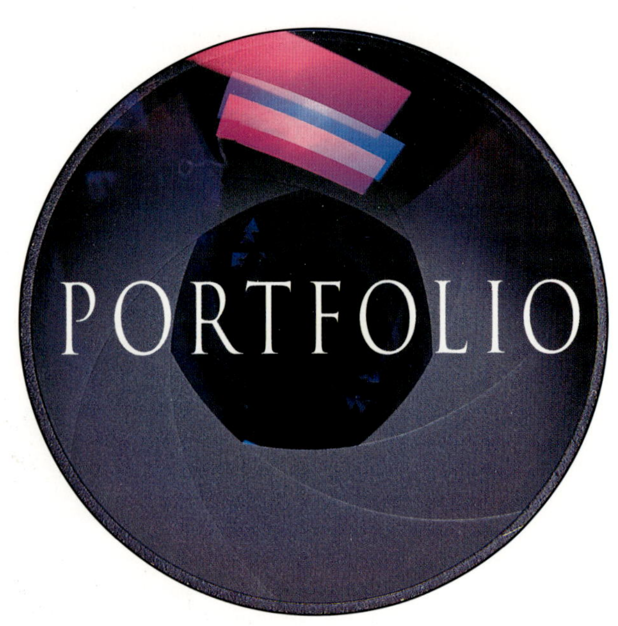

PEOPLE

Many amateur photographers assume, logically enough, that pose and expression are the most critical concerns in photographs of people. Often they aren't. Light actually can make a greater difference because it has so much power over the mood of a picture. Light can make a human subject appear dynamic, intent, strong, sorrowful, penitent, isolated, perhaps even destitute. A good photographer will be just as alert for the opportunities offered by light as by the behavior of the subject. ■

(ABOVE) *Lens iris detail.* CARLTON PHOTOGRAPHY

(RIGHT) *Indoor portrait photography doesn't require strobes or banks of studio lights, and in fact may be more effective without them. Available light from a window warmly and beautifully highlights this saddlemaker's face and work. The underexposed negative space behind him helps express the solitary nature of his craft.* JEFF KIDA

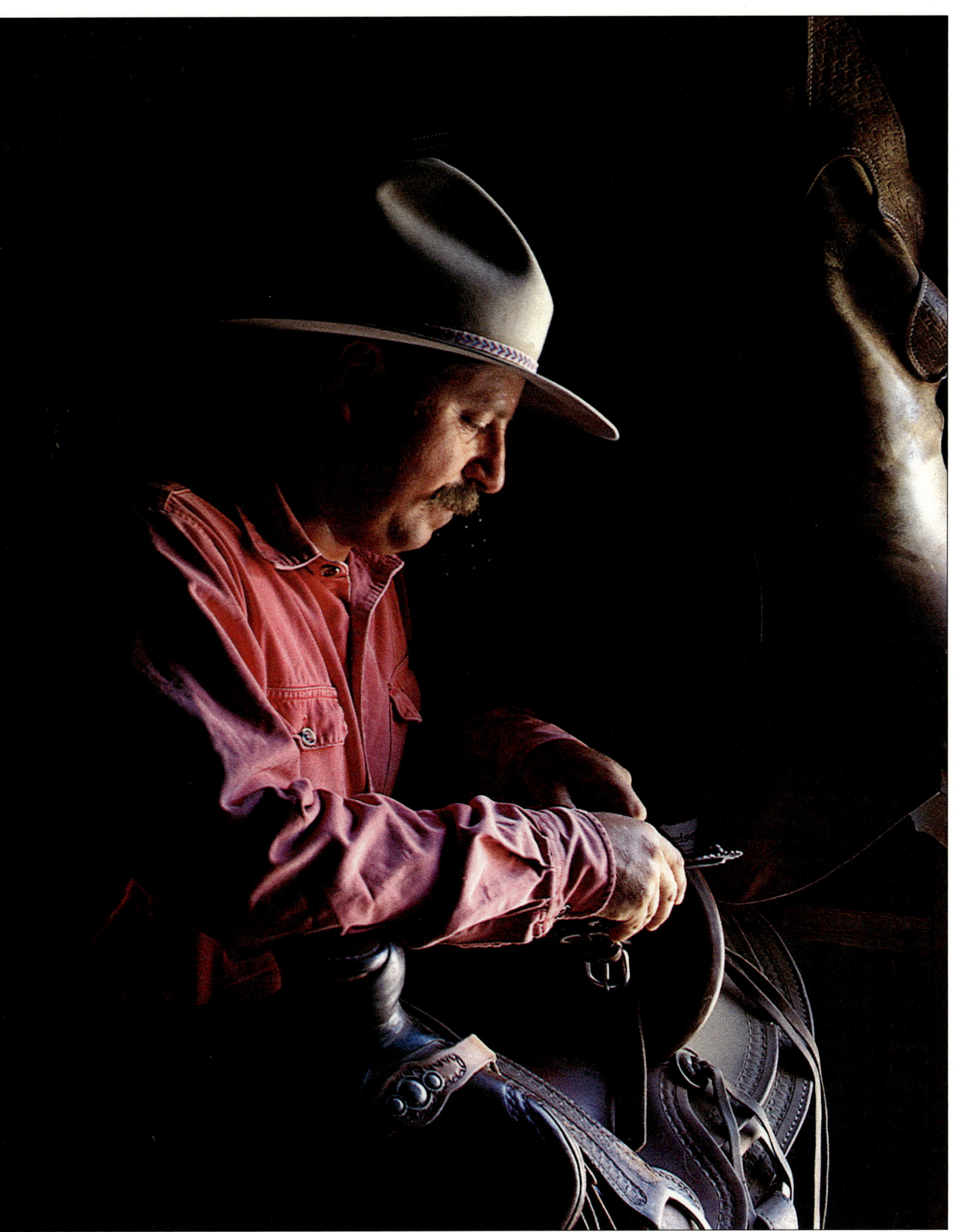

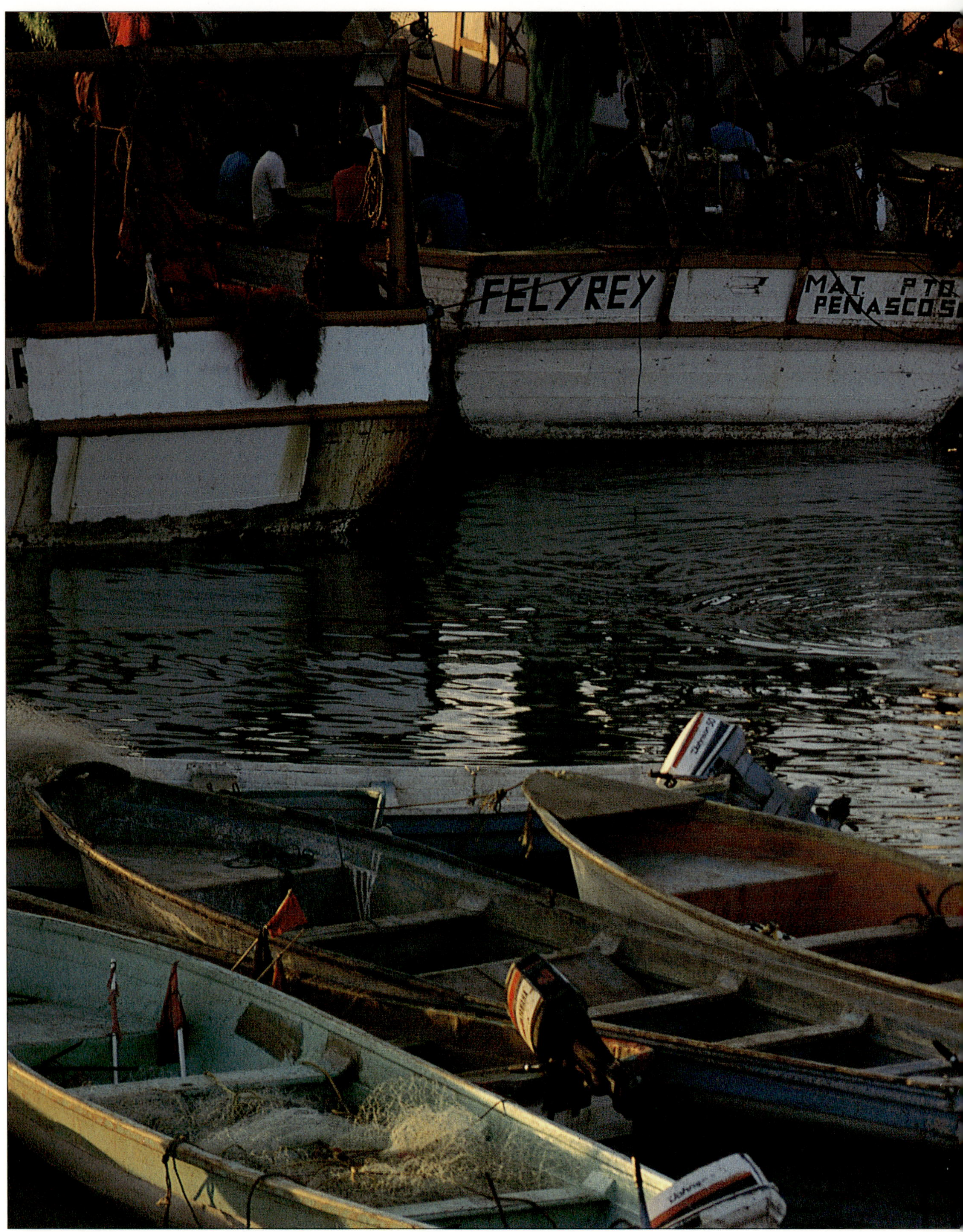
FELYREY
MAT. PTO
PENASCO

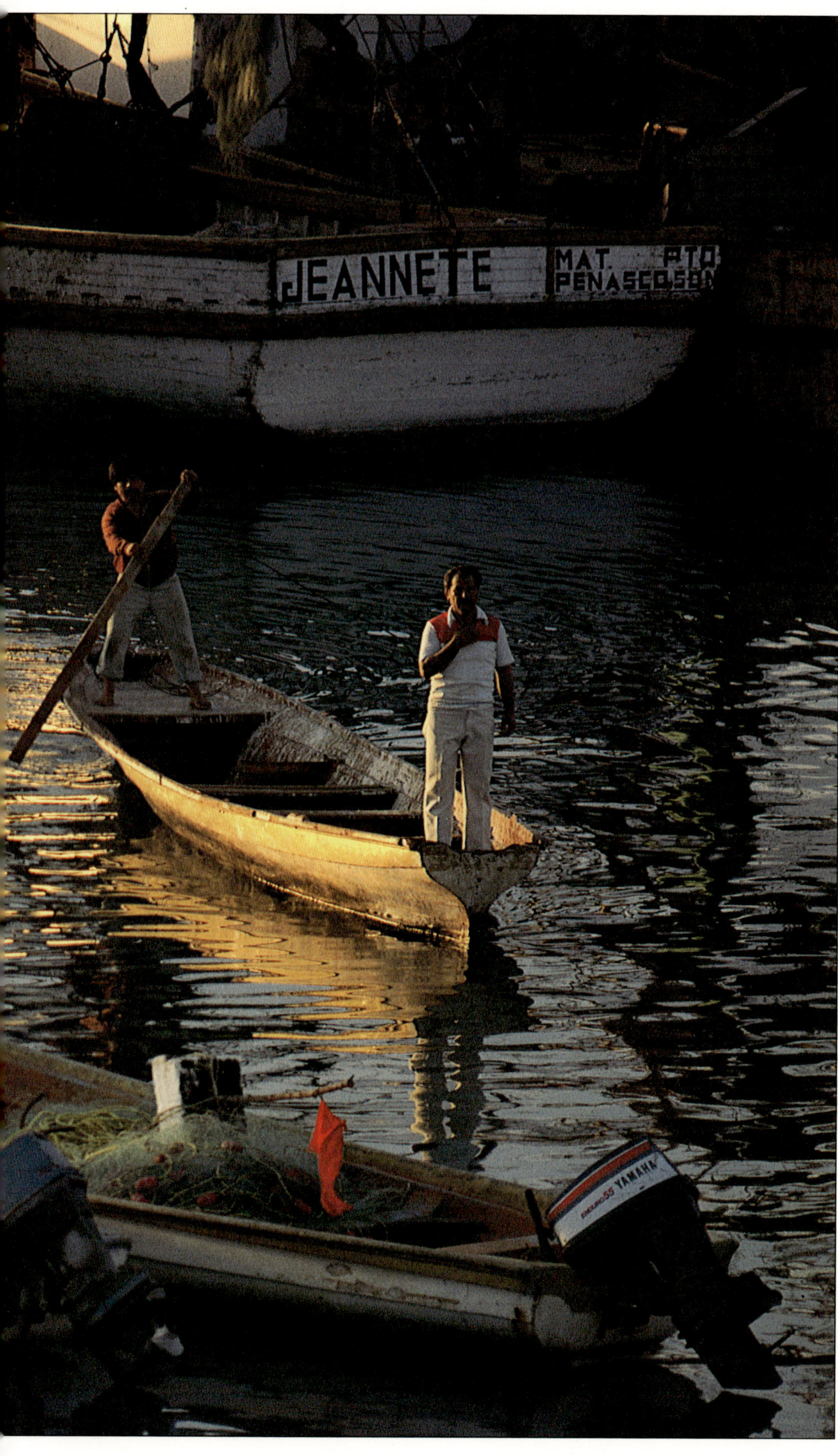

In a setting crowded with plants, buildings or (in this case) harbored boats, a narrow shaft of light from a rising or setting sun may squeeze through to highlight a subject with extraordinary drama. These boatmen and their dinghy in Puerto Peñasco, Sonora, 60 miles south of the Arizona-Mexico border, enjoy an especially warm and selective swatch of afternoon light.
P.K. WEIS

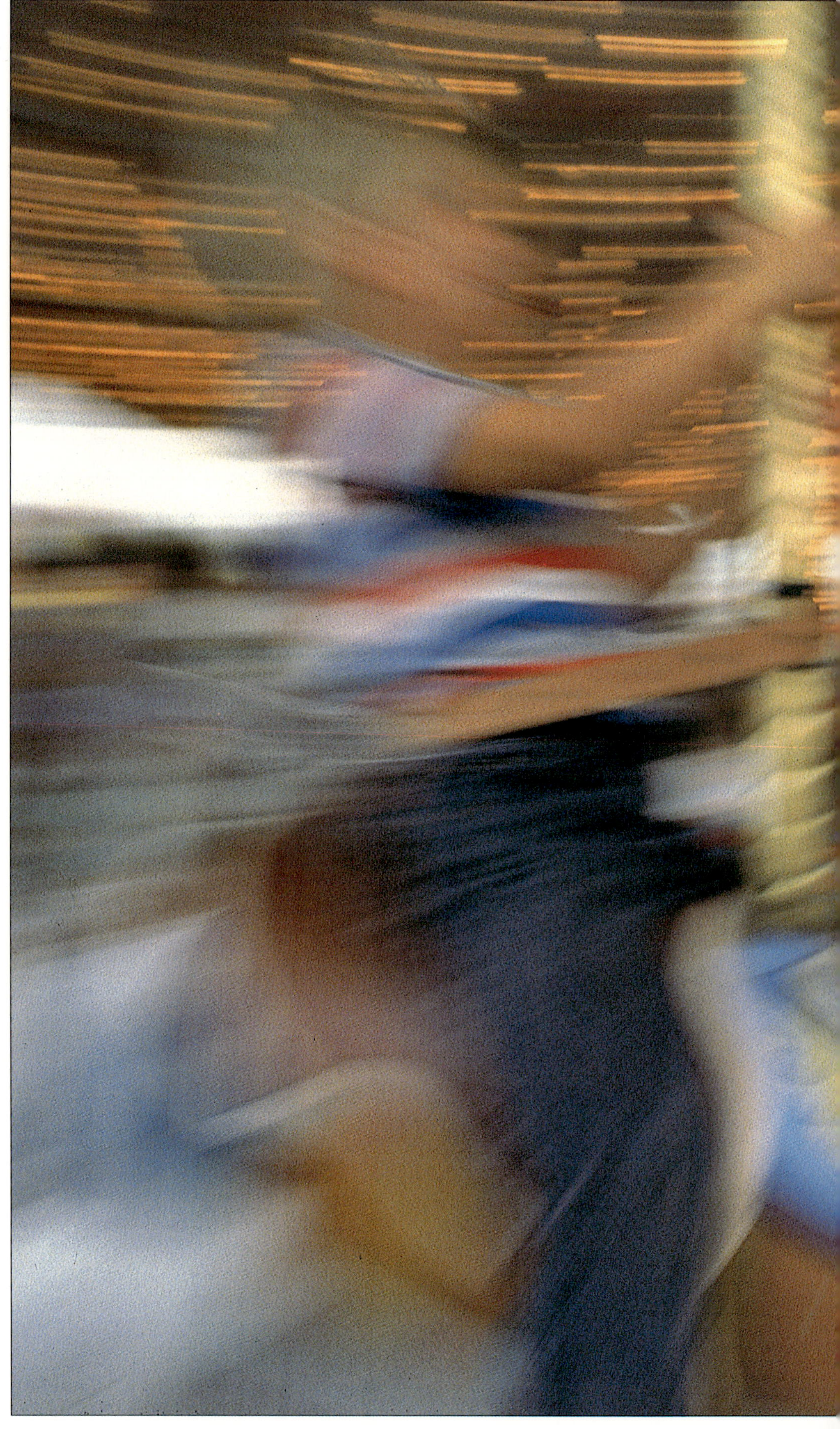

This appealing, quirky photo was taken while riding on an amusement park carousel. One's normal impulse is to track the child, but here the photographer focused on the horse's eye and followed its up-and-down motion. The slow shutter speed caused everything else to blur, especially the background, and imply the sensation of movement. The photo enters the child's world, suggesting the sensations he might be having on the ride.
FRED GRIFFIN

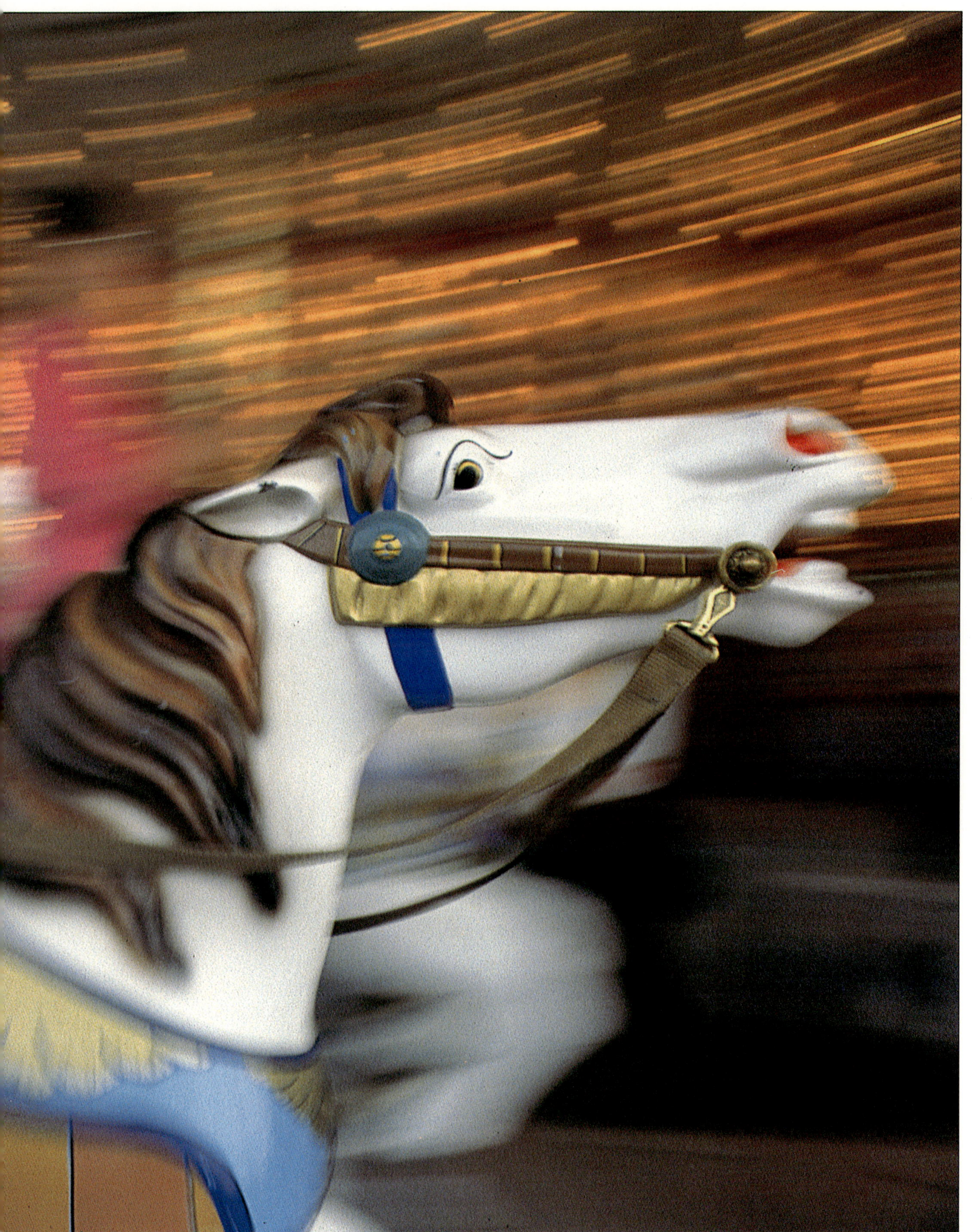

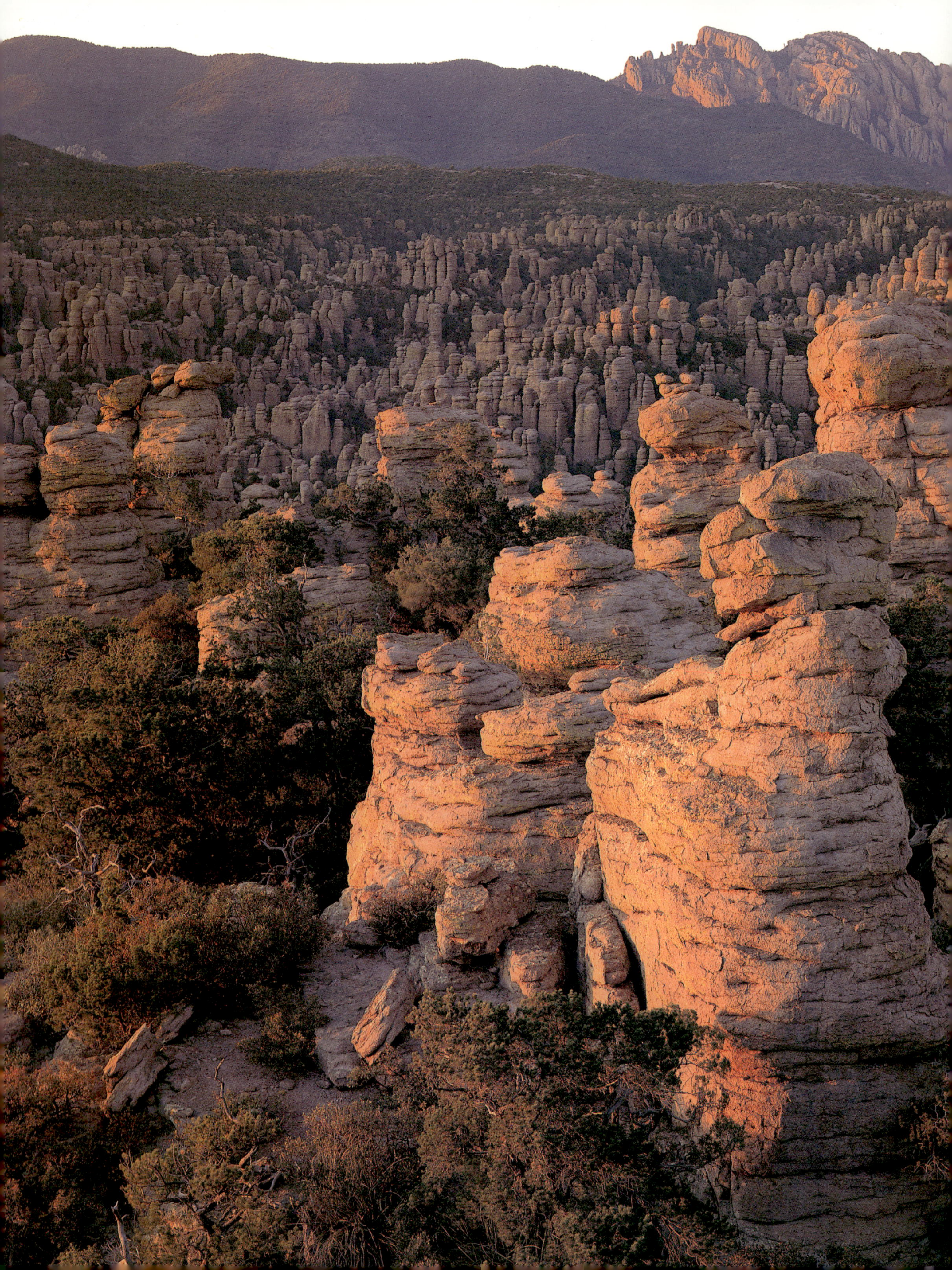

Chapter 3

LANDSCAPE

In Arizona, landscapes can be transcendental. The word is not used promiscuously. Certain views, at the right moments, touch our emotions so deeply that they move us beyond all previous experience. At sunset, sitting on a high rock in the Chiricahua Mountains, Arizona novelist Ray Ring wrote in *Arizona Highways* that "The landscape whispers to me of other realities than my own, other times, other dimensions."

Capturing these emotional whisperings and "other realities" with a camera is what landscape or scenic photography is all about. It is not merely about making pretty pictures. The creative photographer is an artist; he or she is *interpreting* an outdoors scene, recording on film a personal reaction to the landscape. Does it seem heroic? Malevolent? Tranquil? Fragile? Four photographers might photograph the same landscape in these four thoroughly different moods, their interpretations changing through camera placement, choice of lens, composition, light, and weather.

What is scenic photography? Photographic fundamentalists insist that it is *strictly* nature — meadows, streams, mountains, canyons — with the intrusions of humankind banished from the frame. Most of us, though, are willing to admit at least windmills, rustic ranch houses and the occasional *homo sapiens* (for scale or color) into our landscapes. David Muench allows prehistoric ruins into some of his primal Southwestern landscapes because "these people lived and survived in the land, rather than conquering it." But the man-made intrusions do not always have to be pretty to have a point. Scottsdale photographer John Drew shot a Monument Valley picture through the windows of a pickup truck abandoned, appallingly, in this most starkly beautiful of land-

(LEFT) *The rhyolite hoodoos of the Chiricahua Mountains are highlighted by the setting sun.* EDWARD McCAIN

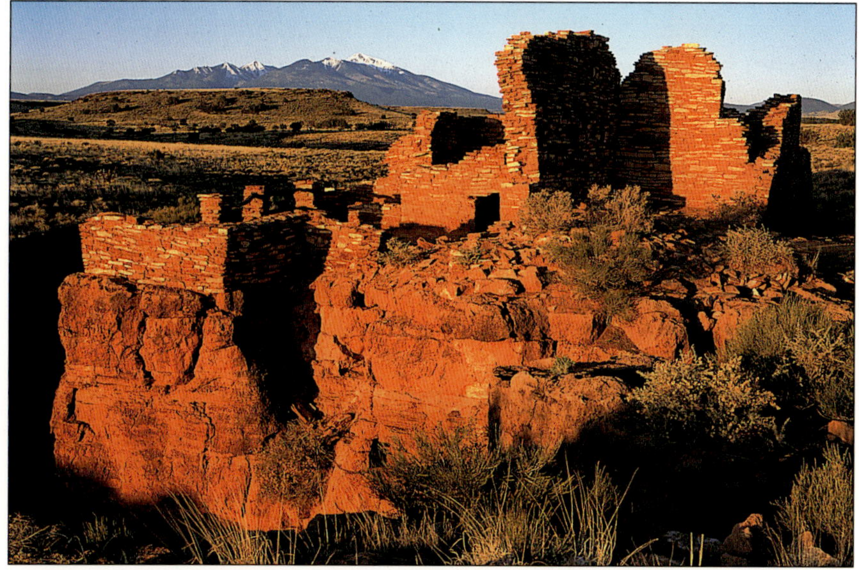

(ABOVE) *Landscape photographers usually strive to keep man-made intrusions out of their frames, but they find prehistoric ruins attractive because they "grow" from their sites with such organic grace. This is the Lomaki ruin at Wupatki National Monument with the San Francisco Peaks in the background.* MICHAEL COLLIER

scapes. As he was shooting, he commented, "It's not an *Arizona Highways* image, but it's a useful one." On one count he was wrong: *Arizona Highways* published it. The story it told was an important commentary on human attitudes toward the land.

Contrast adds interest to the already esthetically pleasing image.
(RIGHT) *A hedgehog cactus in bloom illuminated by a sunburst would make an attractive picture by itself illustrating flowers with their source of life. Incorporating the pine trees adds the ironic juxtaposition of the desert plant thriving in the forest.*
JACK DYKINGA
(BELOW) *A miniature landscape of tiny, delicate, flowering western peppergrass finding nourishment in the rugged hardness of a fissure in a Petrified Forest log.*
JACK DYKINGA

To understand the mood of the land and commit it to film, the first step is to give yourself time to react to it. The best photographers take a great deal of time. In 1944 the acclaimed photographer Paul Strand visited Ansel Adams in Yosemite for a week, taking long walks twice a day, but continually refusing Adams' offer of a loaned camera. "I must get used to the place first," Strand said. Phoenix photographer Fred Griffin says that his favorite images of the North Rim came after he skied cross-country 50 miles to get there. "I could've gone in on a snowmobile, but then the pictures would have been different," he says. "The experiential side of that trip is in the photos in intangible ways." Tucson photographer Jack Dykinga, a tireless

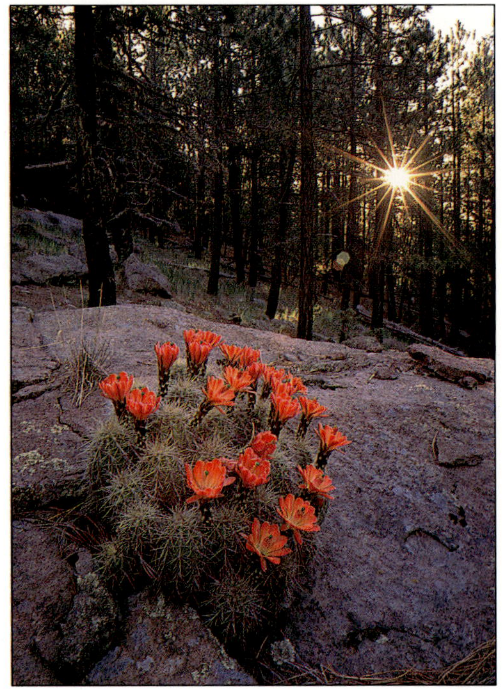

hiker, will tramp around a landscape for days while shooting it, and then will return to the same place year after year. "My philosophy of photographing people is that if you give of yourself, you get back," Dykinga says. "And I think that applies to landscape photography, too. It's hard to show any emotion for a place until you get to know it."

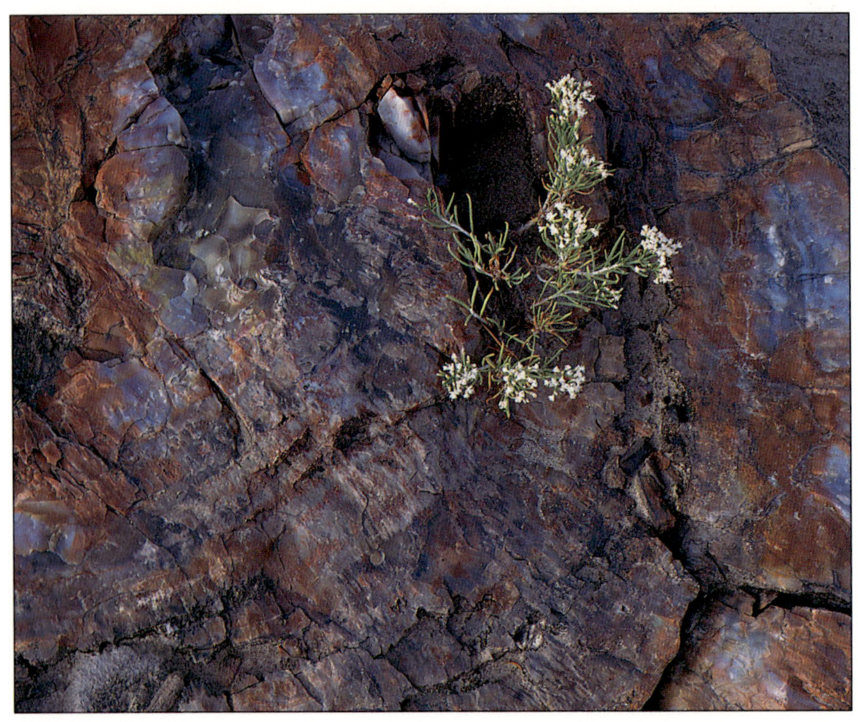

While beginning to know a place, a good photographer is also scouting it. Professionals generally use bankers' hours (9 A.M.-4 P.M.) for this, since the midday light is not often conducive to landscape photography. Look for photographic possibilities, keeping in mind where the light will be coming from when the sun is low on the horizon. What patterns or textures in the landscape seem to have an unusual beauty, or a poignant story to tell? Dykinga looks for juxtapositions — for example, a delicate peppergrass growing through a fissure in a 200 million-year-old Petrified Forest log, or a gnarled Arizona sycamore's exposed roots growing around a boulder, seemingly embracing it. Prescott photographer Jay Dusard looks for "pictures within pictures" — a pattern of saguaros in the foreground, a pattern of shadows on the mountain slopes behind. Whatever they look for, all good photographers look *intently.* The reward is not only better pictures, but a closer and more memorable relationship with their subject, the land.

Early mornings are generally the most productive times for landscape photography in Arizona because the light is soft and tawny, and the air is usually still. (The viewer's eye will tolerate some breeze-induced movement in foreground plants, but not much.) If there are cirrus clouds, the sky usually will light up — for just three or four minutes — with sunrise colors of gold, pink, and magenta, forming a spectacular stage set for almost any kind of large-scale landscape photo. Sunset color tends to last longer and appear more intensely red because of the daytime dust kicked into the air, but wind may be a factor. In either case, be in your scouted location, ready to shoot, *before* the sky begins its Technicolor theatrics. Far better to be disappointed if no color materializes than panicked, scrambling for location and fumbling for lenses, as a world-class sunset evaporates into night.

On mornings and evenings when the sky doesn't cooperate with color, "sunburst" shots are still interesting. If you catch a sliver of the sun peeking from behind a tree trunk or rock formation, a burst of sunbeams will explode radially across the frame. Here the camera lens is creating its own reality, because the human eye doesn't perceive this effect.

Bad weather can be good for scenic photography at any time of day. Before a summer thunderstorm, as gunmetal clouds begin to crowd out the blue sky, a foreground may be brilliantly illuminated by sunlight, while its backdrop is ominously dark. After a storm, low clouds will bump into mountain peaks or droop into valleys and canyons. Fog is fairly rare in Arizona, but be prepared: A desert landscape in fog is one of the most mysterious, yet also strangely serene, images you can commit to film. In any landscape, a photograph in fog accentuates depth.

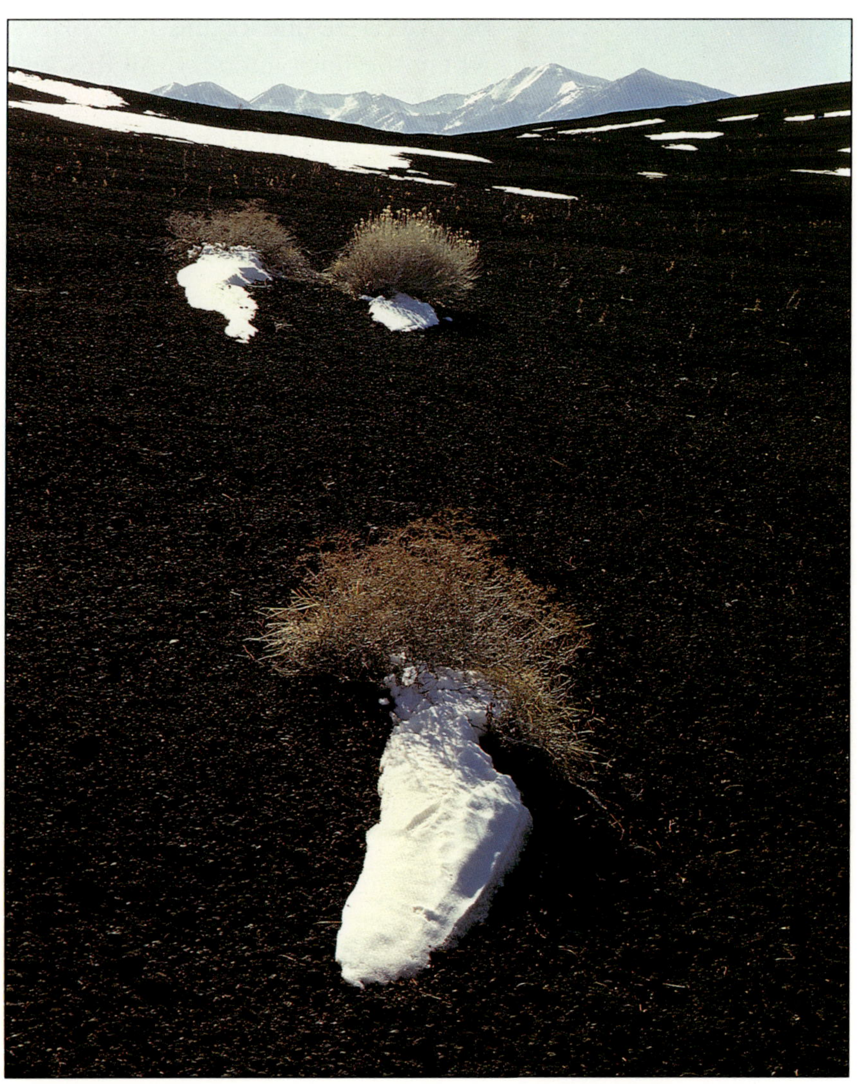

(ABOVE) *Fire and ice. The pattern of snow patches leads the eye across the cinder fields to the volcanic San Francisco Peaks on the horizon.* DAVID MUENCH

Composing a landscape photograph is more a matter of intuition than rules. There is a traditional device worth knowing, however, called the "Rule of Thirds." Imagine the scene in the viewfinder divided by lines into three equal sections, both horizontally and vertically. The horizon, then, should fall within either the 1/3 or 2/3 horizontal area. (If it falls in the middle, the viewer may not know whether the sky or the land is supposed to be more important.) The main subject should be placed at one of the four places where the lines intersect. All this will avoid a symmetrical composition, and usually provide a pleasing proportion of space between the main subject and the edge of the frame. (Too close to the edge generates distracting tension.)

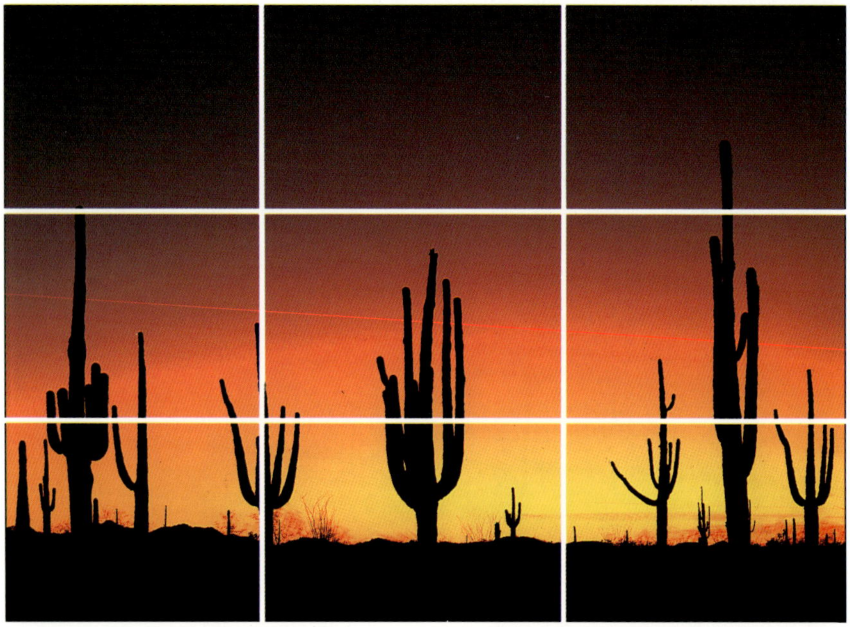

The composition of this image of saguaro cactus silhouetted by a spectacular sunset illustrates the Rule of Thirds by placing the most important feature of the image, the color of the sunset, in the bottom third of the frame.
JACK DYKINGA

A creative photographer, however, may violate the Rule of Thirds all day and have a better shoot because of it. There are more important considerations in composition, although it is hard to express them as rules.

One of those considerations is movement — the direction that the patterns in the landscape lead the eye. To call attention to the main subject, place it at the end or the convergence of naturally occurring lines. If lines and forms seem to lead nowhere, or flow randomly, the composition probably needs more thought.

Another is scale. Since a photograph is just a miniature, two-dimensional reproduction of a landscape, it may not have much impact unless something in it registers size or depth. A picture of a 500-foot-high escarpment by itself conveys little sense of power or grandeur, but place a lonely tree at the bottom, or a lonely hiker on the top, and the great cliff will register with more impact.

Still another is point of view, which is not a rule at all but an opportunity. Most of the time, we see the world from a vantage of three to six feet above the ground. Photographers who routinely use their eye level for camera placement are missing opportunities to portray landscapes in fresh and revealing points of view. What does a meadow look like to a rabbit? (Lie down and shoot over the flower tops.) What do flowering agave stalks look like to a bird? (Find some growing on a mountain slope and climb above them.)

Beware of distractions in the frame. Nearly every photographer, amateur or pro, has at one time or another photographed a companion so familiar that he forgot it was there: his shadow. Camera bags also have a clever habit of migrating into corners of the frame. Less obviously, watch out for bright objects, such as light-colored rocks, at the edges; bright areas in a picture always attract the eye first. Don't let them lead the eye out of the frame. As Dykinga says, "make the corners work *for* you." Not *against* you.

Though he composes intuitively, Dykinga has a useful technique for checking whether he's on target: He will stop down the lens (use the depth-of-field preview on a 35mm camera) until color and detail disappear from the frame. Then only pure form appears, and its harmony and flow — or lack of same — become obvious.

The foreground in a landscape may well be as important, or more important, than the long view. The foreground may be very simple — a tuft of dry grass turned golden by early light, a flowering barrel cactus, a small boulder with an interesting texture. But unless the foreground subject is so important that it wants to be isolated from its environment, the entire picture must be in sharp focus from foreground to back.

This style of landscape photography was cemented into popularity as long ago as 1932, through the influence of Group f/64, founded by Ansel Adams, Edward Weston, and five other major photographic artists. Their manifesto was clarity, sharp definition, and objective reality. Adams termed the opposing photoimpressionists "fuzzy-wuzzies." For 35mm landscape photography today, the doctrine of Group f/64 still stands: slow, fine-grained film (ISO 100 or less), and slow shutter speed paired with a small aperture for maximum depth of field. A tripod is indispensable.

How to be sure everything is in focus? Quite a few photographers have never learned to use two very helpful rows of figures on their lenses. The numbers on the focusing ring are the distance to the subject, usually given both in feet and meters. The adjacent numbers inside the ring are f/stops. Once the camera is focused, estimate the distance to the nearest foreground in the frame, find that number on the focusing ring, and see what f/stop is next to it on the other row. If the distance is three feet and the f/stop f/16, then everything from three feet to infinity will be in focus *if* the lens aperture is set to f/16 or smaller.

In Arizona's high-contrast landscapes, deciding the right exposure can be more demanding than in places where the light is softer and dispersed more evenly. When the Arizona sky is bright, it will fool the exposure programs of most automated 35mm cameras. Their microchip brains don't realize that it's *supposed*

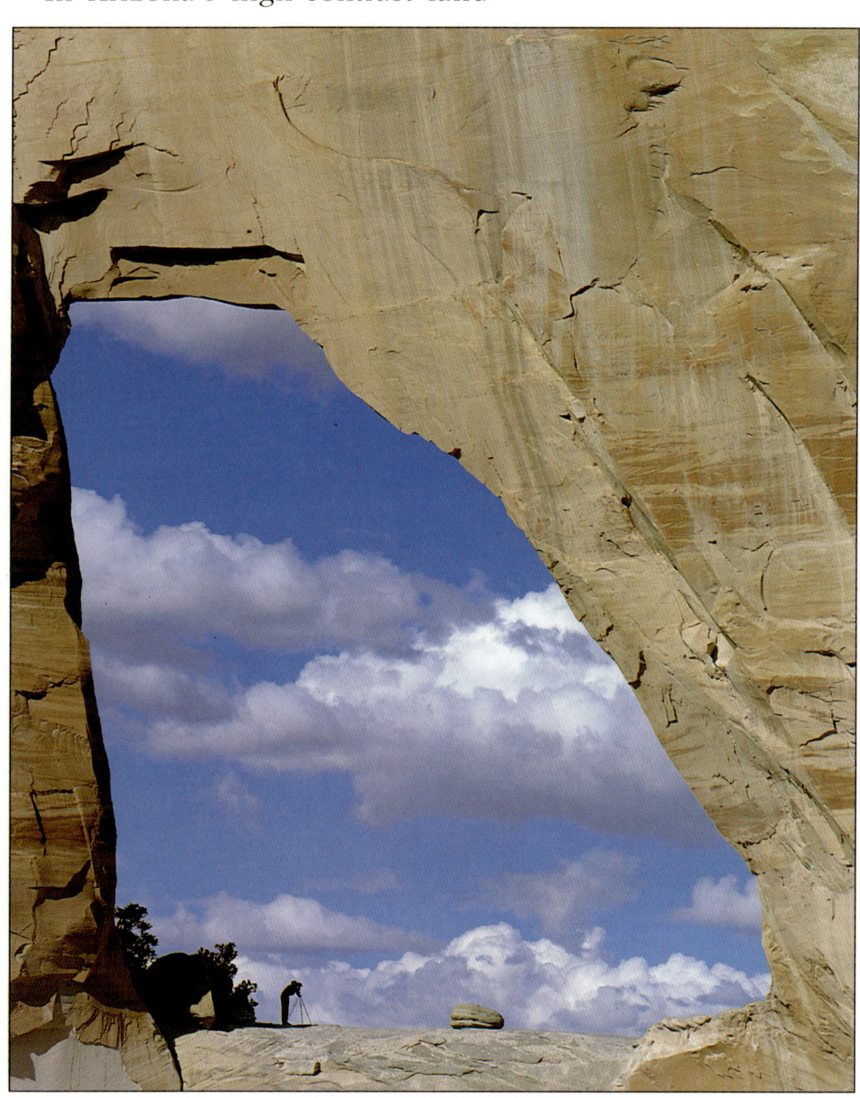

Humans occasionally have their place in landscape photography. Here the tiny photographer, dwarfed by the immensity of White Mesa Arch, provides scale.
MICHAEL FATALI

to be bright, so they will choose a smaller aperture or higher shutter speed than they should. The result is an underexposed picture. If you're planning to include bright sky in a landscape, set the camera on manual exposure, and point the camera down a bit for a better average light reading for the frame. Often it will be at least one f/stop wider than the camera recommends. Sometimes, however, the sky itself may be the main subject of the photo. In that case, meter it and expose the picture accordingly.

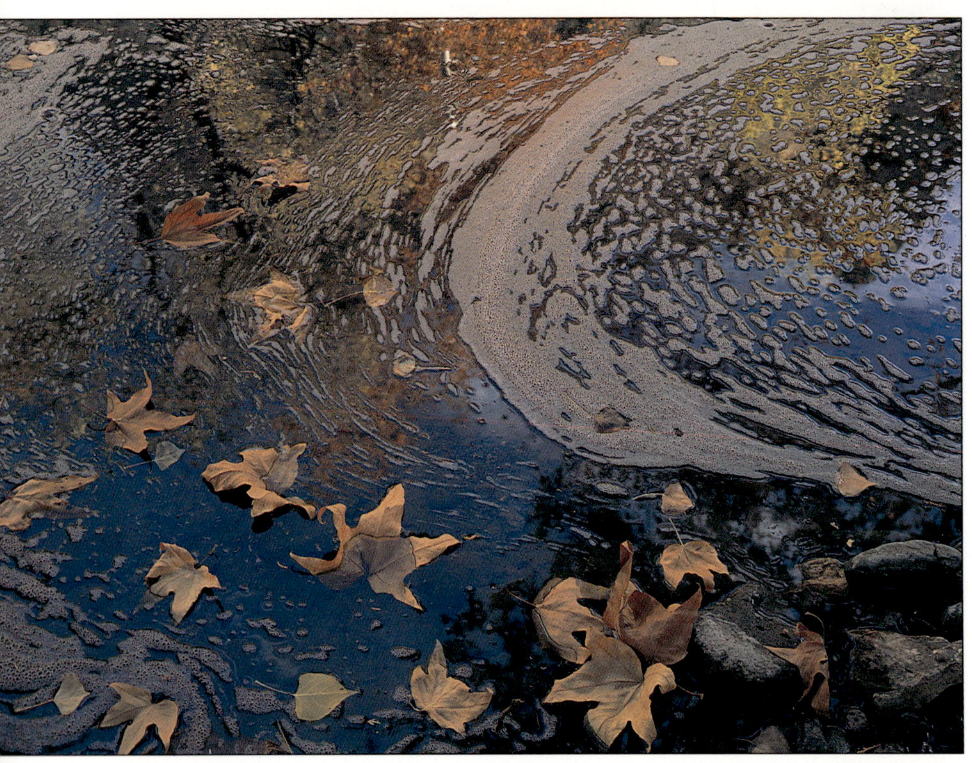

The images on these two pages show a contrast of moving and static design in intimate landscapes. **(ABOVE)** *Dry sycamore leaves, a curling pattern of foam, and fall color reflected in a slow-moving creek create a flowing and near-abstract intimate landscape.*
JACK DYKINGA

For Arizona's famous sunsets, meter a layer of color off to the side of the sun rather than directly on it, and then bracket. This will give a median exposure for the sky's light.

Backlit landscapes present thornier problems, but the images — particularly in the desert — reveal so much structure, depth, and warmth that they're well worth the effort. Generally, the camera will want to meter the light source and underexpose the picture. One defense is to take the camera off the tripod, look for a nearby object with what appears to be diffused light falling on it, and meter that. Another is to meter several readings over the entire landscape and average them. Whatever the metering strategy, *always* bracket backlit exposures. Use a lens hood to prevent those glowing polygons called "iris flares" in the finished picture. Walk around to the front of the camera and look at the lens. If direct sunlight is striking it, you have a problem. If you don't have a lens hood, try shading it with a hat.

Other exposure tips: When photographing something such as a yucca in silhouette against a sunrise or sunset, expose for the sky, not the plant. But try to choose a median value for the sky's light, not its brightest layer—otherwise, you'll lose the rich subtleties of the darker tones. When making a "sunburst" exposure, however, meter for the object in front of the sun (and bracket—this is tricky!). In fog, open up 1/2 to 1 1/2 stops over the meter reading — the meter will read the reflective mist as a medium gray.

The best advice in scenic photography, finally, is simply this: experiment. In the 35mm format, film is the least expensive instruction you can buy.

INTIMATE LANDSCAPES

We huddle in the car, watching the day's second summer monsoon batter the Chiricahua Mountains and erode our views of its rocky skyline into ghostly oblivion. "We'll be looking for intimate landscapes today," says my hiking companion, photographer Edward McCain.

Many amateur photographers, at this point, would be looking only for the road down off the mountain. The experienced pro, however, is undaunted by most bad weather. Bad weather often means good pictures, if you're creative enough to make them. McCain doesn't care to slog directly into this storm — there's lightning dancing all around us — but summer thunderstorms in Arizona almost always pass over quickly, and the rest of the day, even if it remains overcast, should offer good material for those "intimate landscapes."

What are they? The opposite of the grand, sweeping, rim-of-the-world vistas for which Arizona is famous. An intimate landscape may take in only a few square feet, or a few hundred, of land, trees, rocks, or water. It has the power to draw the viewer into a close, emotionally dynamic relationship with a place. Arizona is rich in intimate landscapes, and not only when the weather turns too somber to include the sky in the picture. Hike in the desert a few days after a winter snow in nearby mountains, and you'll frequently come across temporary ponds or minuscule rivers carrying the runoff away. A picture of a foot-wide stream gently rippling through a grove of backlit cholla and prickly pear tells a story about life's renewal that is almost Biblical. A portrait of one of the hundreds of little waterfalls in Arizona's mountains reminds one that this land is not only about grand gestures, but also miniatures.

The practical value of the intimate landscape is that it allows you to keep shooting in conditions that make large-scale landscape photography useless: dull and overcast skies, flat midday sunlight, dusty or humid air that obscures distant features, smog on the horizon, or even enveloping fog. Or there may be permanently unwelcome features in the larger landscape, such as power lines, that need to be excluded. In all these cases the pros' suggestions are: Close in. Think small.

After the storm lifts, McCain and I set off on the Echo Canyon Loop, one of the loveliest trails in Chiricahua National Monument. After half an hour we come to a perfect

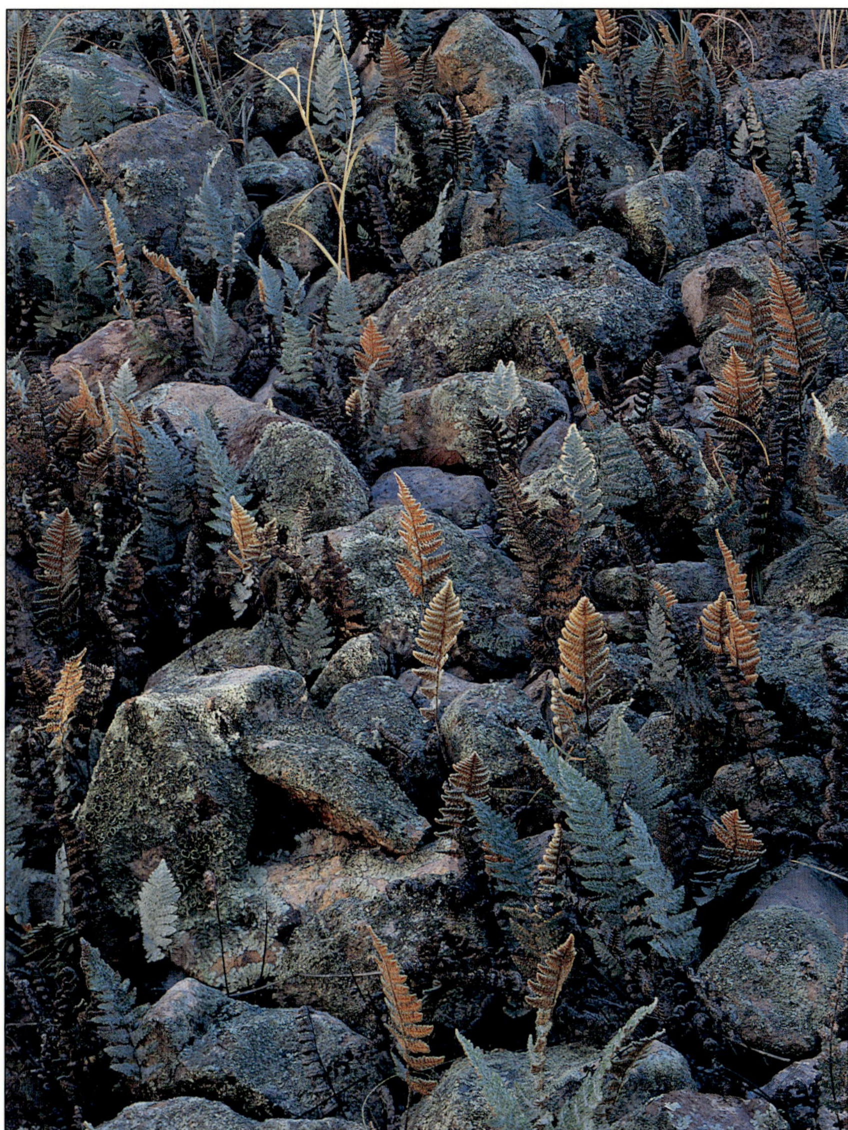

A gray, damp day in the Chiricahua Mountains rules out grand skyline vistas. But the soft, bluish light is ideal for letting the eye explore the detail of Nature's arrangement of ferns, lichens, and rocks.
EDWARD McCAIN

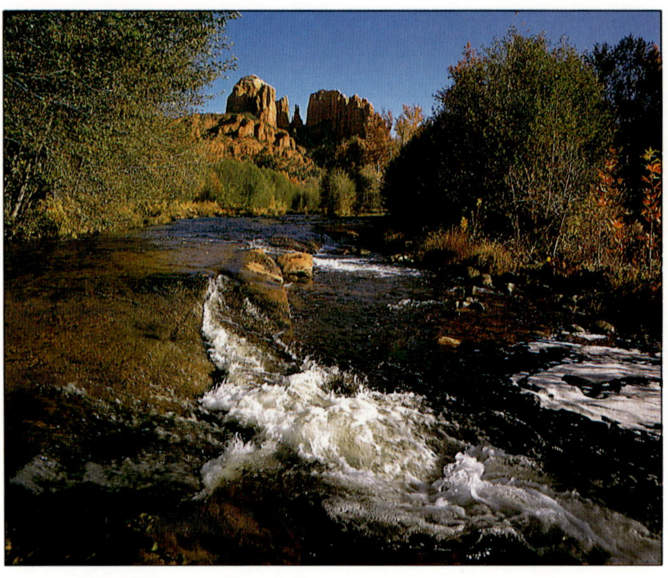

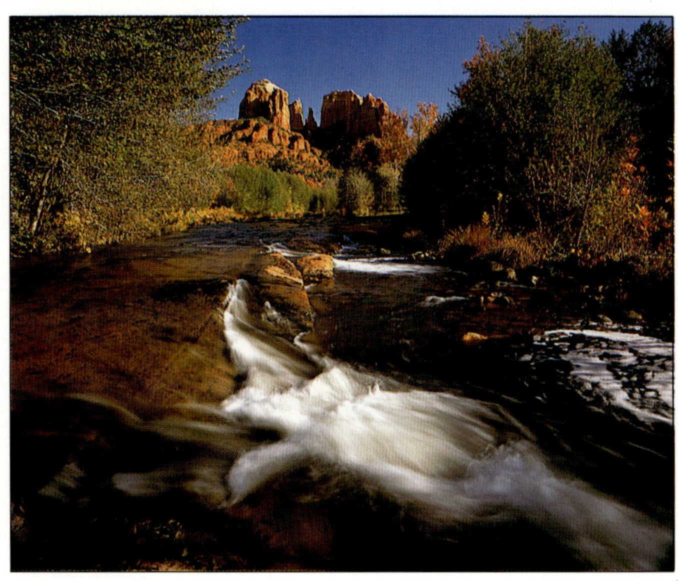

(ABOVE) *At a shutter speed of 1/125, the water's motion in Oak Creek appears hard, almost frozen in the frame.* **(RIGHT)** *At 1/2 second, the moving water appears smooth and milky. It is up to the photographer as an artist to decide which is best. A shutter speed of 1/2 to 1/15 probably would be the speeds of choice for this appearance.* BOTH BY JERRY JACKA

intimate landscape: a natural grotto of several rooms, formed by a series of eroded apertures that look almost like Gothic arches. A wedge of soft light is filtering in from a natural skylight, painting a small section of the grotto's floor. The picture has a distinctly medieval mood, like a twisting, shadowy alley in an ancient Tuscan village. It's the overcast sky that lends it this vaguely spooky character; a bright sun would have burned away all the implication of mystery.

"If we had a bright sun, this would probably be an unmanageable picture," McCain adds. There would be more than five f/stops' difference between the sunlight and deep shadow in the frame, and with color slide film, the darker areas would go completely black.

Composing intimate landscapes takes more care than grand vistas because the details are so prominent. First, look carefully for visual distractions and do a little of what Cave Creek photographer Jerry Sieve calls "photogardening" — erasing footprints, tire tracks, and certainly removing any broken glass or cigarette butts ("the detritus of *Homo disgustus*," as Sieve puts it). Landscape photographers are fiercely protective custodians of nature, and they will not remove or damage a living plant to improve the composition of a photograph.

Intimate landscapes often show little or no sky. If it's overcast or bleached by the midday sun, no sky is preferable — it will read as a pale white blotch in the picture, drawing the eye away from the important elements. If some sky seems good to have, remember that the center of interest — a glistening boulder, a cascade of water, a clump of flowers — is more important than the issue of where to place the horizon. Depth of field is also critical. In an intimate landscape the foreground is likely to be quite close to the lens, so you will want a slow shutter and small aperture. (However, try to avoid using the smallest aperture available, usually f/22 or f/32, because even the highest-quality lenses lose sharpness at their extremes.)

If there's moving water in the picture, the balancing of aperture against speed becomes a little more involved. You may want to show movement in the water, but not so much that it turns shapeless and white, like pouring milk. An exposure at 1/250 will freeze fast-moving water, while 1/15 or more turns it completely to velvety fuzz. In most cases, exposures from 1/15 to 1/2 second will preserve the best sparkle and shape while suggesting motion in running or falling water. So, bracket. If the water is backlit, you may *want* to freeze it, to capture the sparkle and show droplets splashing in the air. To capture pond ripples you will need a shutter speed of 1/60 or faster. Again, bracket.

An intimate landscape is easily spoiled by trying to draw too much into it. Be wary of bright, distracting things, like sun-splashed autumn leaves, that are away from the center of interest — unless the eye is naturally drawn toward them by the flow of the composition. When in doubt, edit, clean up, pare away. Keep it simple and clean. In the intimate landscape, less is more.

RUINS, THE CANYON, & MONUMENT VALLEY

These three Arizona landscapes present special opportunities and problems, so they're worth a few paragraphs' further contemplation.

Arizona's Sinagua and Anasazi ruins, dating mostly from A.D. 1050 to 1300, can seem difficult to photograph at first because they are invariably built of the same stuff — sandstone, generally — as their surroundings. They are the same color and texture as their immediate environment, and they blend into the landscape so perfectly that it is sometimes hard to tell where nature ends and architecture begins.

The first key to success is light. Soft, indirect light, perhaps on a slightly overcast day, will reveal subtle differences between the texture of the masonry walls and surrounding cliff faces. The second is to take the time, before setting up the camera, to understand the relationship of the building to its site. There is a natural inclination to shoot the ruin close up (or with a telephoto lens) to reveal as much structural detail as possible, but this may not tell the most effective story. Many Anasazi and Sinagua ruins huddle, tiny and timorous, in coves at the bases of towering canyon walls. Many successful pictures exploit this relationship, illustrating the vulnerability of prehistoric humans in a beautiful but unforgiving land. In Arizona, photographing

White House Ruin at Canyon de Chelly National Monument seems fragile and lonely when an expanse of the vast canyon wall is included in the composition. The encroaching shadows enhance the drama of the scene.
DAVID MUENCH

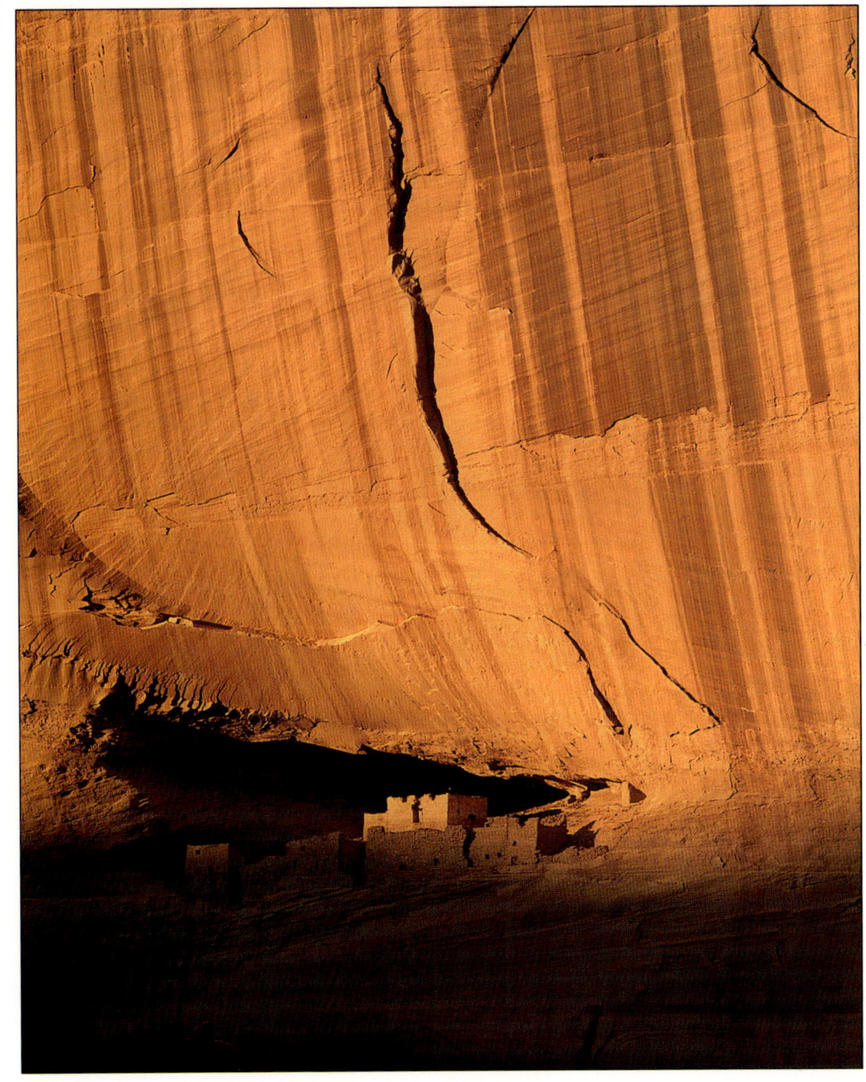

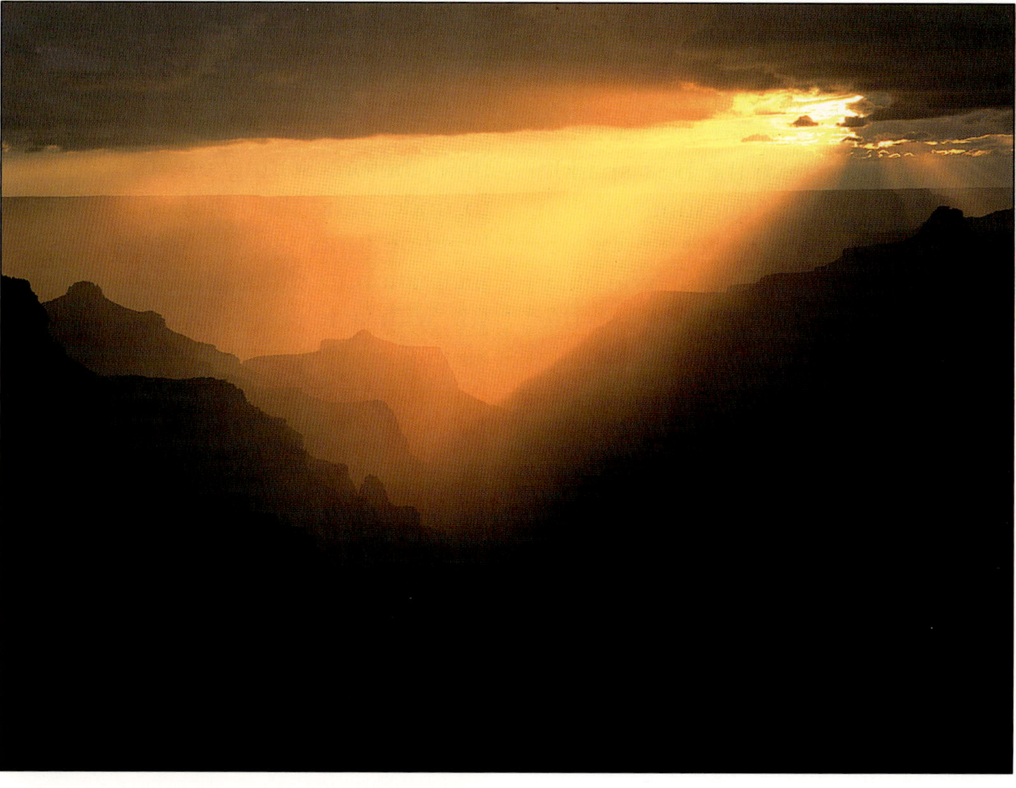

(RIGHT) *A "bad day" at the Grand Canyon turns to gold as the setting sun lights up a passing rainstorm and the ridges below Cape Royal. Overlapping planes of color help define the immense space and distance within the canyon.* JACK DYKINGA

(BELOW) *With a partial overcast and a rising sun at Maricopa Point, the canyon exhibits three tonal characters in one picture. Compare the lighting in the foreground, middle distance, and the opposite canyon wall. The low-hanging cloud emphasizes the spatial dimensions of the shot.* KATHLEEN NORRIS COOK

ruins is more landscape than architectural photography.

The Grand Canyon is not necessarily difficult to photograph, but it is intimidating. Even the most accomplished professionals, including Dykinga, admit sometimes feeling overwhelmed by it.

Once again, advises Dykinga, the first step is to get to know the place. "I'd been there 20 or 30 times and still didn't feel I knew it," he admits. "Finally, I blew an entire day of flat-light time driving to every overlook on the South Rim, from Desert View to Hermit's Rest, and walking a hundred yards in each direction. This got some of my composition problems out of the way, and the rest was up to nature."

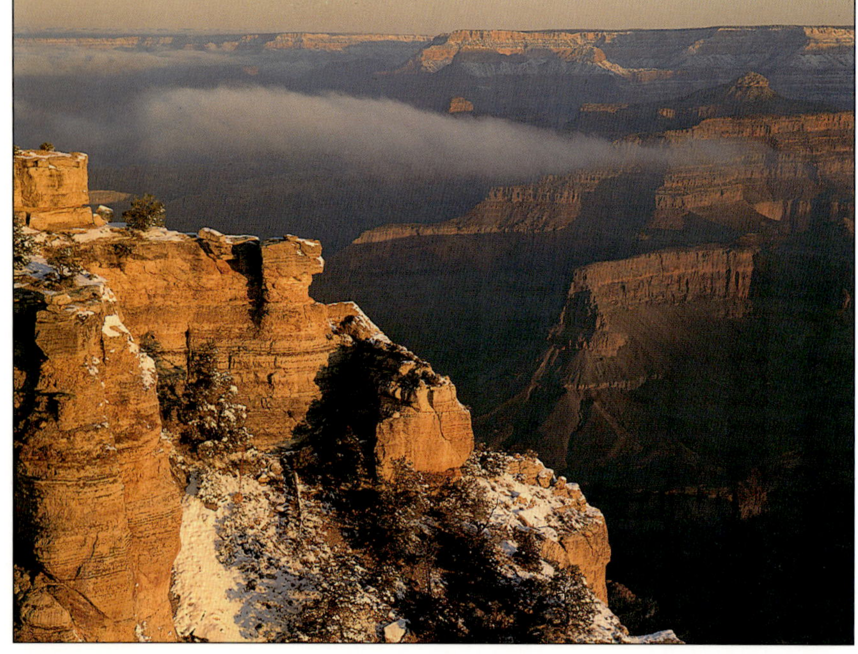

And nature — meaning weather — is the key. Photographer Michael Collier once heard a canyon visitor comment, "I'm so glad the IMAX theater is here, because now there's something to do on a bad day." Photographers pray for bad days in the canyon. They produce spires poking out of low-hanging clouds, new colors appearing as if by magic in the canyon walls, rainbows, snow, and more. In any kind of weather, one productive strategy is to put away the wide-angle lens and concentrate on foreground details, such as wildflowers, while the great chasm yawns in the background. Remember: keep everything sharp.

Collier, a master of aerial photography, advises that shooting the canyon is possible for the amateur on a commercial air tour, but there are a few caveats. You should book a flight in a high-wing plane and sit where struts won't interfere with sight lines into the canyon. ("It doesn't matter how wonderful the canyon looks, if the photo has airplane parts in it, it's no good.") Take the first or last flight of the day; flat light over the canyon is even worse than flat light *in* the canyon. Use high shutter speeds to eliminate shake from the plane's vibration. And finally, watch the horizon line — a skewed horizon, says Collier, is no more welcome than airplane parts.

Even more than the Grand Canyon, Monument Valley challenges the photographer to come up with fresh images. And this place is a good teacher of the photographic art. It's so demanding that when you fail, you fail miserably. When you succeed, it's spectacular. Both are useful.

Sunrise and sunset are times not to miss in the valley, even when it means lumbering out of bed at 5 A.M. on a frosty April morning. The colors of the buttes and spires are both fantastic and unpredictable — they may go from amber to crimson to rust in a span of five minutes. In any light, be aware of patterns in the landscape other than the obvious. Leading a Friends of *Arizona Highways* photo tour on a day of indolently flat light, the observant Gary Ladd managed a delightful shot of a wind-rippled expanse of sand in the lee of Left Mitten Butte. The patterned sand filled three-fourths of the frame. Other photographers on the same tour cleverly framed the monuments in the crooks of the valley's wind-twisted juniper trees, editing out much of the boring sky.

One morning on that tour, Ladd took the participants to a ridge for sunrise shots. The best picture seemed obvious, so the two dozen enthusiasts erected their tripods in a virtual line along the ridge, aiming their cameras toward the famous monoliths, silhouetted in an amber sky. After a few moments, Ladd interrupted to explain the "180-Degree Rule" of photography: Periodically, turn around 180 degrees to see what's happening behind you.

The "180 Degree Rule" led to this intriguing photograph. On a Friends of Arizona Highways *photo tour to Monument Valley, photographer Gary Ladd turned away from the sunrise everyone else was shooting and photographed the reflection of the group in the windows of the bus.*
GARY LADD

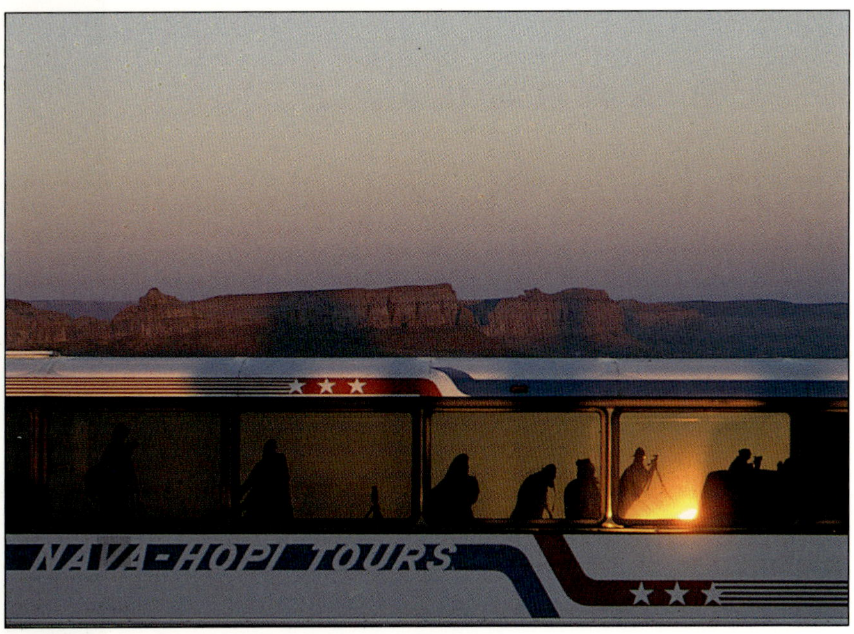

The participants did, and saw a ghostly image of themselves, huddled over tripods, reflected with the rising sun in the windows of the bus that had brought them to the ridge. Ladd's photo made *Arizona Highways.*

Ladd's excellent admonition to the photo tour participants: "One of the hazards of situations like this is that you'll come out here with a good idea of what you want to do, and stick with it." ■

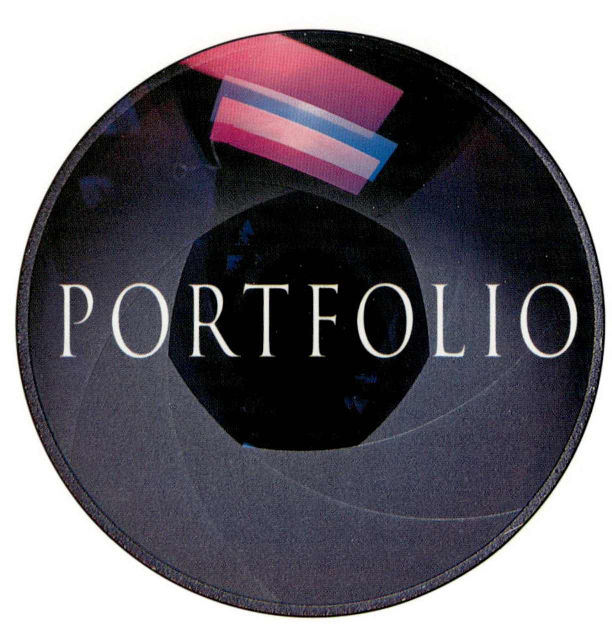

LANDSCAPE

A landscape photographer is a hunter, and his prime quarry is the unusual, the unfamiliar, the unexpected. Sometimes a quirk of weather provides a fresh revelation on a commonplace landscape. At other times a natural occurrence, such as a fallen tree, offers a design element that can give direction or intrigue to a landscape photograph. Human figures and familiar manmade objects, such as ancient ruins or even an abandoned pickup or broken-down fence, sometimes can add scale or a compelling photojournalistic story line to a landscape. ■

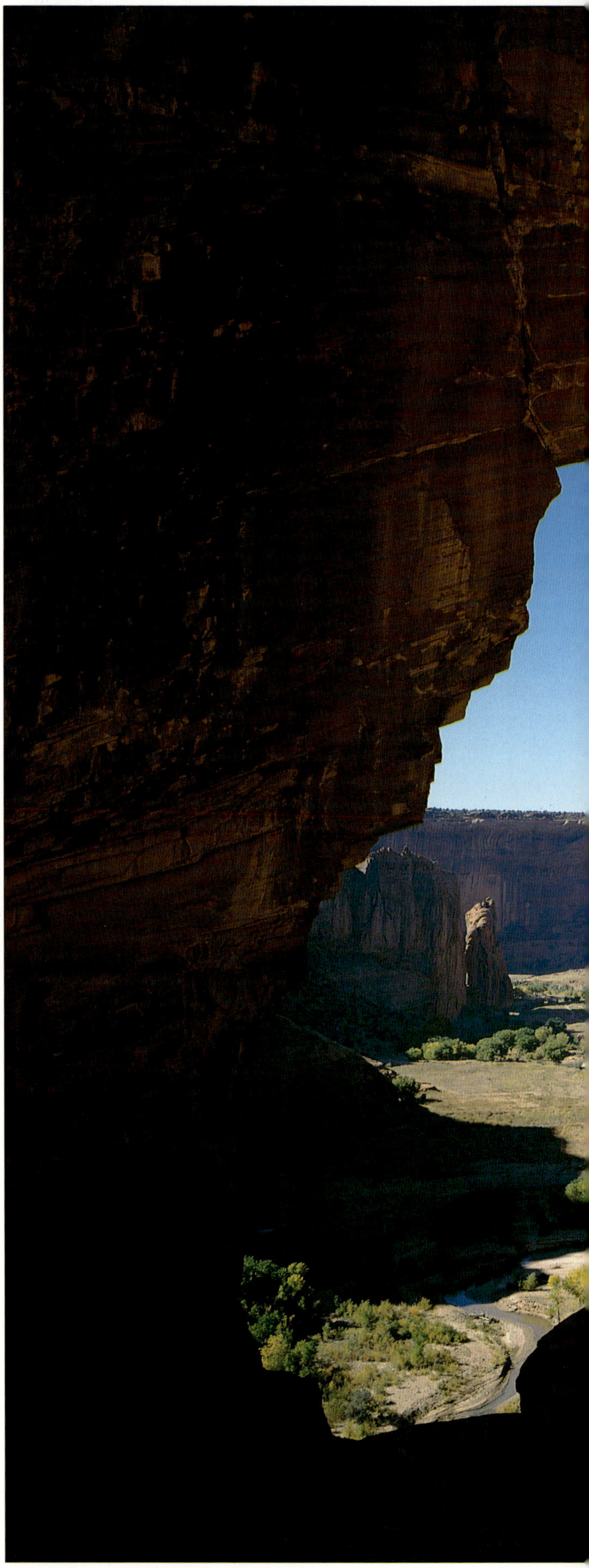

"The Window" in Canyon de Chelly is a difficult shot in lighting conditions of deep shadows and bright highlights. Advice from the photographer: walk through the arch and take a light reading off the canyon floor. Then step back and meter the relatively dark arch at close range. Shoot a frame at each of those exposures, then take a third shot halfway between. JERRY JACKA

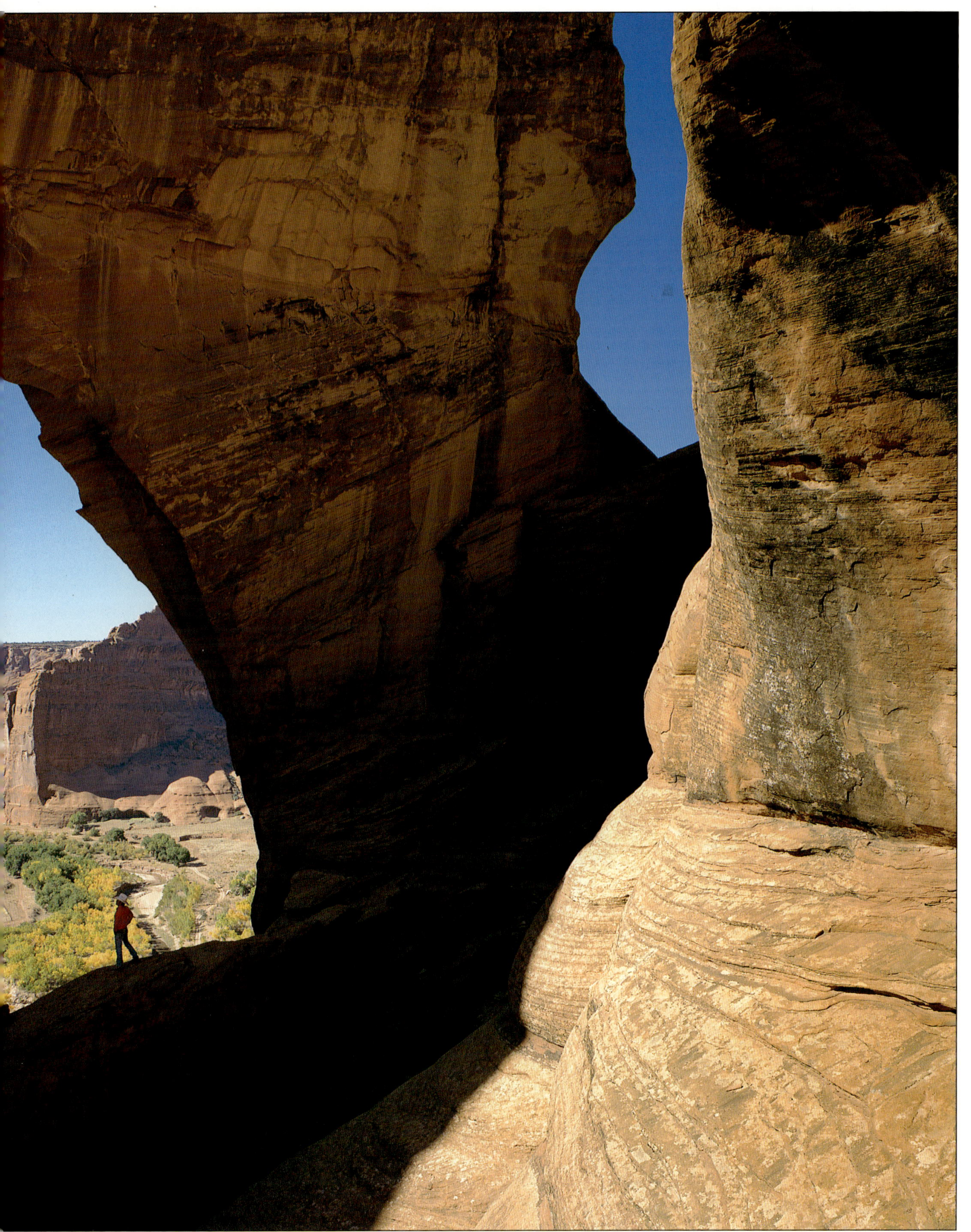

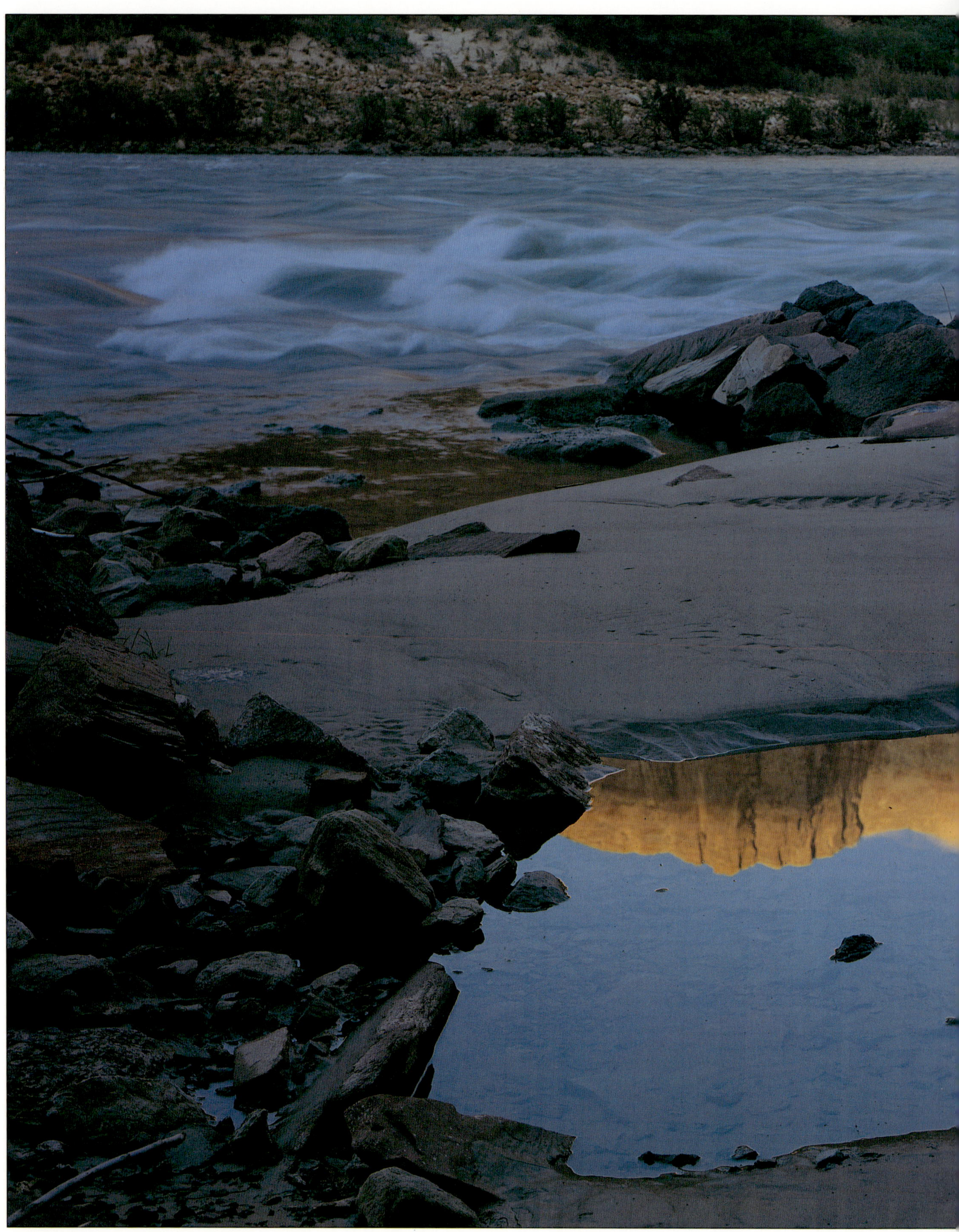

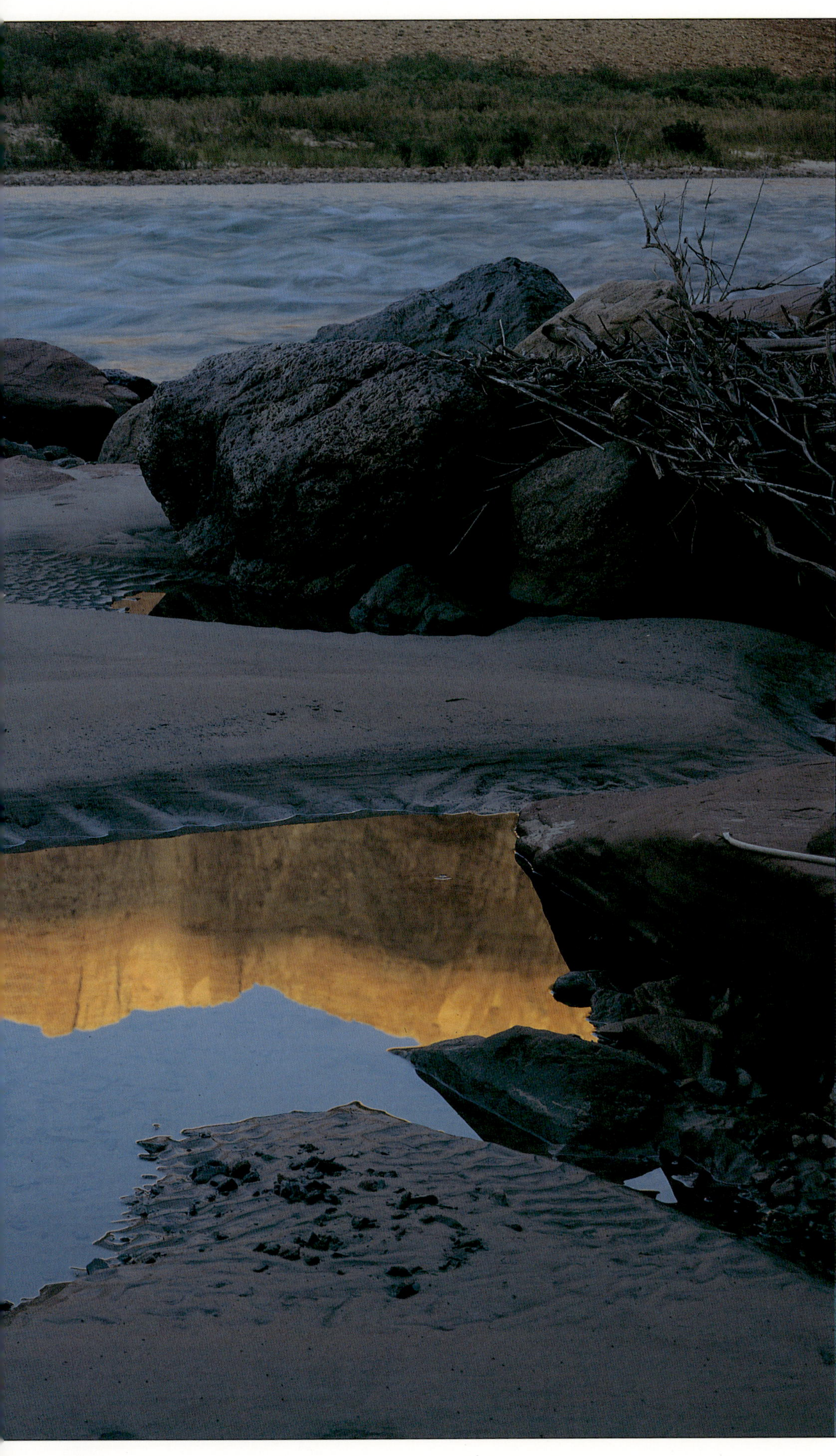

A fresh and colorful image from the floor of the Grand Canyon: Desert Palisades illuminated in the sunset and reflected in a pool, with the cool blue Colorado River surging past in the background. Note the use of the Rule of Thirds: the brightest area of reflection from the cliffs lies on an imaginary line through the bottom third of the frame.
GARY LADD

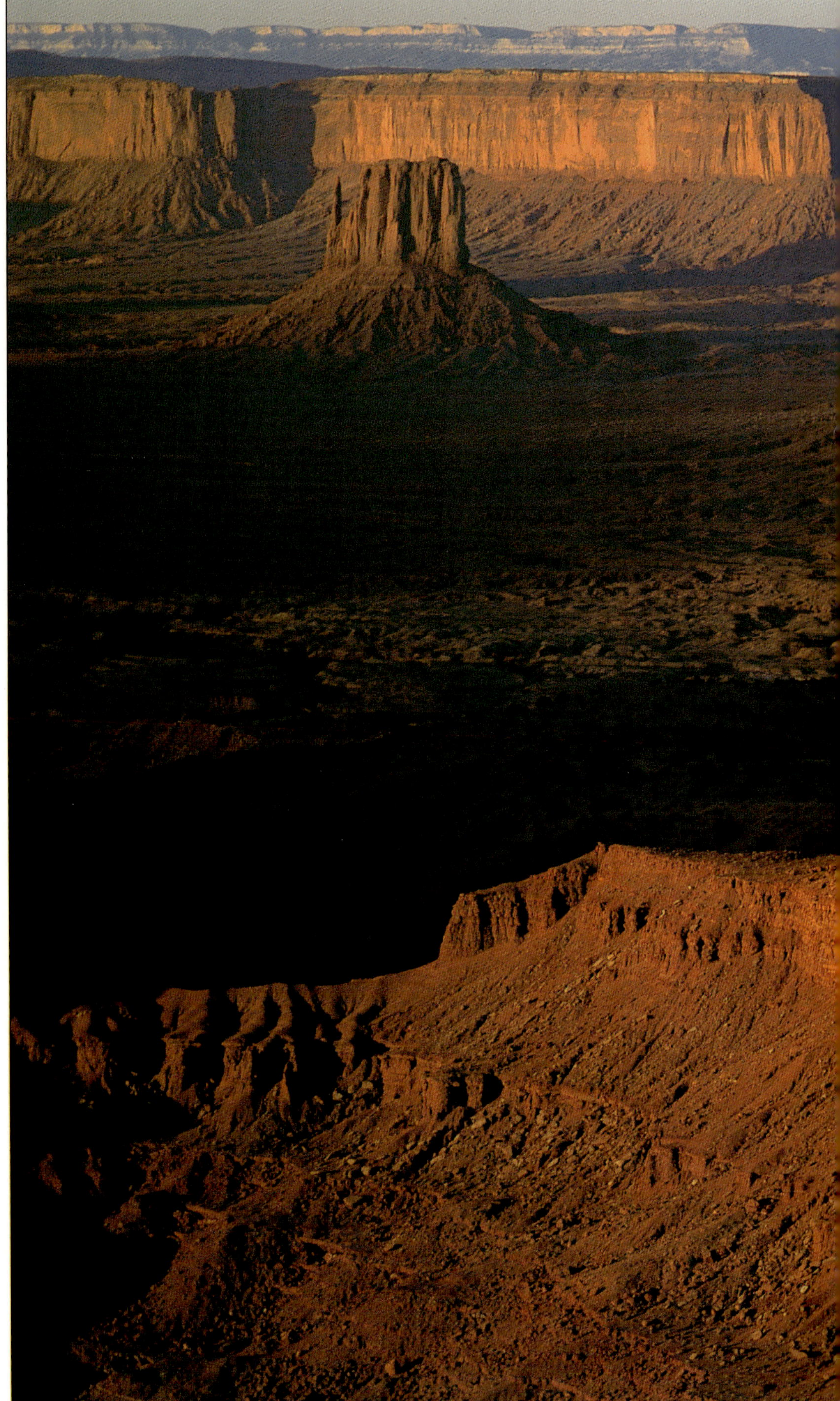

Aerial photography, like earthbound landscape photography, is almost always enhanced by early or late sun, which favors the Arizona landscape with soft and gold-to-red-tinted lighting. The long shadows in this aerial photo of Monument Valley also enhance the picture, providing contrast and suggesting great distances between the monuments.
MICHAEL COLLIER

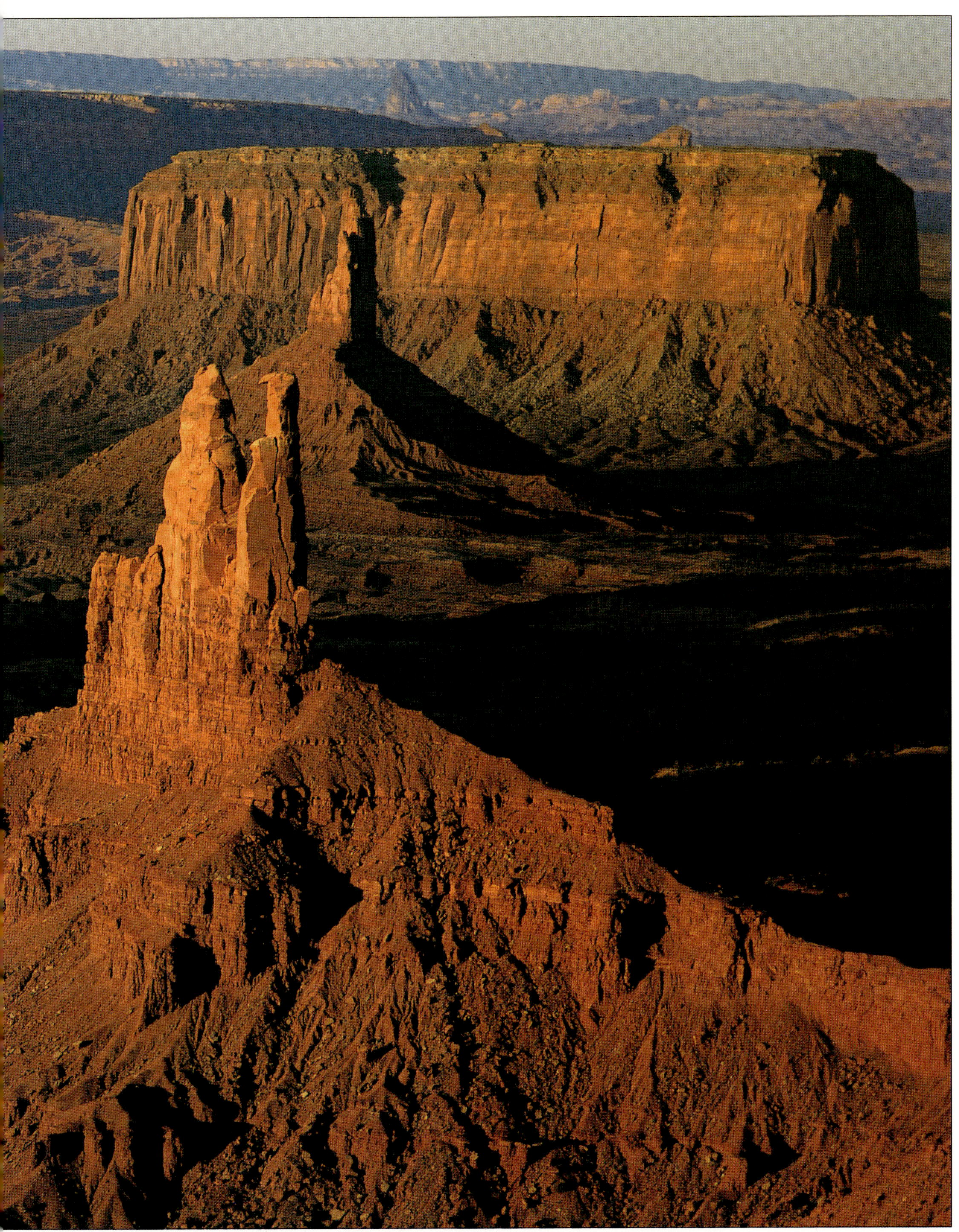

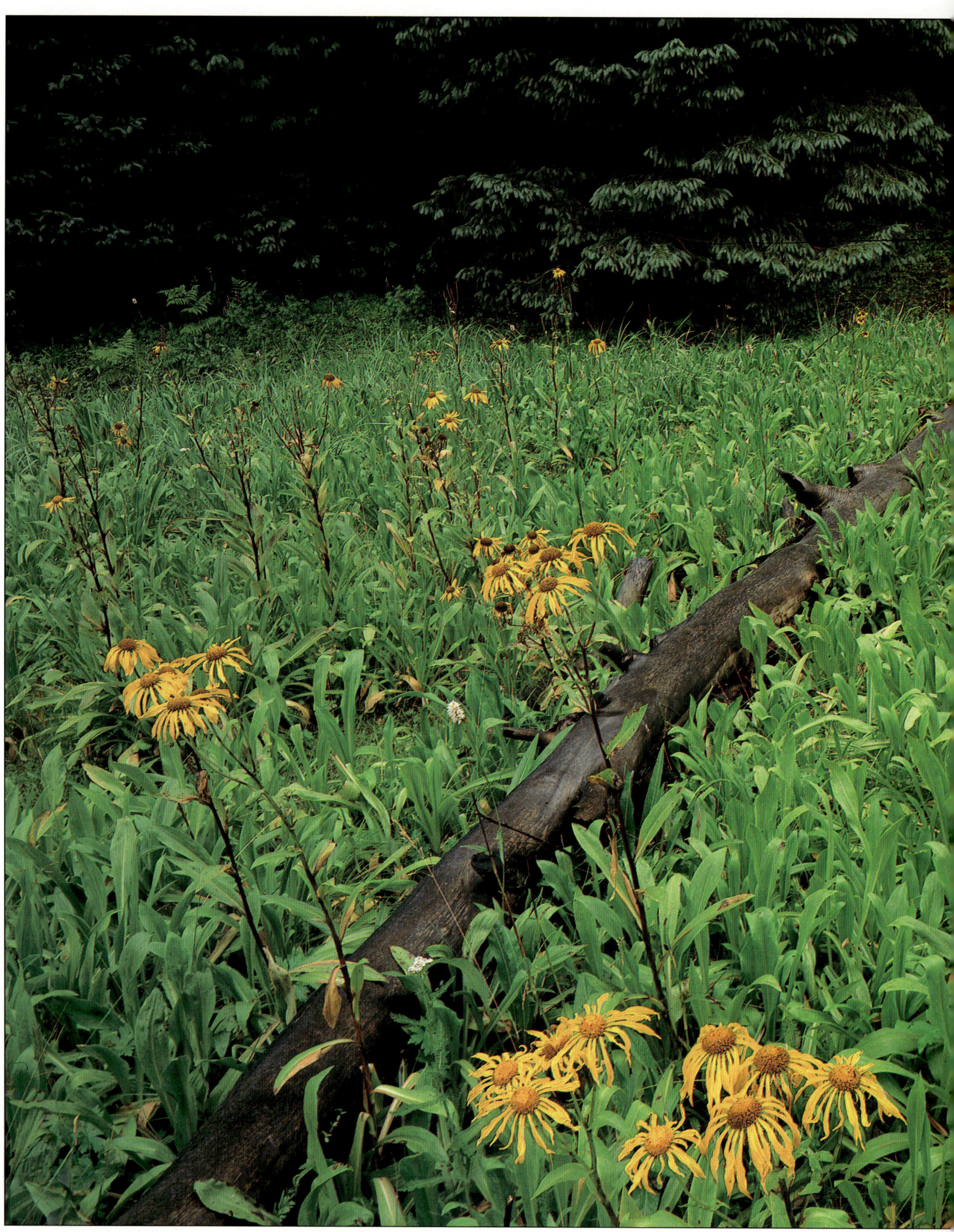

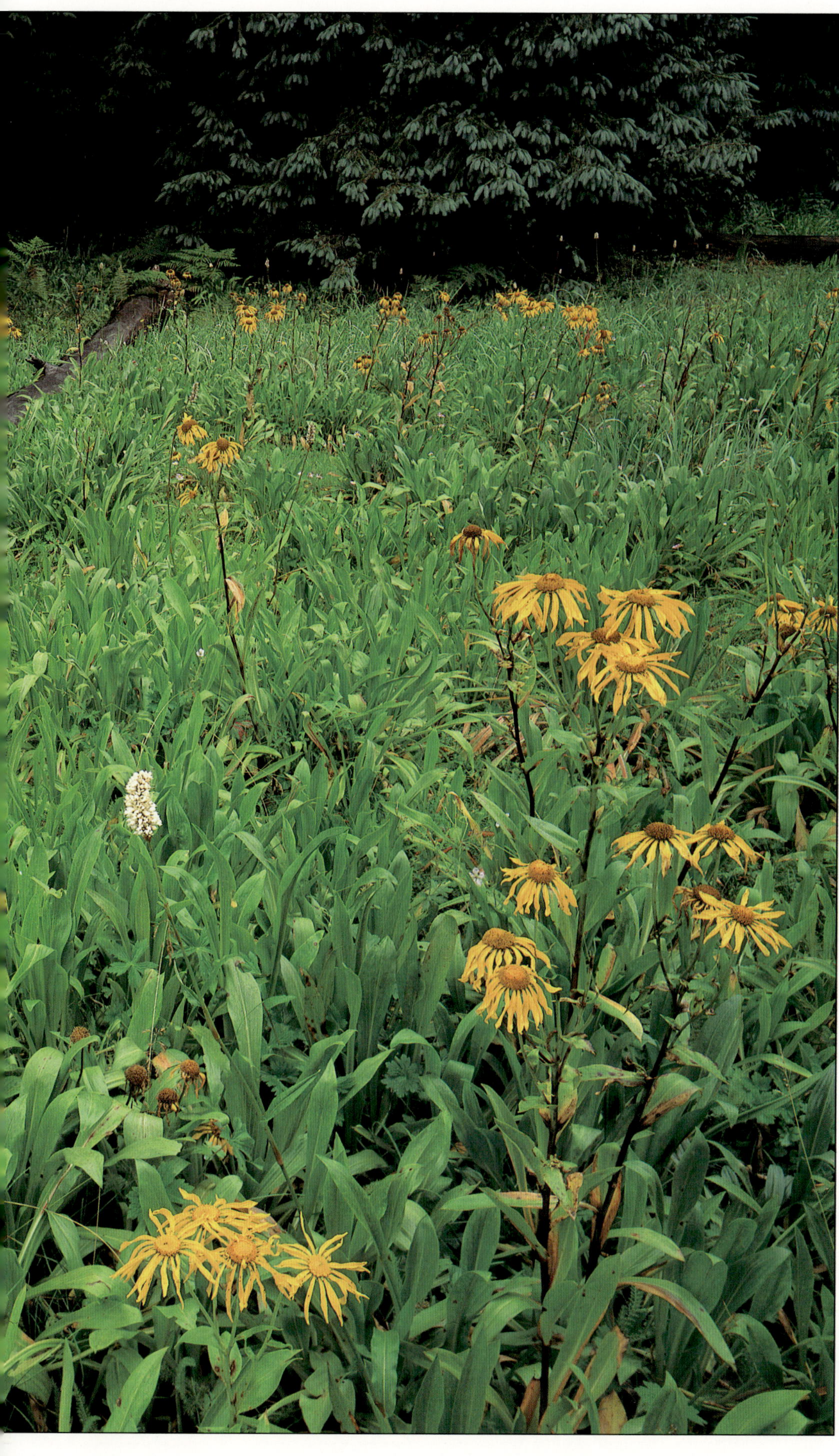

Soft daylight envelops this field of sunflowers near Hannagan Meadow. The fallen log stretching diagonally through the frame is a critical design element, leading the eye from foreground to forest's edge and giving the picture some dynamic thrust. Cover the log with your hand and notice how the composition becomes rather ordinary— a merely pretty picture, nothing more.
EDWARD McCAIN

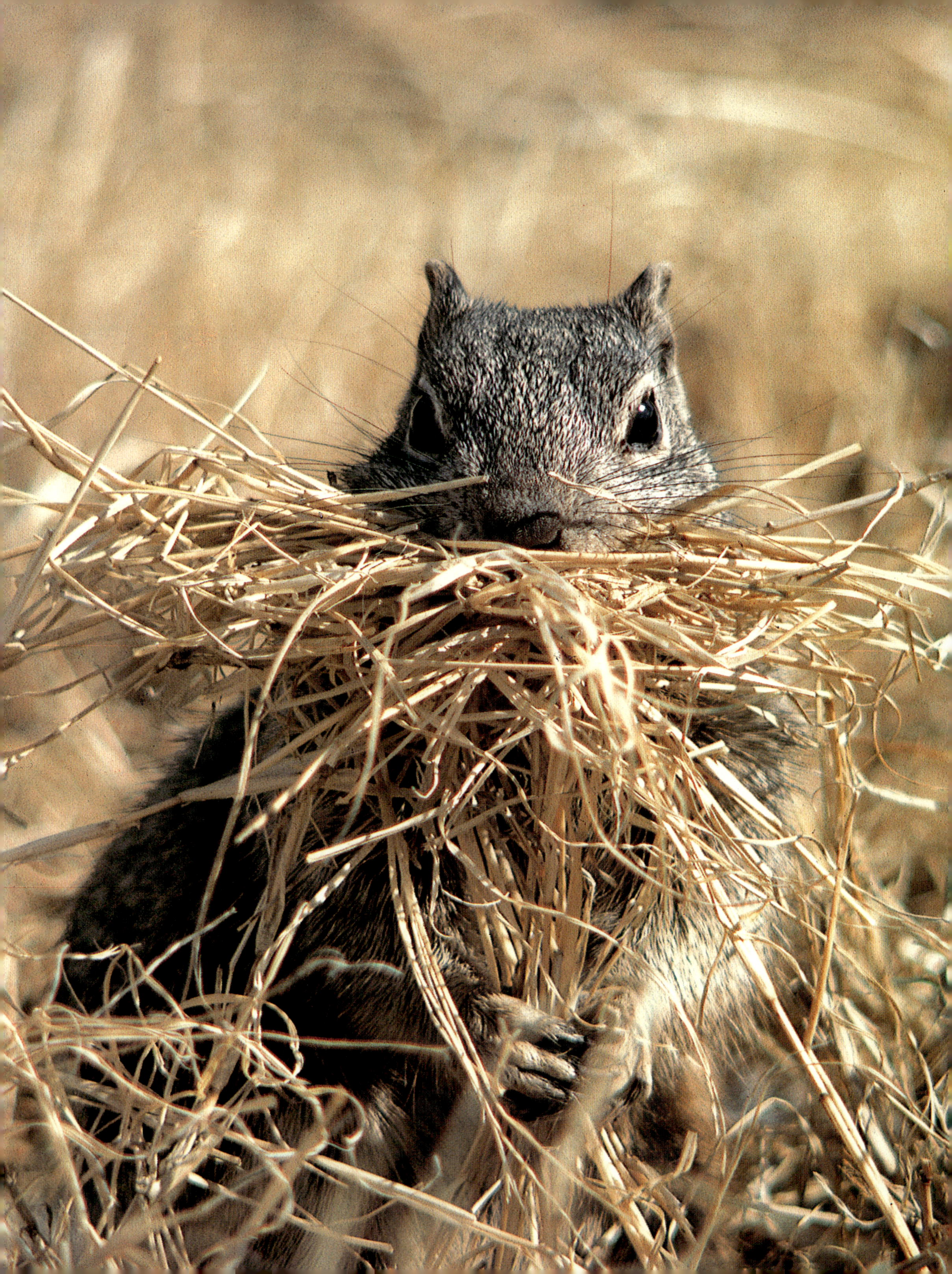

Chapter 4

NATURE

In perfect synchronization, the four elk grazing at the forest's edge snap their heads upright and stare, saucer-eyed, at the two strange predators rolling to a stop in the Honda. The elk's fur, backlit for a moment by an afternoon sun dodging a patchwork of rain clouds, looks like silvery fuzz. Their expressions, in our anthropomorphic delusions, seem divided between alarm and intrigue. If they will stay put for just a few more seconds this will make a wonderful photo.

I kill the engine. In a full day of photographic elk hunting in Apache-Sitgreaves National Forest, this is the closest that photographer Edward McCain and I have approached any of these wary beasts. McCain slowly lowers the passenger window, braces his 400mm lens on the sill, composes the picture and fires a motor-drive burst. The noise shoots across the quiet meadow and startles the elk. They look at each other, voting. Consensus: That didn't sound like a gun, but humans are bad news in general. Let's split, guys. In perfect synch, again, the animals switch ends, moon us with their great white rumps, and bound into the woods.

In Arizona, hunting with a camera yields extraordinary prey. The state's climatic and topographical diversity means that it also harbors amazing zoological diversity, from black bear and elk in the ponderosa woodlands to javelina and Gila monster in the low deserts. Insects are abundant and outrageously colorful; while hiking in the Chiricahua Mountains on another occasion McCain photographed a study of color harmonics in an orange-and-black cicada clinging to a slender stalk of pale yellow bear grass.

James Tallon, as versatile a photographer as is to be found in Arizona, says that wildlife "is the most fun to

(LEFT) *A common rock squirrel becomes an uncommon portrait when photographed from a squirrel's eye view.*
JAMES TALLON

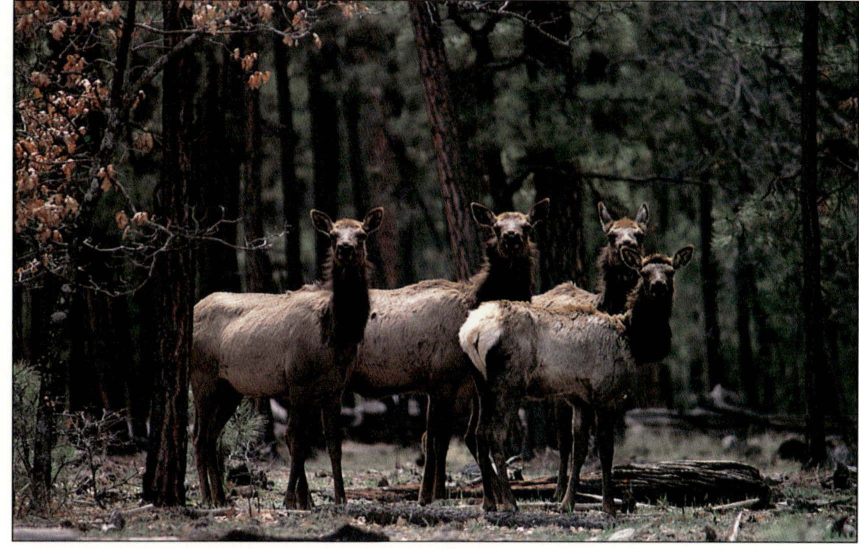

(ABOVE) *A quartet of elk near Hannagan Meadow pauses for a moment before bolting. Being more decisive than the elk, the photographer gets the picture.*
EDWARD McCAIN

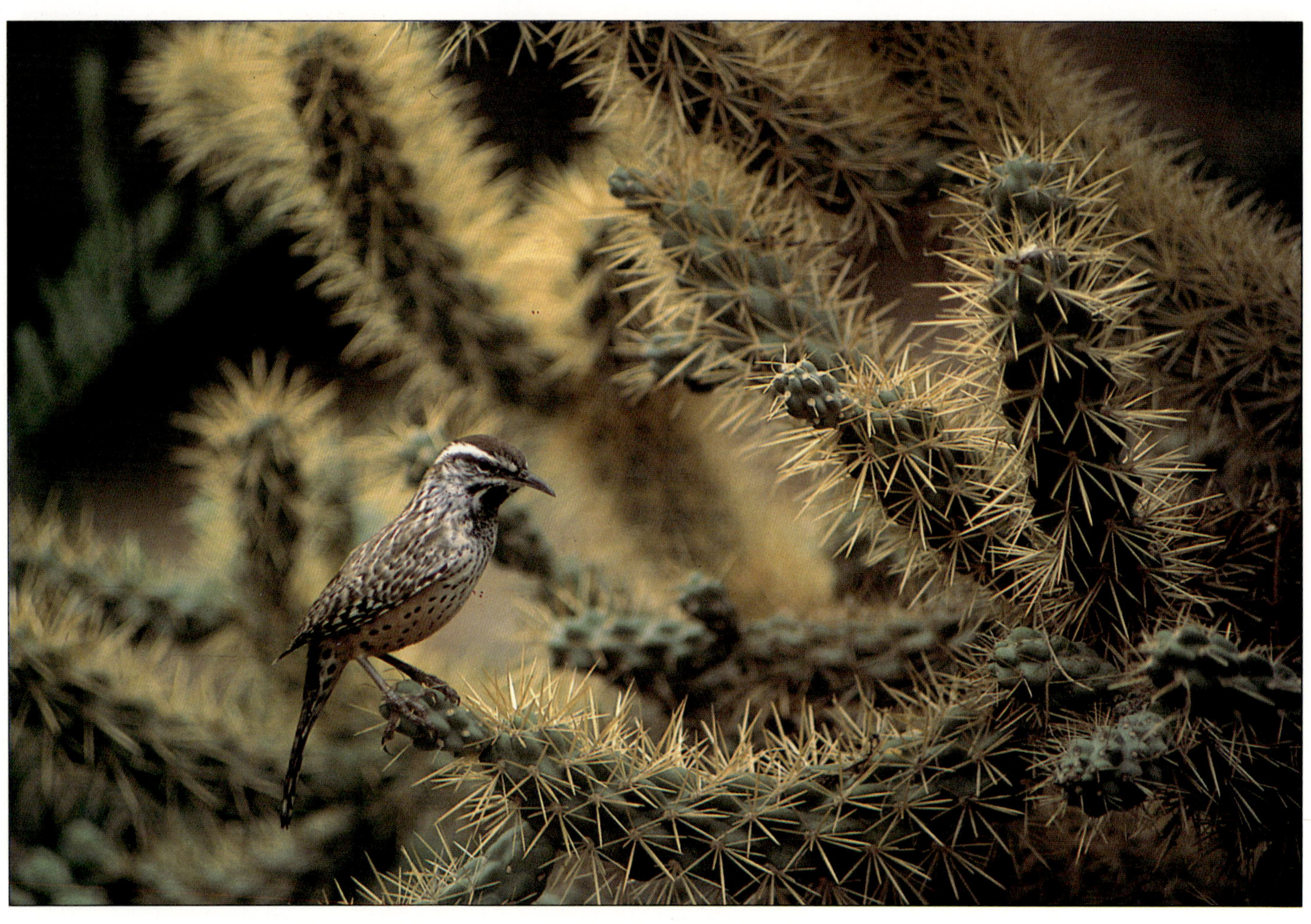

The limited depth of field of a long lens isolates a cactus wren in sharp focus from the out-of-focus cholla forest in the background.
JAMES TALLON

photograph of anything." Tallon also believes it is easy. And it is — but only after quite a few basics are absorbed.

The first problem in photographing animals is, of course, finding them. Begin by collecting field guides, which give locations where each species is most common. (The guides also help you identify what you've photographed.) In the deserts, avoid the midday heat; most animals do likewise. In the mountains, picnic areas (on quiet days) are often productive: Animals come to forage for scraps, and they may be somewhat accustomed to human presence and easier to approach. Some photographers summon wildlife with calls, available at outdoor or hunting supply stores. Tallon, a virtuoso on the wounded-rabbit call, has had coyotes all but run into him. Another technique is to use bait — seed for birds, sardines or tuna for skunks and raccoons, and nuts for squirrels.

Approaching some animals takes skill and deception. If the shot looks good from inside the car, take it — don't get out. If you're approaching on foot, hunch over as you walk (animals are less afraid of something that doesn't quite look like a biped), don't look it in the eye, and don't walk straight toward it. Move in a deceptive meander, gradually edging to where you want to be for the shot. Avoid rattling keys or camera equipment. Speaking of rattles and the snakes that are attached to them: There are a few Arizona animals that definitely should not be approached closely. With these, it is the biped's turn to be wary.

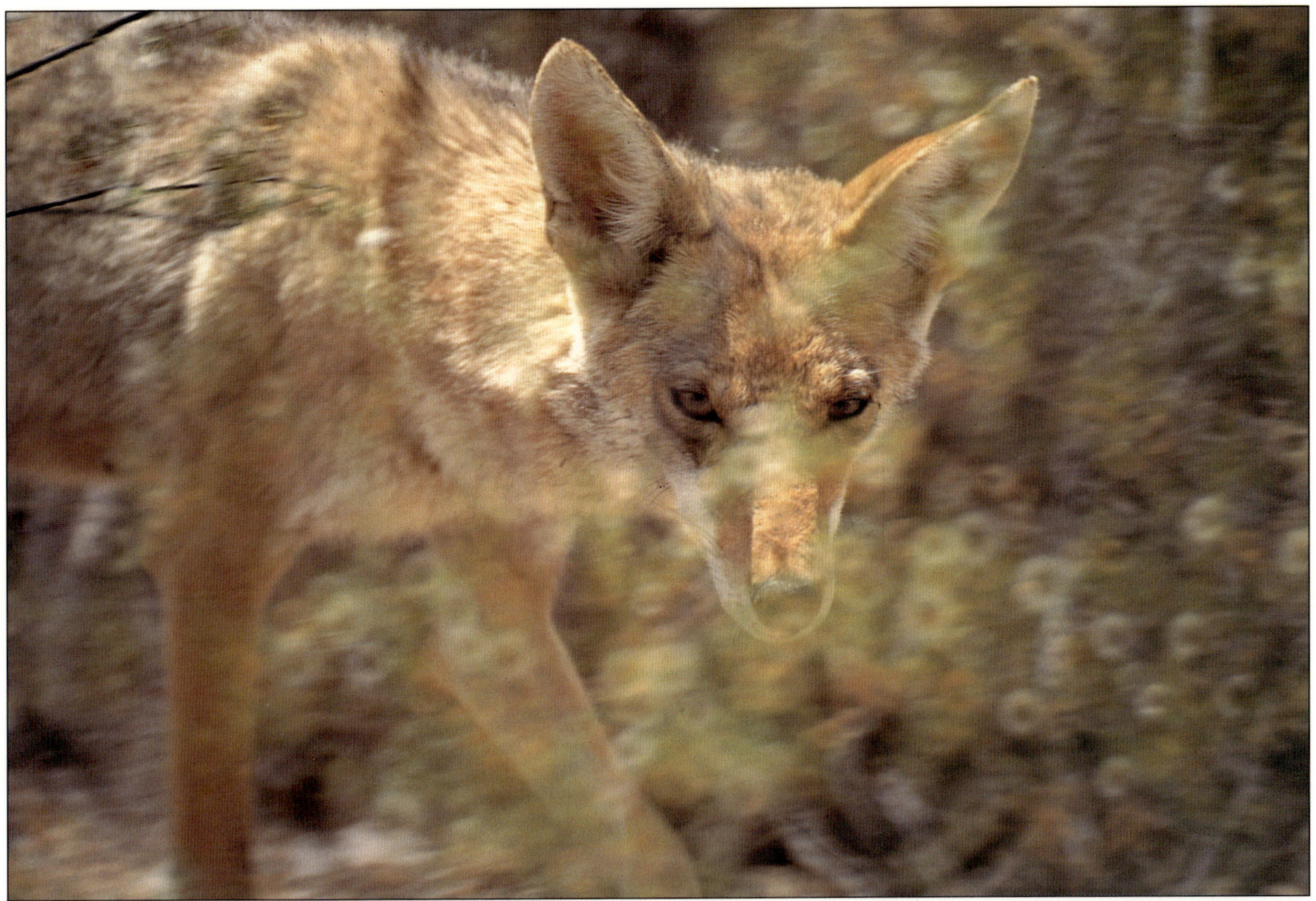

If shooting with a long lens (200mm or more), steadying the camera is the next challenge. A tripod may work in some situations, but the commotion of setting it up will usually spook the prey. A monopod is a good compromise; a careful photographer using one with a 200mm lens can usually get a sharp picture at as leisurely a shutter speed as 1/30. Practice helps. Lacking a monopod, use whatever natural braces are available — trees, boulders, etc. — for your body, lens or both. If you can shoot without glasses, that is an added advantage, because you can press the camera body against both your nose and forehead, providing an extra point of stabilizing contact. If you have a motor drive, fire off three or four continuous frames; the later ones will usually be sharper because your squeezing pressure on the shutter button has stabilized.

Why not solve the camera-shake problem with ISO 400 film and shutter speeds of 1/250 or faster? For the photographer who's satisfied with small prints, this is indeed the perfect solution. But few photographic trophies look more impressive on the wall than a framed 16x20-inch print of a great blue heron in the wild, or of a butterfly 10 times life size, and for that you need relatively slow film. ISO 100 is probably the best all-around compromise for wildlife photography.

The next step is focusing the camera and composing the picture. The longer the lens, the shallower its depth of field, which means that it may be impossible to focus a com-

A variation from the opposite page, here the in-focus desert coyote is isolated from the out-of-focus foreground. The coyote's intent eyes and alert ears suggest he is on his way to dinner.
JAMES TALLON

plete animal from head to tail. This is one of the wildlife photographer's enduring curses. If a choice must be made, always focus on the eyes. This same limited depth of field, however, also is an advantage in helping isolate the animal in its environment. Surrounding cactus or trees in sharp focus are a distraction and may camouflage the subject. It's good, though, to compose the picture so that some of the animal's environment remains in the frame, however soft in focus it may be. If a coyote fills the whole frame, there is little color and no sense of place for it. Environmental portraits of animals, like people, nearly always seem to have more to say.

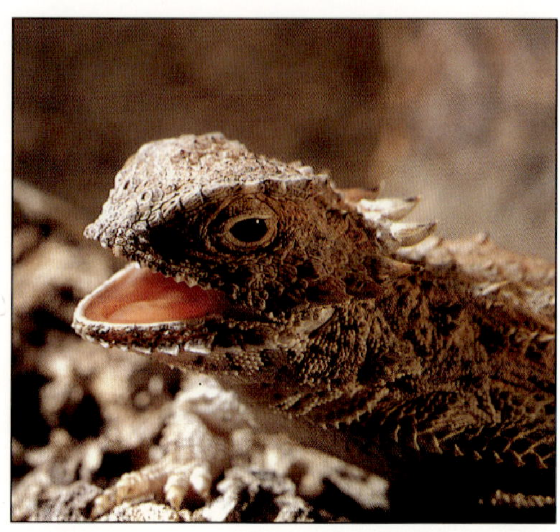

(TOP RIGHT) *The eyes are the focal point whether photographing a portrait of a person or an Arizona horned lizard. The patience to wait for the opened mouth pays off with a vibrant spot of color.*
ROBERT CAMPBELL

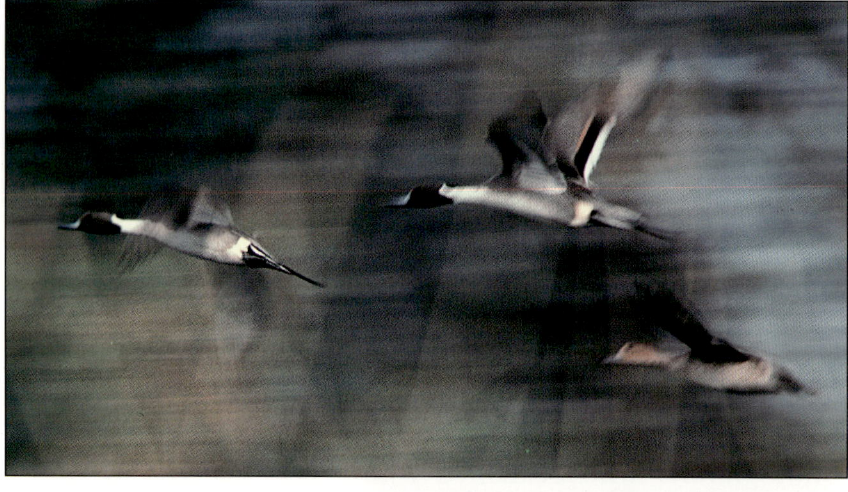

(ABOVE) *A trio of pintails are captured in flight. A relatively slow shutter speed blurs the wings and background as the camera pans to follow the birds.*
JAMES TALLON

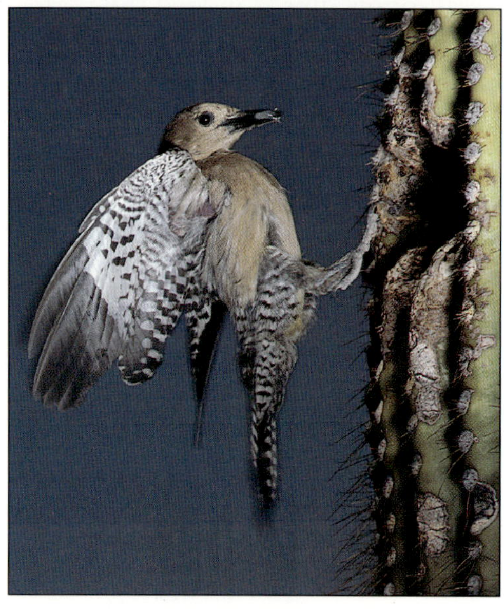

(RIGHT) *This Gila woodpecker was photographed at dusk with a slow shutter speed as a strobe stops the movement of every feather.*
ROBERT CAMPBELL

A telephoto lens, incidentally, makes it possible to photograph zoo animals through cage wires, as long as the wires are thin and no sunlight is striking them directly. Select a wide lens aperture, and the wires disappear. On hot days in the desert, however, this same helpful lens becomes a nuisance, picking up atmospheric distortion caused by rising heat waves. Count this as another reason to neglect hot-weather wildlife photography.

Miscellaneous tips from Arizona professionals to enhance your pictures of animals:

When shooting small creatures, such as ground squirrels or tarantulas, don't be reluctant to get prone and dirty. Almost all animals are more interesting when portrayed from their eye level; this is how the photographer enters their world. Speaking of eyes: Wildlife photographer Robert Campbell of Tucson often uses a flash, even in bright daylight. "The animal tends to look dead unless there's a little brightness in the eyes, either from a flash or reflected sunlight," he says. In his experience, the flash doesn't spook his subjects; they're accustomed to seeing flashes of light from other sources, such as headlights. Campbell also likes photographing action in the animal world: feeding, nursing, flying, chasing, fighting. He points out that some animals that have rather amorphous shapes and dull colors, such as javelina, are pictured most effectively if caught with some sort of facial expression, like yawning or snarling. These are not commonplace wildlife photos, but they are worth waiting for.

When shooting any animal, patience is your best companion. For example, the most visually spectacular wildlife in the Santa Catalina Mountains north of Tucson are bighorn sheep. The rams, with their outrageous arcs of horns, like to stand on rocky outcrops, boldly silhouetted against the sky, surveying their landscape like woolly barons. Yet they are only rarely photographed, or even seen. Bighorns are sharp of eye and extremely wary. Successful bighorn spotters report that you have to be willing to sit quietly in a secluded spot for hours and endure some disappointment in exchange for a chance at one of Arizona's most spectacular living creatures.

Finally, a word about ethics. Professional wildlife photographers are invariably protective of nature, and they do their best to avoid disturbing or altering the behavior or habitat of what they photograph. All of us should do likewise: Never, for example, approach a bird's nest for a close-up that might frighten the mother away. Unfortunately, most photography of living creatures, animal or human, is intrusive. (The elk who were spooked back into the forest by the whir of a motor drive, for example.) The trade-off may be that the more excellent wildlife photography we have, the more we *Homo sapiens* may come to respect our companions. ■

PHOTOGRAPHING ARIZONA FLORA

Desert claims two-thirds of Arizona. But our most prominent desert, the Sonoran, is the world's most lush, and all the state's arid lands exhibit fascinating, even bizarre, forms of plant life. Only in Arizona can one photograph several kinds of succulent desert forests — yucca forests in the Chihuahuan Desert, saguaro, cholla, and mesquite in the Sonoran, and Joshua tree in the Mohave. In the Great Basin Desert, which droops into the Navajo Reservation in northern Arizona, ancient, wind-twisted juniper trees provide some of the most elegantly tortured geometry found anywhere in nature. In the Sonoran Desert of central and southern Arizona, a winter of above-average rain will trigger a spring outbreak of wildflowers in every imaginable color. In the forested canyons and mountains of northern Arizona, every fall delivers a color-slide festival of gold, orange, and red aspen, sycamore, and maple leaves.

Morning is usually the best time to photograph plants and flowers: the light is soft and the air is calm. Here the rising sun backlights organ pipe and cholla cactus at Organ Pipe Cactus National Monument.
DAVID MUENCH

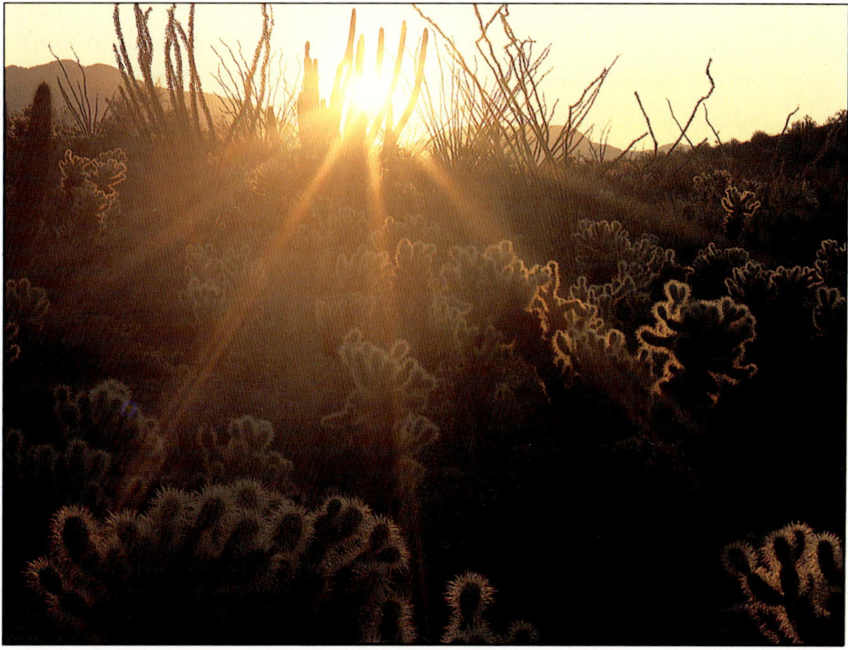

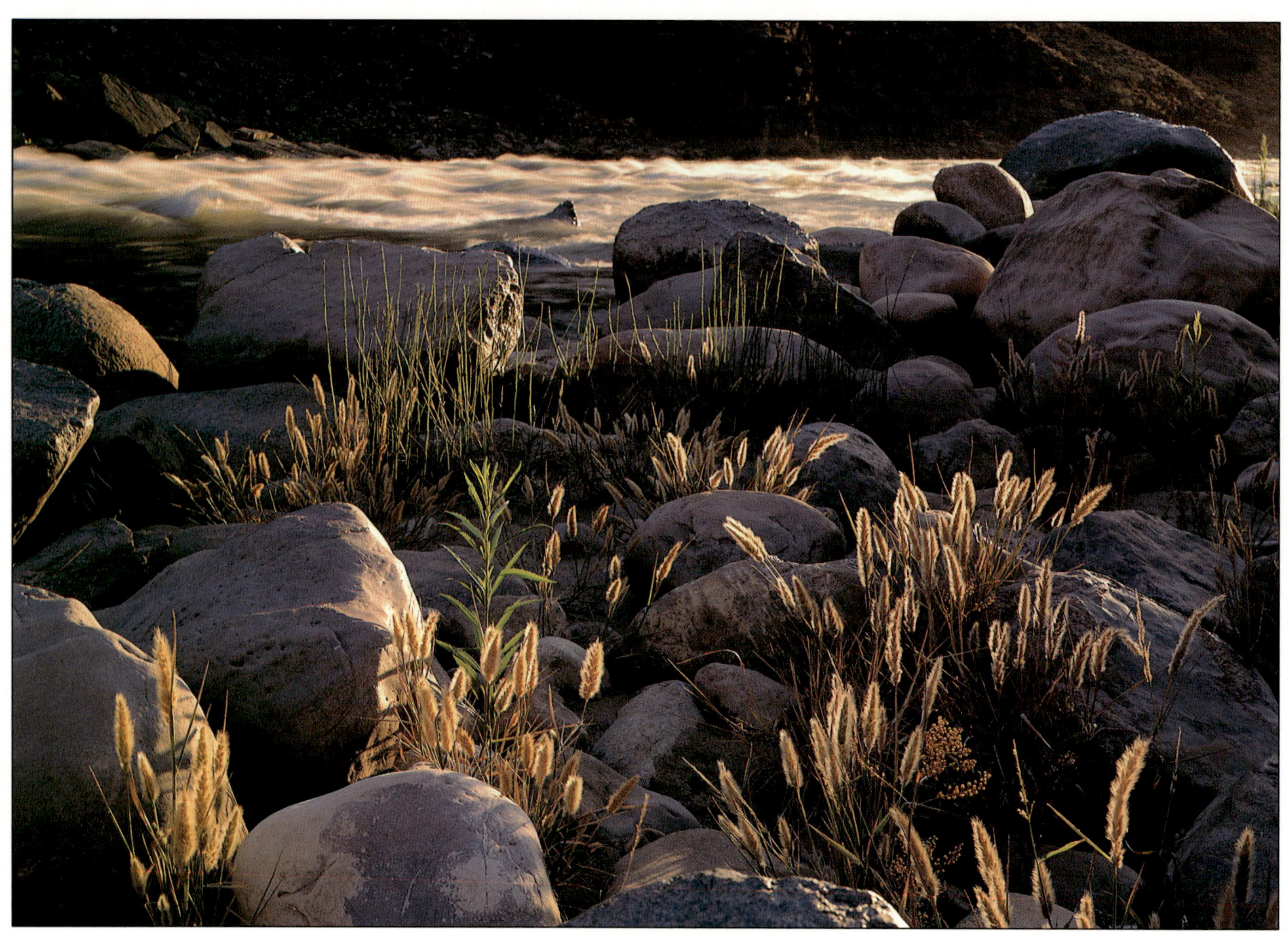

The evening air doesn't often allow delicate plants to stand still enough for long exposures, but these were sheltered — on the floor of the Grand Canyon. Strong side lighting illuminates ordinary grasses with a golden glow.
GARY LADD

The most important word to remember in photographing Arizona botanical life is: morning. *Early* morning, before the breeze begins to exercise stems, flowers, and branches into rumbas photographable only with a video camera. Morning also brings the possibility of glistening dew, which enhances all manner of plant pictures.

Two more words form a key to superb plant pictures: Think small. This may seem like odd advice in a land where saguaro cactus poke as high as 50 feet into the Sonoran Desert sky. But as nature photographer Gary Braasch wrote in his superb book *Photographing the Patterns of Nature*, "Small details are often what lead your eye and mind to an understanding of the big picture." Consider the barrel cactus, which in late summer erupts in a resplendent display of flame-like yellow and orange buds. A close-up of these buds, held in fiercely protective custody by the barrel's claw-like spines, may tell a better story about this cactus's character than would a portrait of the whole plant. It also provides the viewer of your photograph with a fresh and intriguing image, since the frame of reference — the cactus's body and surrounding desert — are removed. For photographing plants and flowers, a macro lens is essential.

A number of desert plants are wonderfully photogenic when backlit by a low sun; their filigree of thorns or spines will glow like a golden halo outlining the plant. If you want to avoid repeating the nearly inevitable backlit-saguaro shot, try prospecting for other backlit desert plants. In late summer, after the seasonal rains leave, an ocotillo's leaves will brown before falling off, but with an early sun shining from behind, they form patterns of glowing green and gold. In the winter, stands of dead wild grasses, a simple subject usually overlooked in the flat light of midday, can be utterly radiant a half hour after dawn. Don't overlook the expressive power of monochromaticism. Those dead grasses may be entirely beige or buff-colored, but with low backlighting they may glow as if with an inner golden light. At such a moment there may be no need to draw in the blue sky or green leaves to complete the picture.

A few other thoughts on Arizona flora from the pros:

As with wildlife photography, be willing to get dirty. Drop down on hands and knees and look for the miniature landscapes you normally miss as a biped. Inveterate crawler Inge Martin once found a spider web jeweled with dew this way; the resulting photo became a full page in the August 1983 *Arizona Highways*. When photographing flowers close up, consider sprinkling them with a bit of water from your canteen. The droplets will reflect sunlight, adding sparkle and new points of interest to the picture. (A few professionals consider this cheating, but the view here is that you're doing nothing that doesn't regularly occur in nature.) After rain, fog, or morning dew is an excellent time to photograph plants and intimate landscapes, even if the sky remains overcast. Leaves are glossier, colors more saturated. And after a rare desert snow (it won't happen in Phoenix, but Tucson actually receives an annual average of one inch) the photographic opportunities are — well, a picture is worth all the words anyone could spend on the subject. ■

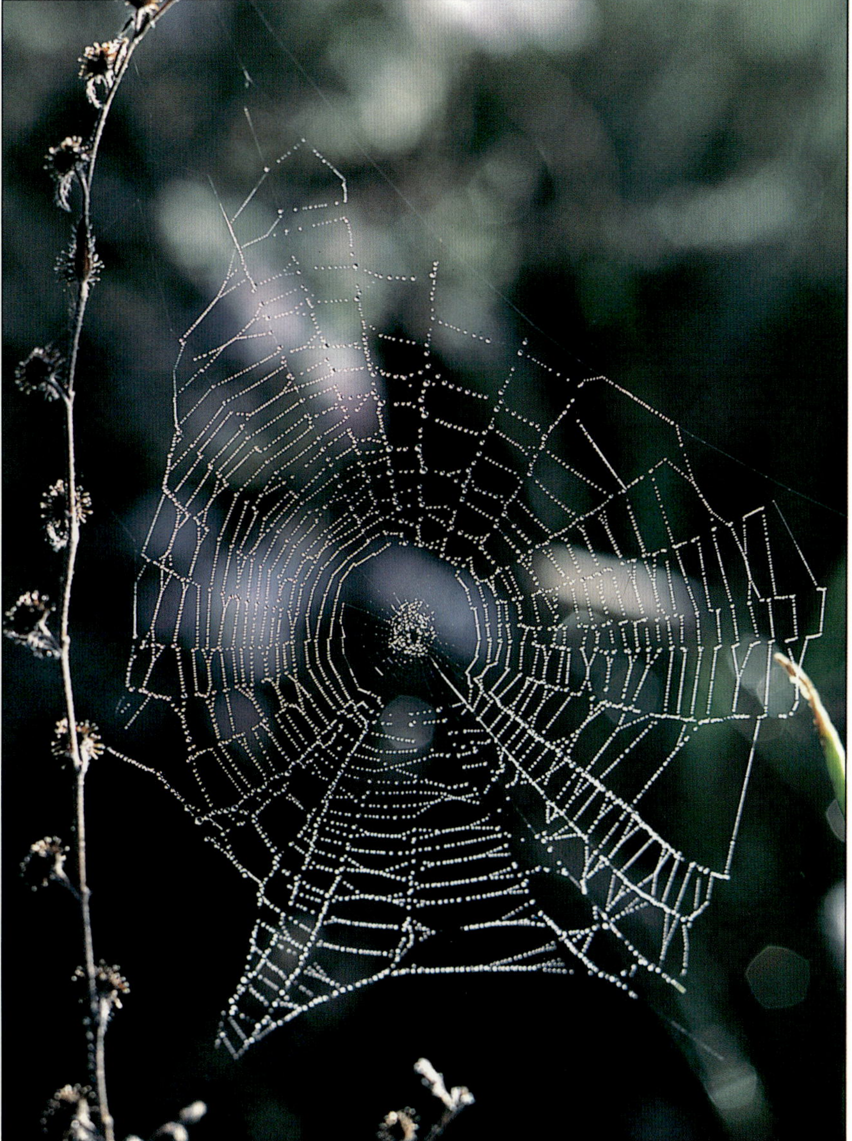

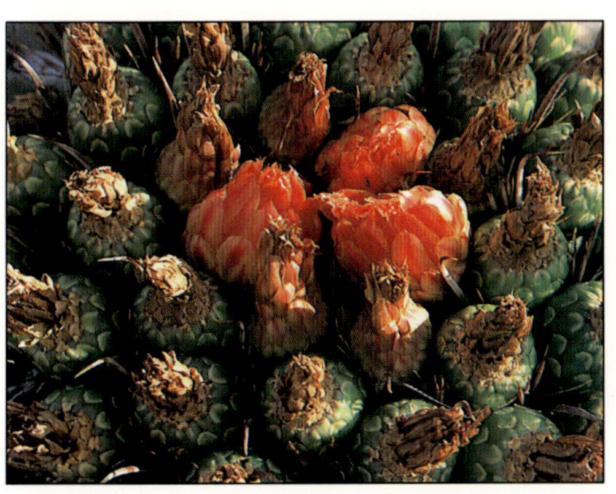

(ABOVE) *Morning dew and backlighting dramatically highlight this spider web at Sunset Crater Volcano National Monument.*
INGE MARTIN

(LEFT) *In this closeup, a backyard barrel cactus becomes a counterpoint of delicate buds and vicious hooked spines. A macro lens is preferred for photographs such as this and the spider web above.*
LAWRENCE W. CHEEK

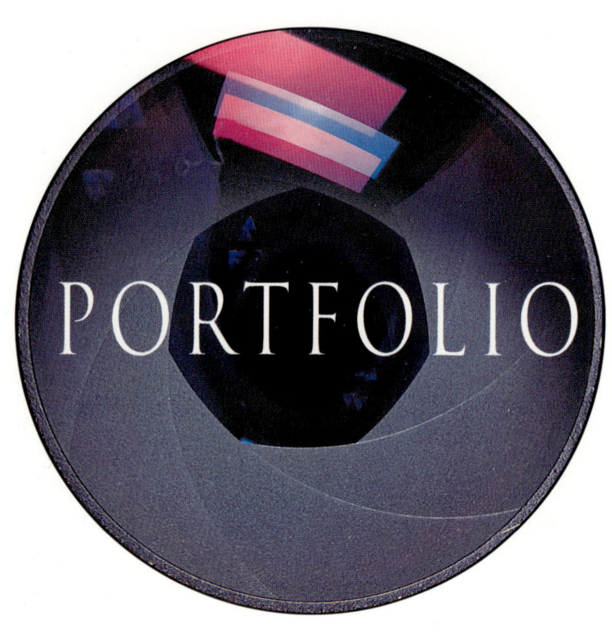

NATURE

A picture of a deer or coyote 50 yards away taken with a normal 50mm lens is all but pointless; the image of the animal will be vague and tiny. The serious nature photographer uses imagination, stealth, and long telephoto and macro lenses to invade the private worlds of the animal, the bug, or the dewy leaf. As photographer James Tallon says, this is the most fun in all photography — but it is not necessarily easy. Of all the genres described in this book, nature photography demands the largest investment in equipment and perseverance. It may also deliver the greatest satisfaction. ■

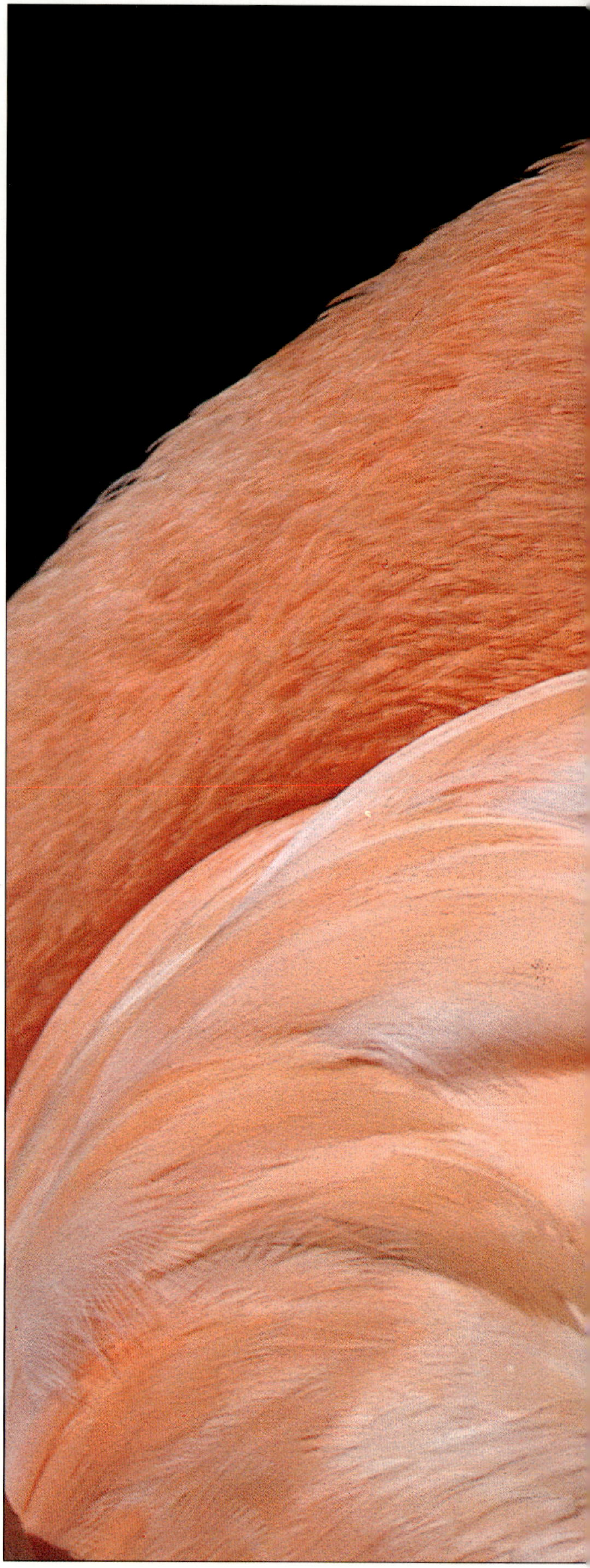

Thanks to their color, flamingos are a favorite photographic subject at the Phoenix Zoo. Fresh images are always welcome, however. In this unusual portrait, a 200mm telephoto lens brings the viewer in intimate contact with the bird's eye and the striking patterns of its feathers. JAMES TALLON

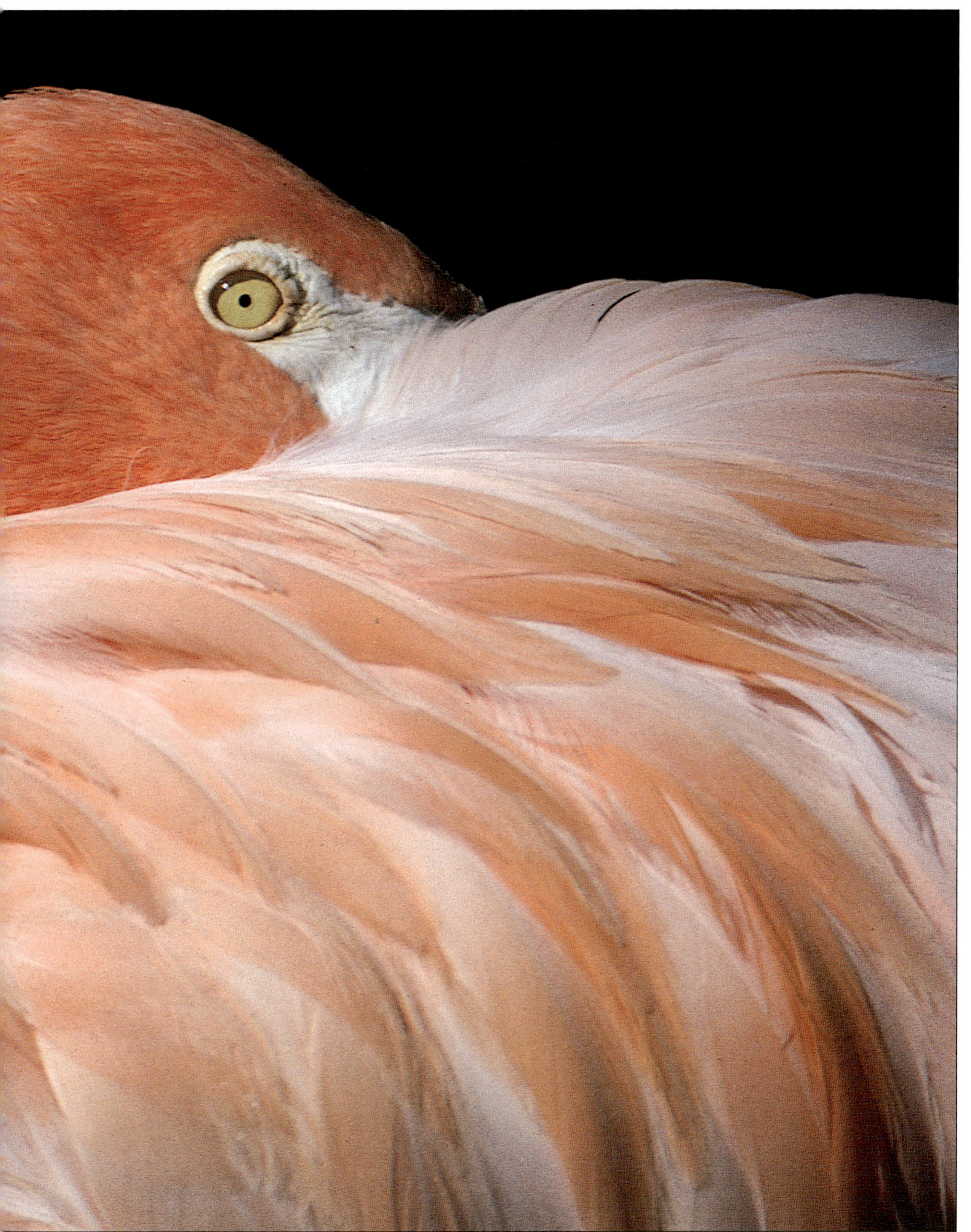

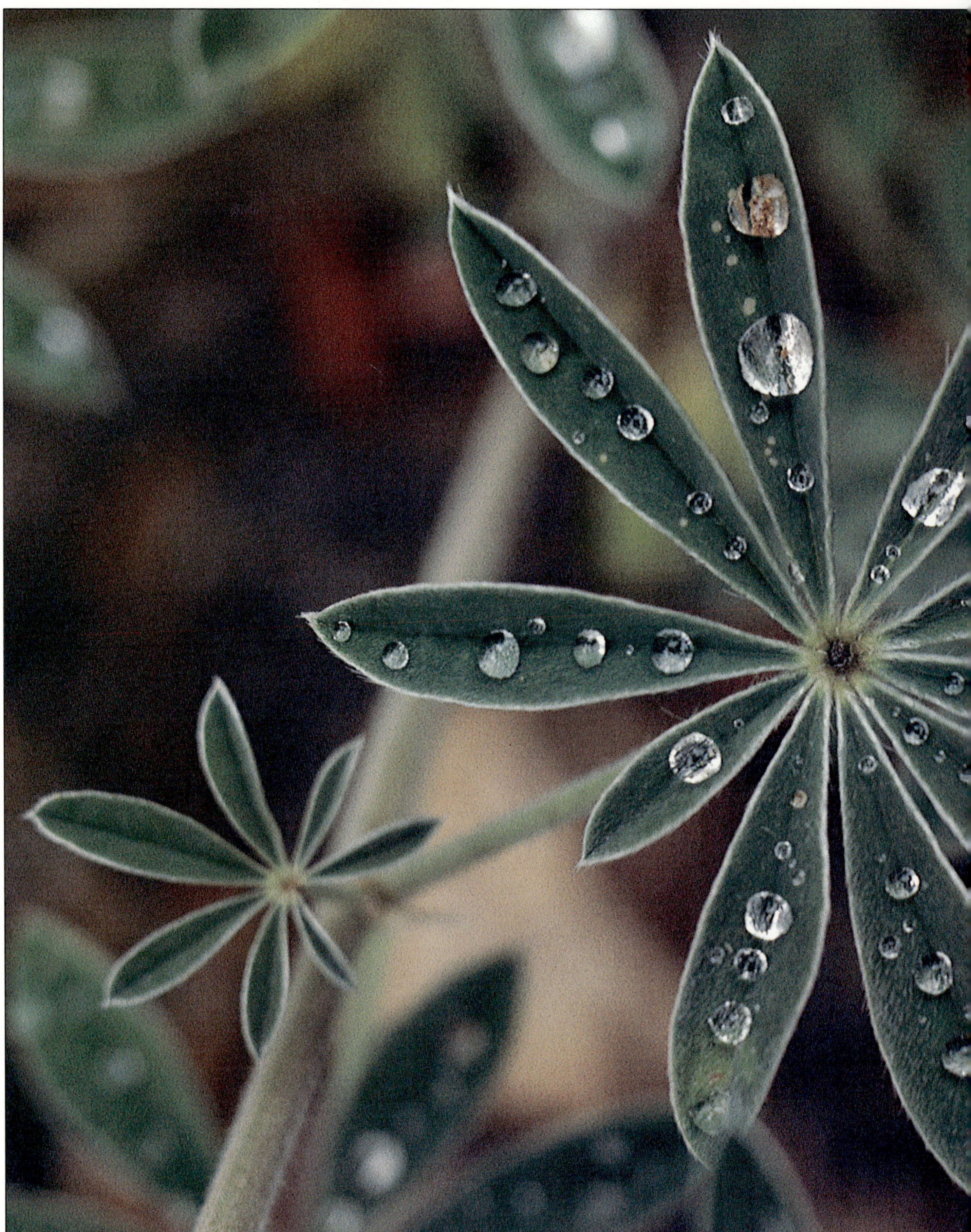

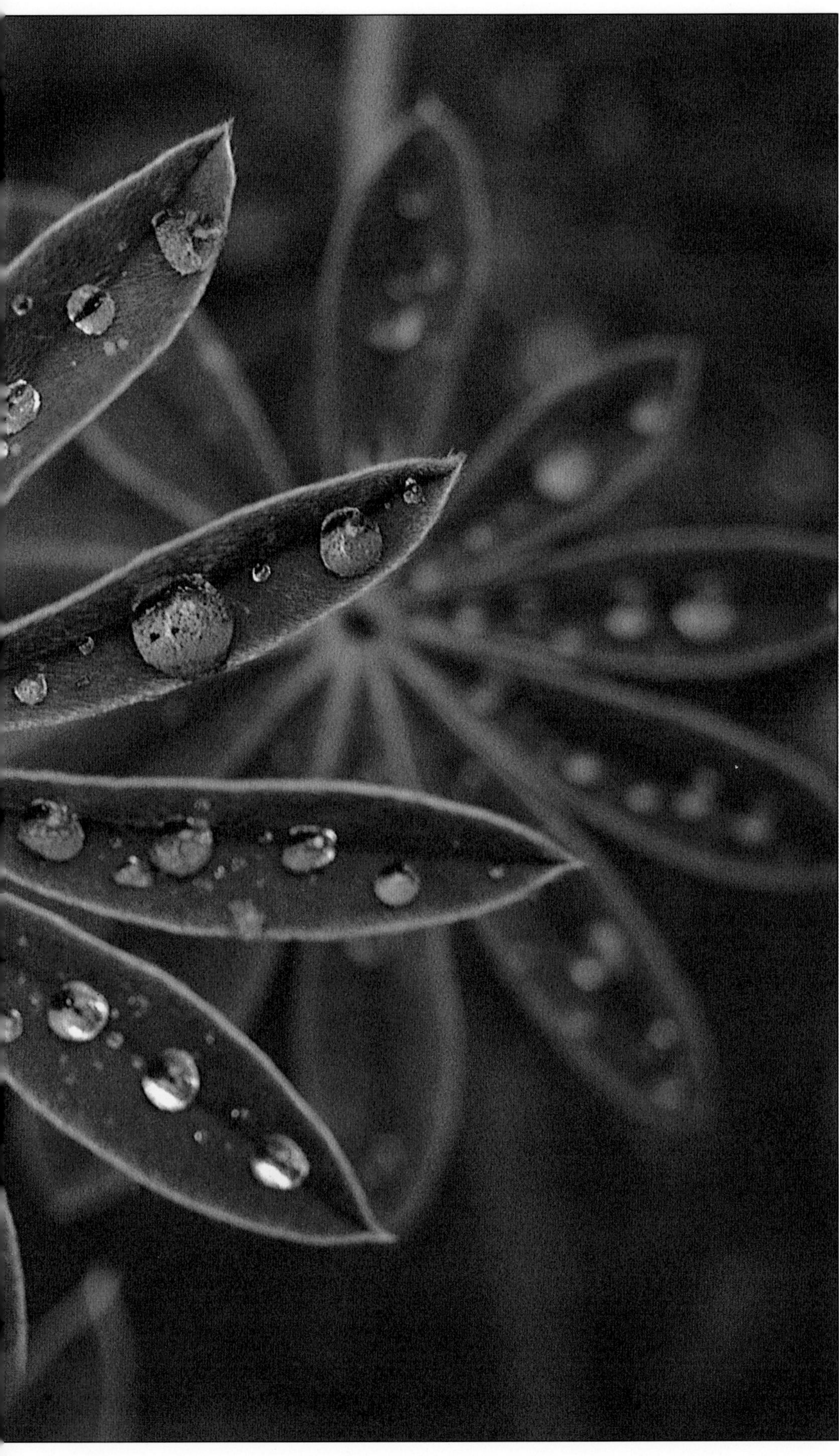

The geometry of nature in flowers and leaves can make delightful close-up photographs. In this photo of a lupine leaf at the Grand Canyon, a second pattern appears in the form of raindrops gathered in remarkable order. The photographer used a shallow depth of field to avoid cluttering the picture with competing patterns.
INGE MARTIN

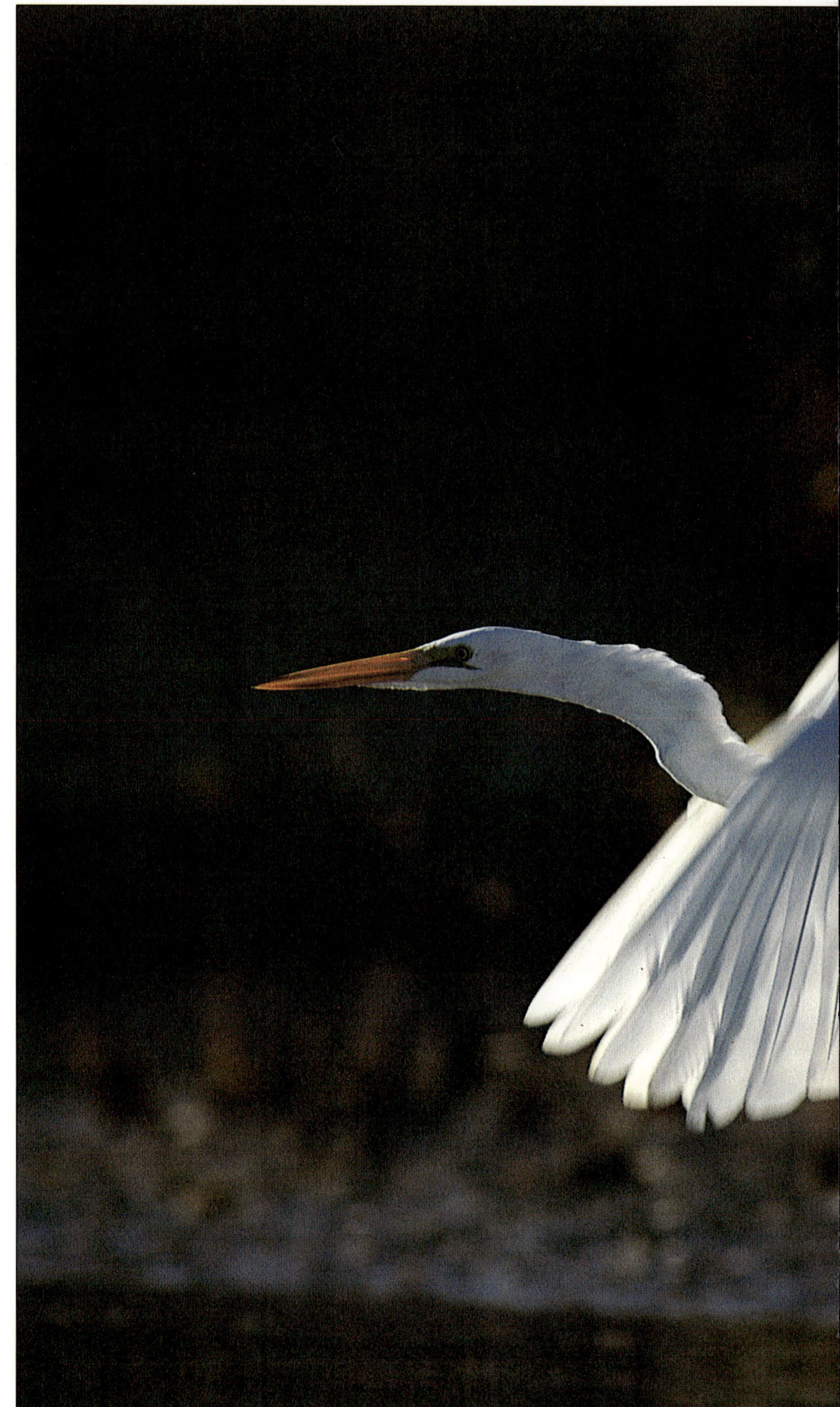

A long telephoto lens brings this spectacularly sunlit egret close enough for a portrait filled with grace and energy.
ROBERT CAMPBELL

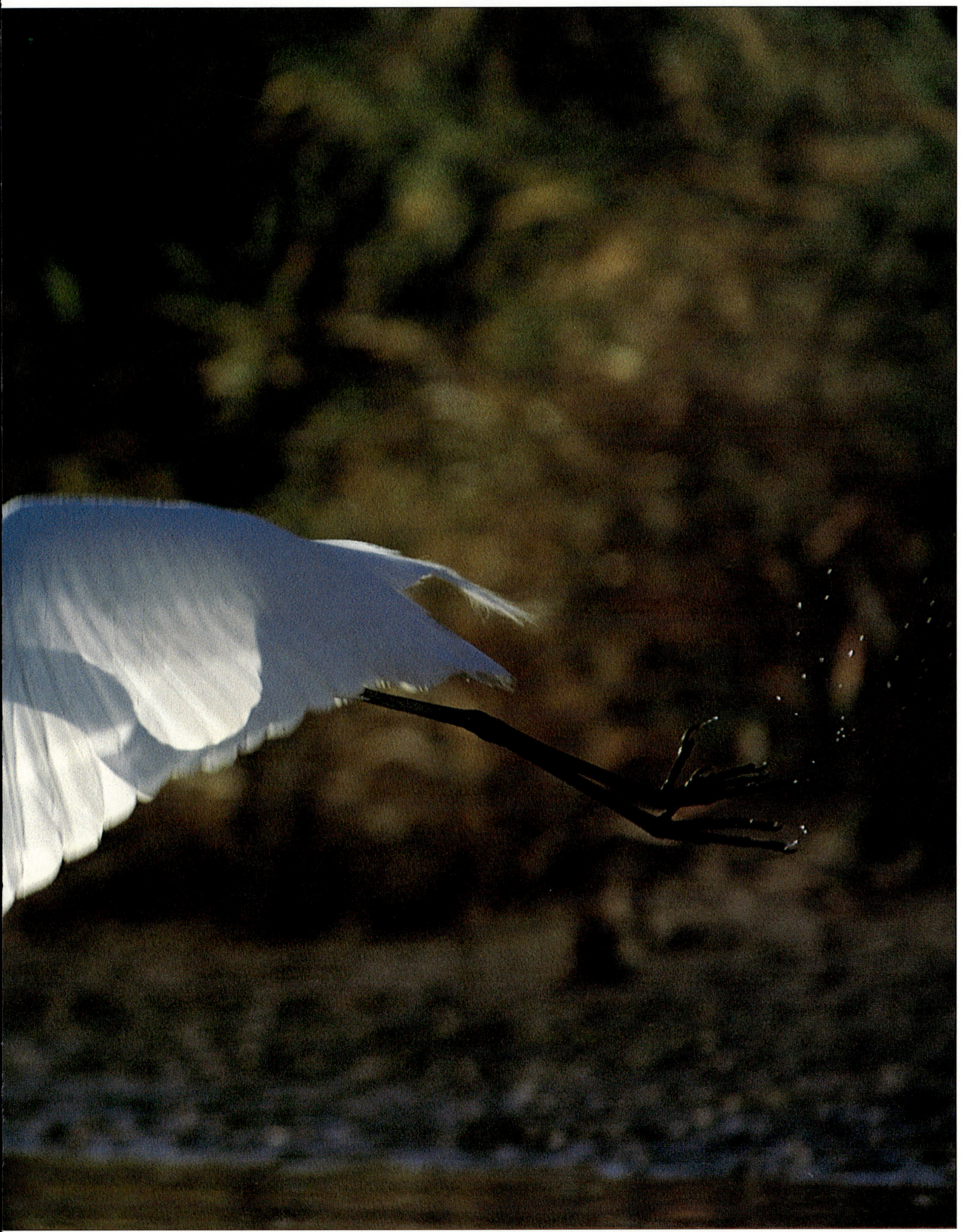

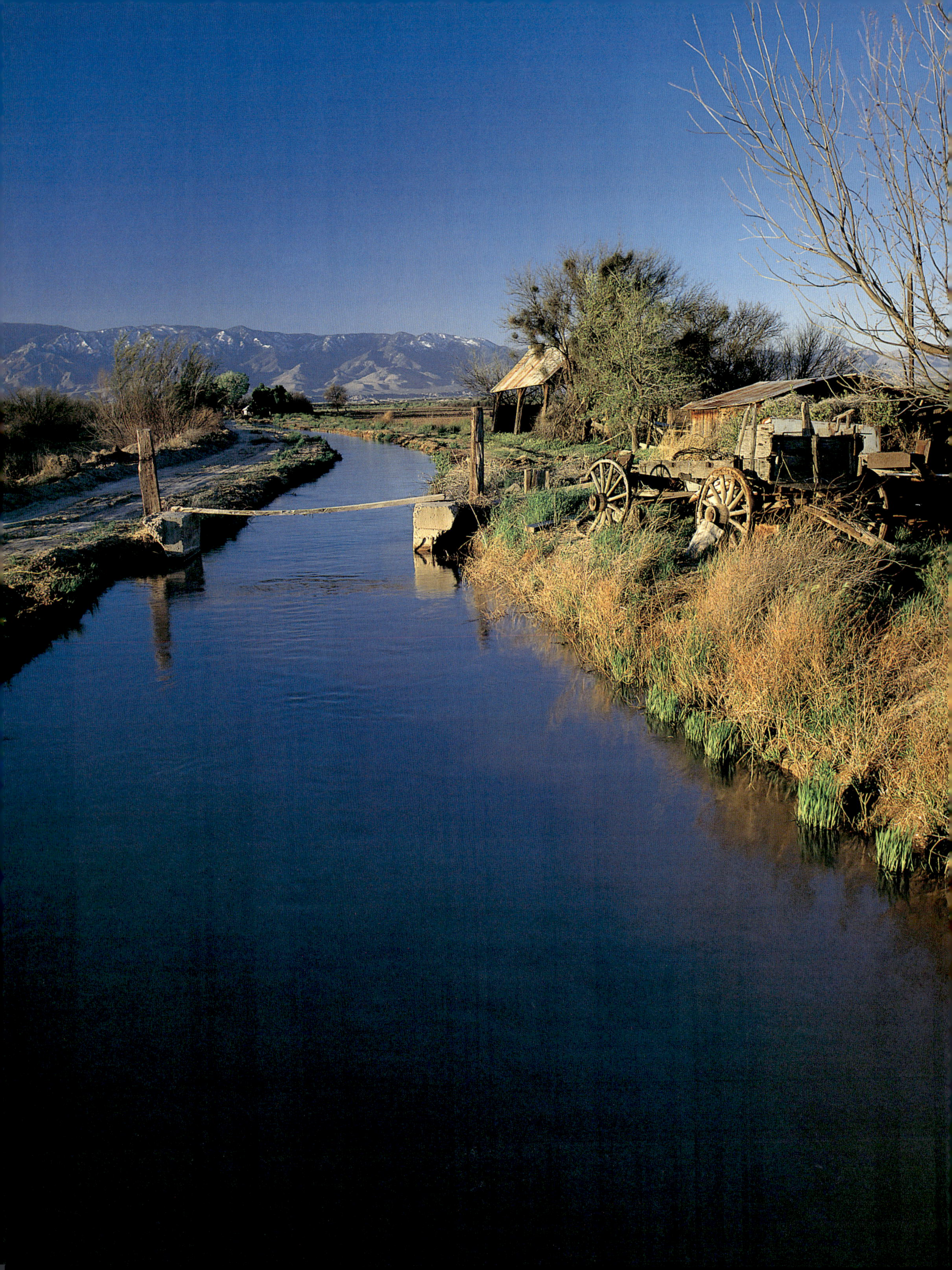

Chapter 5

UNDEREXPOSED ARIZONA

One of my favorite photographs of Arizona is a portrait of an irrigation ditch. I vividly remember the circumstances in which it was taken, because they seemed so unpromising at the time.

Photographer Jerry Sieve and I were developing a story on the Gila River Valley for *Arizona Highways.* It was an unusually difficult assignment for both of us, because this peaceful, agrarian valley did not strike us as rich in scenery, and there were few obvious attractions for a travel writer to mine.

Early on a clear, crisp, and frosty spring morning Sieve and I bounced along a dirt road in his pickup, prospecting for pictures. There appeared to be few possibilities. Without warning, he stopped suddenly after crossing a bridge over a snaking canal flanked by an abandoned and rusting steel-roofed shed, some biodegrading ruins of a wooden wagon, and an overgrowth of brown weeds. For more than an hour, as Sieve fussed with his camera equipment, I stood around, bored and freezing, wondering why on earth such a skilled artist was bothering with such a yawn-inducing scene.

Sieve's photo of this workaday canal became the cover of the October 1987 issue of *Arizona Highways.* And it was gorgeous. The gentle S-curve of the surprisingly blue water led the eye toward the snow-crusted Pinaleno Mountains in the background. The dormant weeds glowed like filaments of gold in the morning's tawny light. The rustic, abandoned debris of a farm on the right bank provided a nostalgic

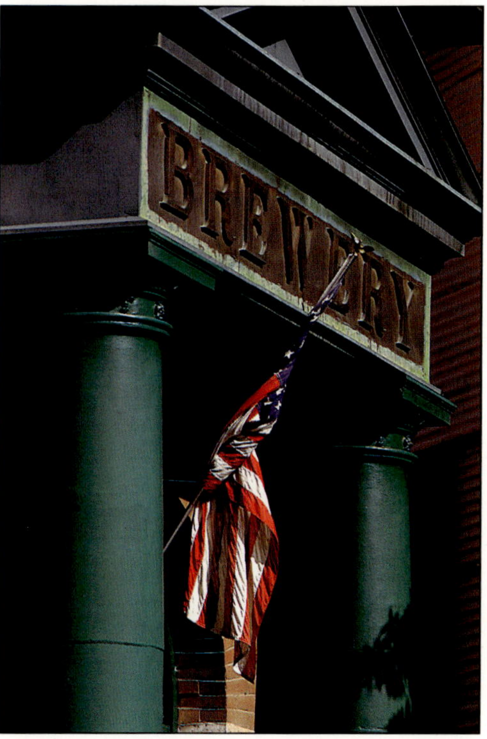

(OPPOSITE PAGE) *Surely the most romantically photographed irrigation ditch ever to appear in* Arizona Highways, *this Gila River Valley canal appeared on the October 1987 cover. The reasons: light and composition.* JERRY SIEVE

(LEFT) *Bisbee, a mining boom town at the turn of the century, venerated its brewery enough to celebrate it with a Greek Revival portico. Such architectural details can tell a town's story as readily as photographs of its people.* JEFF KIDA

counterpoint to the robustly flowing canal, and together the two implied a story line: Even amid abandonment and decay, the artery of renewed life — the canal — flows on.

The point of this anecdote is that first-class photography of Arizona is hardly limited to the obvious — the classic saguaro silhouetted in the sunset, a storm over the Grand Canyon, autumn color embracing Oak Creek. There certainly is nothing wrong with capturing these lovely images on film; there is good reason why they are reproduced time after time in magazines and books published worldwide. Take the pictures of "Obvious Arizona," as Vladimir Nabokov called it, and get them out of your system. Then begin to think about returning home with travel photos that will cause viewers to exclaim, "I didn't know anything like that existed in Arizona!"

Bisbee, a retired Cochise County copper mining town six miles north of the Mexican border, is an example of a wonderful lode of unexpected photographic treasures. The amateur (or professional) photographer is immediately drawn toward the striking architecture left over from Bisbee's turn-of-the-century wealth: the Italianate Victorian Copper Queen Hotel, the Greek Revival portal of the Muheim Block, where the word BREWERY is cast prominently into the frieze. But this is only the surface, the Obvious Bisbee. The creative photographer will roam the terraced streets in search of pictures that tell unpatented stories about this quirky and engaging town. Textures, for example: vines crawling over an old stone wall, stairways ascending the steep sides of Brewery Gulch and slowly crumbling into oblivion — things that photographer Jeff Kida cites as illustrations of "nature retaking the town."

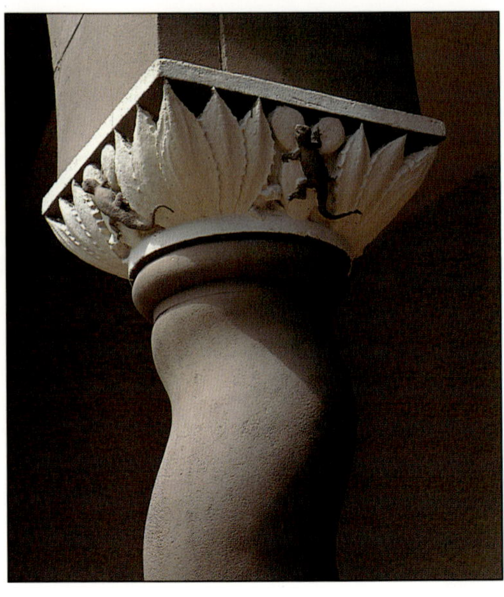

(RIGHT) *Concrete lizards crawl across carved agave leaves in this unusual column and capital at Tucson's old YWCA. Such details are often more interesting than photos of whole buildings.*
LAWRENCE W. CHEEK

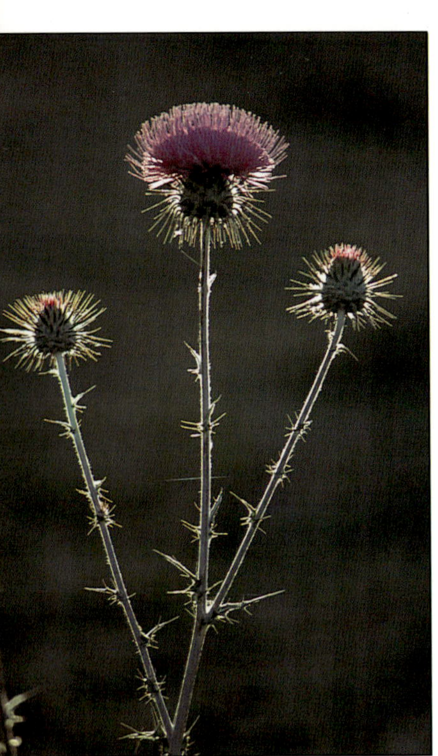

(BELOW) *Lighting and composition make the ordinary exceptional. A thistle backlighted before a dark background.*
INGE MARTIN

Bisbee is also rich in human character. On one photographic excursion, Kida discovered Walter Swan, a 75-year-old retired plasterer who runs Bisbee's One-Book Bookstore, selling, indeed, just one book (which he wrote and published). Swan was delighted to be photographed in his peculiar store. Kida also wandered through the Central School Project, an artists' cooperative, knocking on doors, introducing himself to artists at work, and photographing them with their work or amid the eccentric clutter of their studios. Kida is a pro, but every picture he took in a couple of days of prowling the town would be available to the amateur willing to make the effort. (See Kida's Bisbee photographs on page 71.)

Interesting pictures are everywhere, even in less obviously picturesque places. To find them, we must teach ourselves to look. One of Jay Dusard's favorite Arizona images is of the latching device at the back of an old truck he found rusting away near Prescott. It is almost abstract, and it is strangely compelling. Dusard's advice for learning to see such possibilities: Don't merely look for pictures; look for underlying design relationships in the natural and man-made landscape. Also, remind yourself that even in a state famous for its scenery, good photography is about much more than scenery. In downtown Phoenix, Inge Martin looked at mirror-glass skyscrapers until she found a wall where one pane was slightly bowed, which caused an appealingly quirky distortion in the reflection of a neighbor building.

In the Pinal county seat of Florence, soft early or late light falling on the old Sonoran-style adobe houses paints them with an alluring romance. The pictures I have taken of them are not really architectural at all, but are all about light and texture. In Tucson, I was captivated by the humorous variation on a twisted column at the west entrance to the old YWCA building. Instead of the proper Corinthian acanthus leaves, its capital sports agave leaves with lizards crawling about them. A very simple picture, it still tells the story of how architects in early Arizona were working to invest their buildings with a sense of place in this unique land.

The Grand Canyon is surely Arizona's most overexposed scenic attraction, and even some professional photographers will admit they have a hard time coming up with fresh images of it. Arizona, however, is torn and furrowed by thousands of canyons from the Mexican border to Utah, and many of the little-known ones can be as photographically rewarding as the Grand one.

Michael Fatali's photographs of a slot canyon near Page reveal an otherworldly landscape where sculpted, light-splashed formations dance and glide and collide with astonishing grace and power. (See page 68.) In a photo essay in *Arizona Highways* Fatali called it a "symphony in sandstone," a fine description.

In Romero Canyon, 20 miles north of downtown Tucson, a foot-wide seasonal stream laboring for thousands of years has carved a sluice into what looks like a gallery crowded with Henry Moore sculptures.

After a rain in the Chiricahua Mountains' Echo Canyon, miniature waterfalls appear, some only a couple of feet high — but as seductive, in their intimate way, as the well-known cascades of Havasu Canyon.

Underexposed landscapes are everywhere in Arizona, and there are photographic possibilities even in those that seem, at first, to be dull or mundane. Along with his irrigation canal classic, Sieve has successfully photographed many lovely riparian woodlands beside what seem to be piddling, insignificant desert creeks. As he works, cars streak by over nearby bridges, their occupants never dreaming that landscapes of secret beauty lie just a few steps away. ■

Finding the unique: The Valley Bank Center in downtown Phoenix is Arizona's tallest building, and it has been photographed countless times. A reflection in a bowed pane, however, yielded a fresh and quirky image.
INGE MARTIN

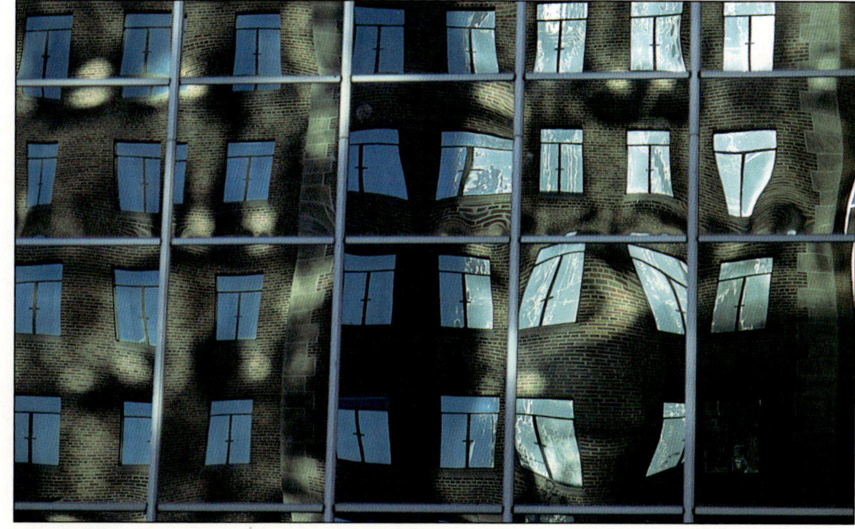

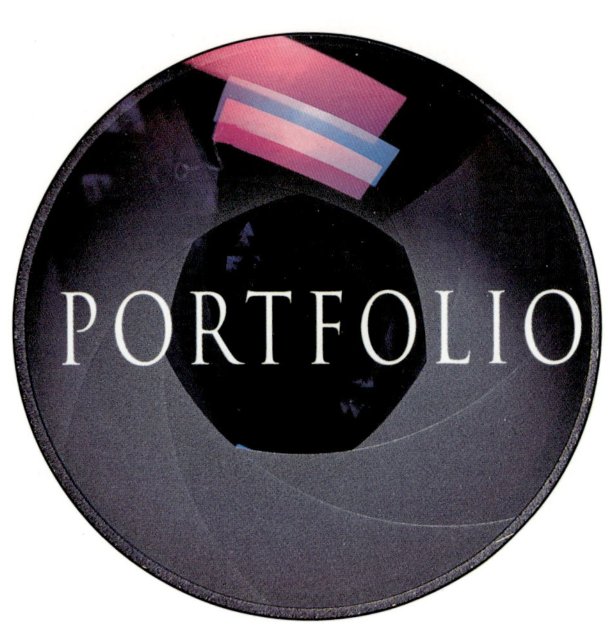

UNDEREXPOSED ARIZONA

How to find fresh photographic images in overexposed Arizona? Explore. Climb, clamber, or crawl into places everyday tourists never see. Look, then look again even more intently. Experiment, even with ideas that seem unlikely to work; film is the cheapest resource any photographer has. Take chances, ignore rules, defy convention. Try taking familiar sights out of context. For example, consider shooting a landscape with no sky in it. Take out your camera in a town that at first glance seems anything but photogenic and look for the unique shot that explains the place. Any destination in Arizona can yield good pictures; only the photographer's ambition and imagination limit the results. ■

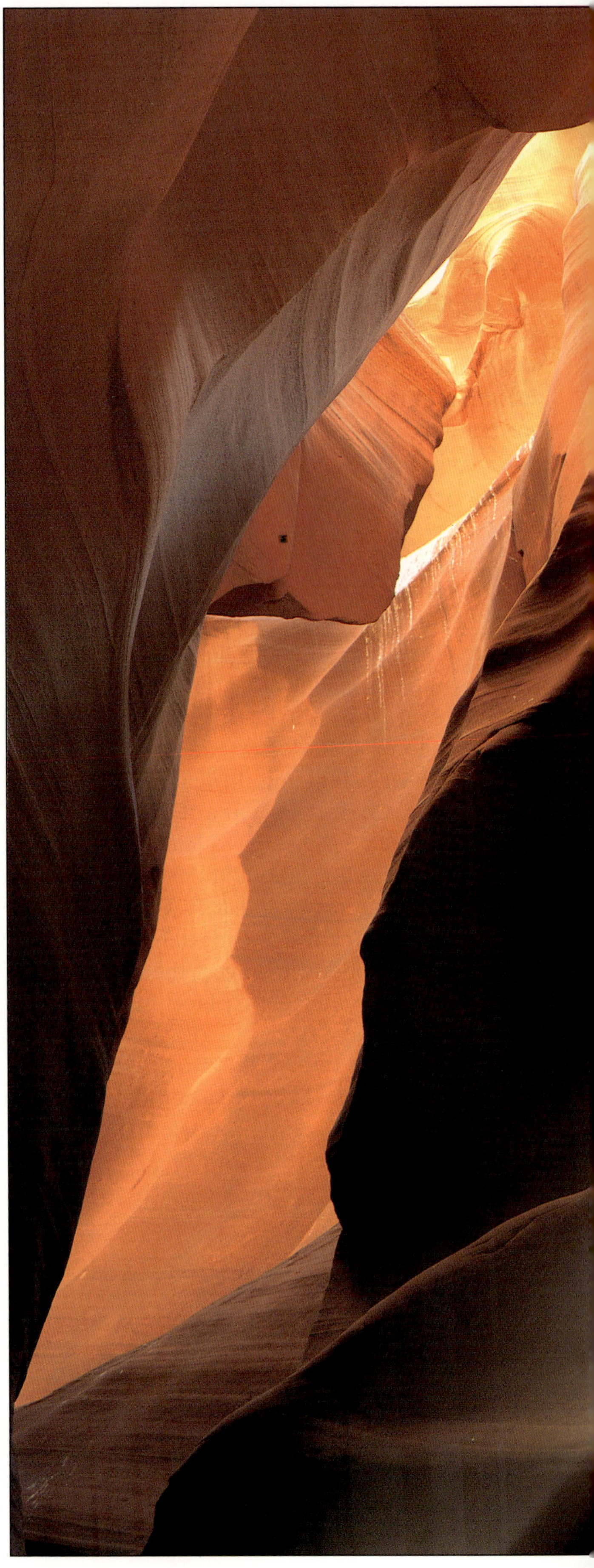

Some Arizona landscapes are so strange that they invite the photographer to make them into virtual abstract art, with no clues for the viewer as to scale or location. Such a place is this slot canyon near Page. MICHAEL FATALI

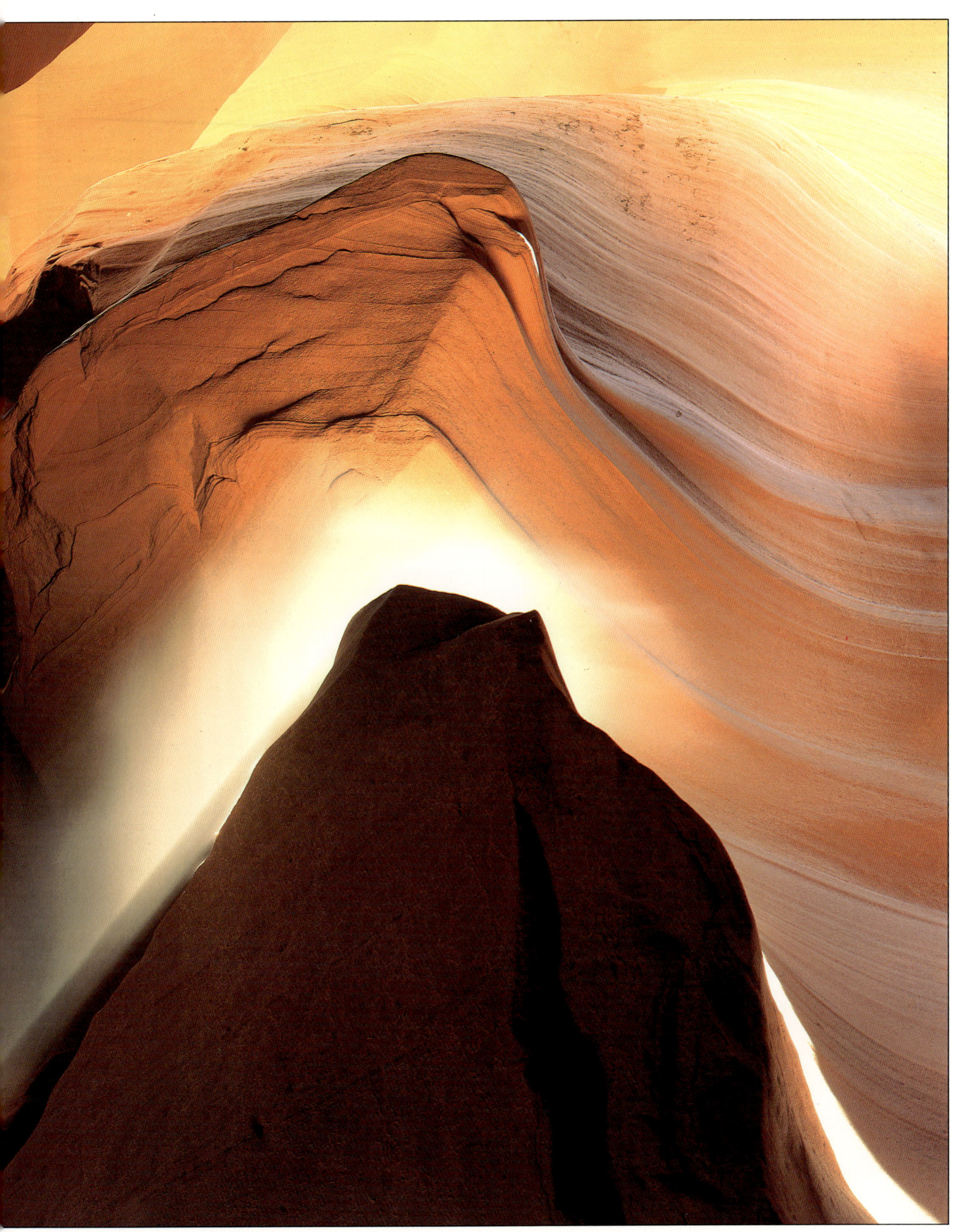

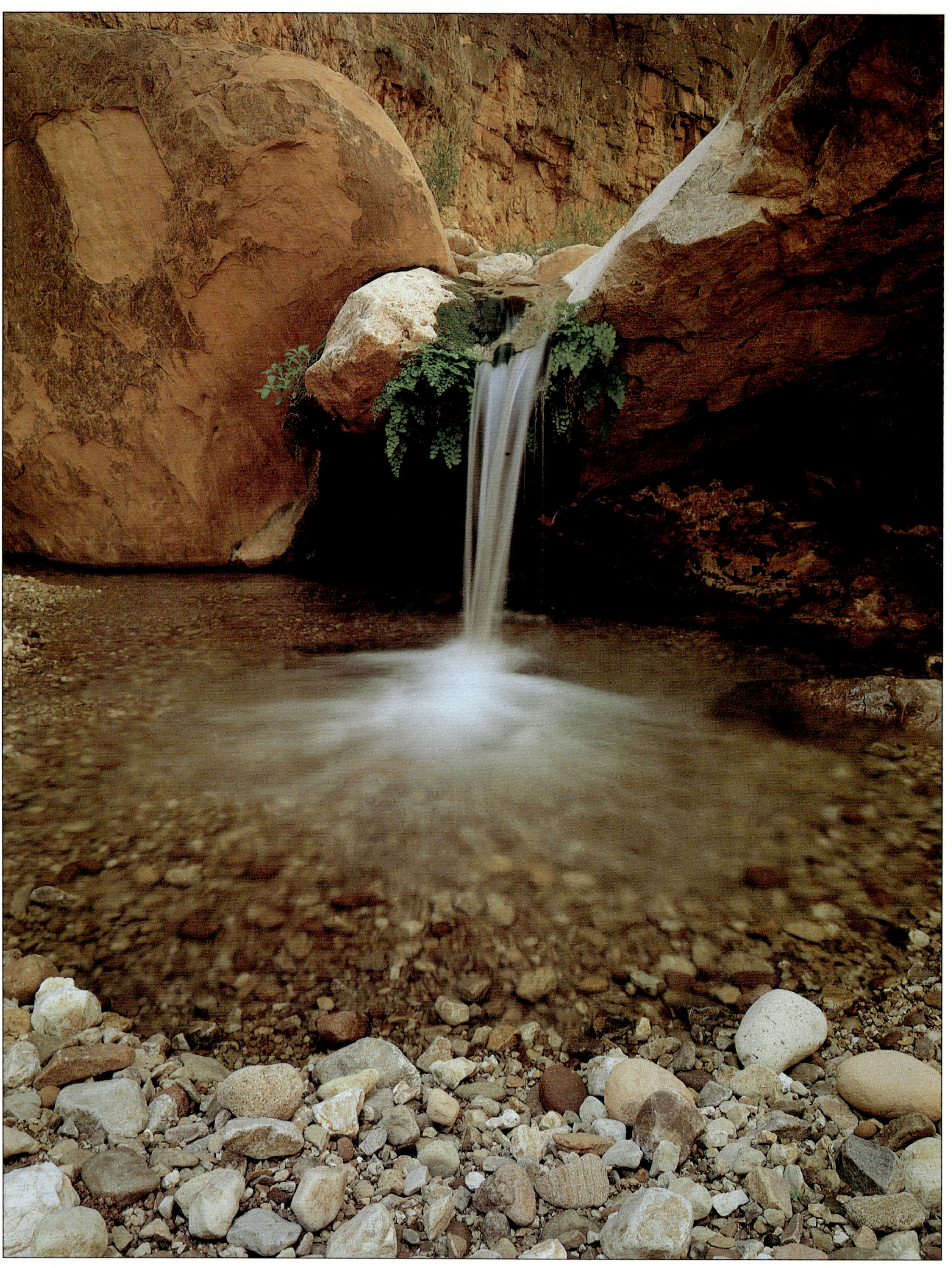

(LEFT) *Exploring another facet of the Grand Canyon's "personality" leads the photographer to this two-foot high fern-fringed waterfall at Scottys Hollow.* GARY LADD

The mining industry left Bisbee in 1975, but the charming, quirky town remains a rich lode for photographers.

(RIGHT) *A partly cloudy day places the background hill in shadow, increasing the apparent brilliance of the sunlight splashing the town.*

(FAR RIGHT) *Retired miner Toby Valdez leads tours of the old Copper Queen Mine; his face is a study in pride and dignity.*

(BELOW) *La Vuelta de Bisbee, a harrowing professional bicycle race through Bisbee's steep and narrow streets, is a festival of speed and color. Blurring of the cyclist in the lower right corner gives the photo a sense of movement up and to the left, the direction of the race.* ALL BY JEFF KIDA

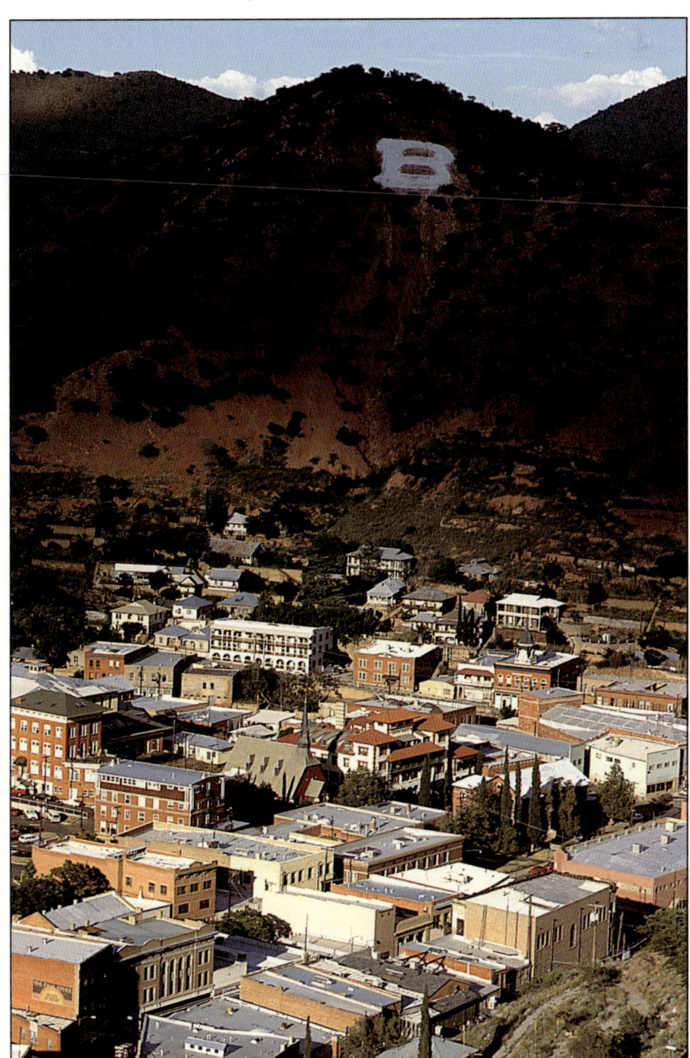

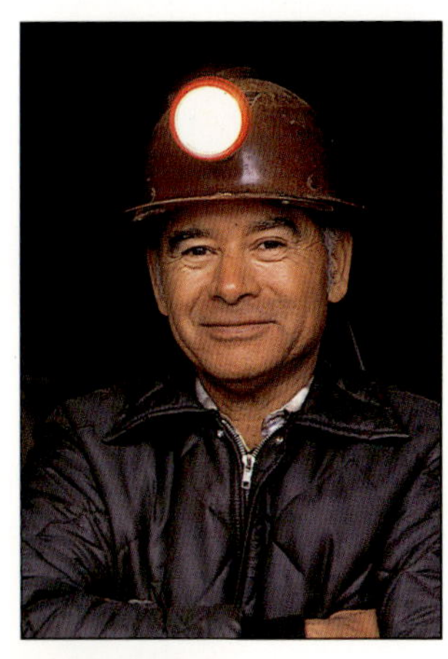

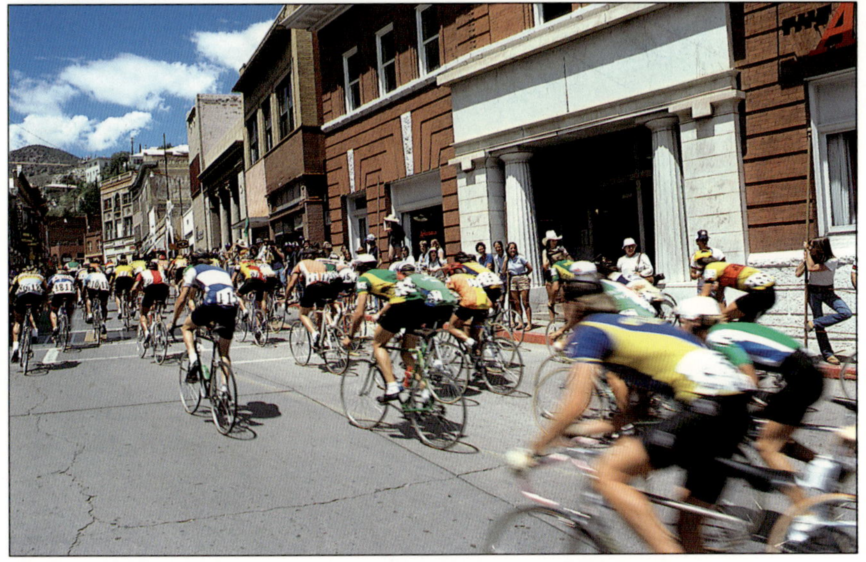

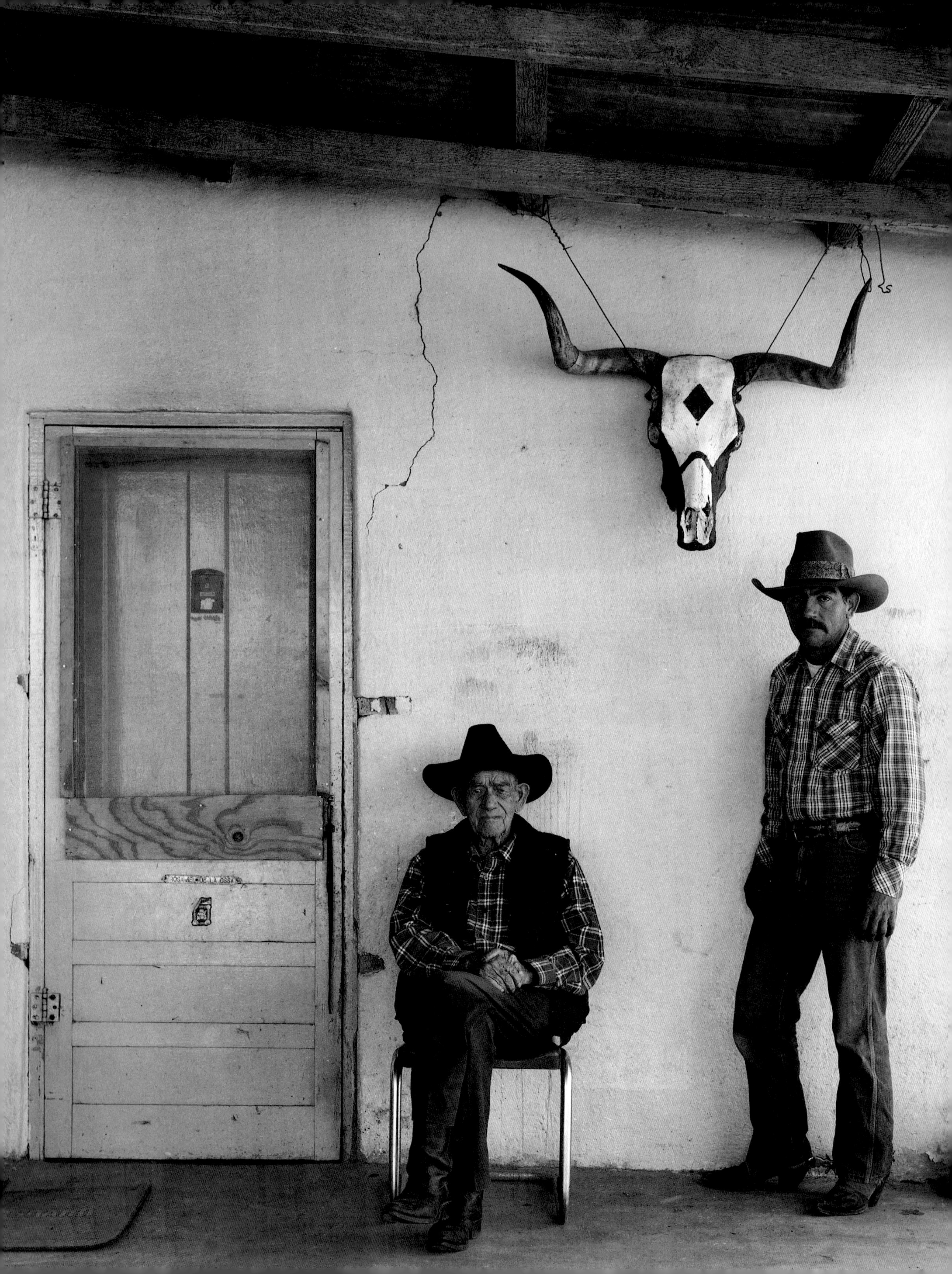
ROSAMEL DE LA OSSA

Chapter 6

PHOTOGRAPHIC INSIGHTS

In population, Arizona ranks 24th among the states. In photographers per capita, we crowd the top. Terence Pitts, director of the University of Arizona's Center for Creative Photography, says that this state is among the five richest in the production of professional photography — ranking with much larger California, New York, Illinois, and Massachusetts.

This tradition is more than a century old. Beginning as early as the 1870s, photographers from the East journeyed to the newly opening West to document its largely unknown wonders — its canyons, badlands, ruins of vanished civilizations, contemporary Indians, and before long, alas, the wars against those Indians. Some of these 19th-century images are unforgettable. A Tombstone-based photographer named C.S. Fly took an astounding series of portraits of Geronimo, his family, and warriors, usually armed to the eyelids, sometimes staring directly into the camera with unfathomable intensity and throttled fury. Fly either earned the Apaches' trust or appealed to their vanity; few other white men ever witnessed such displays and lived to describe them.

In the present century, travel to Arizona soon became commonplace, but the impulse to commit its images to film never lagged. Ansel Adams went back time and again to photograph Canyon de Chelly and its people. "Canyon de Chelly ... is an extraordinary experience," he wrote in *An Autobiography*, "made more intense by the presence of its Navajo residents, who demonstrate that man can live with nature and sometimes enhance it .... Some of my best photographs have been made in and on the rim of the canyon."

Beginning in the 1930s, two decades before he first ran for public office, Barry Goldwater undertook a personal project to portray his

(LEFT) *Cowboys Rosamel and Ramón de la Ossa are posed with a spatial precision that belies their relaxed moods* *(see page 84).* JAY DUSARD

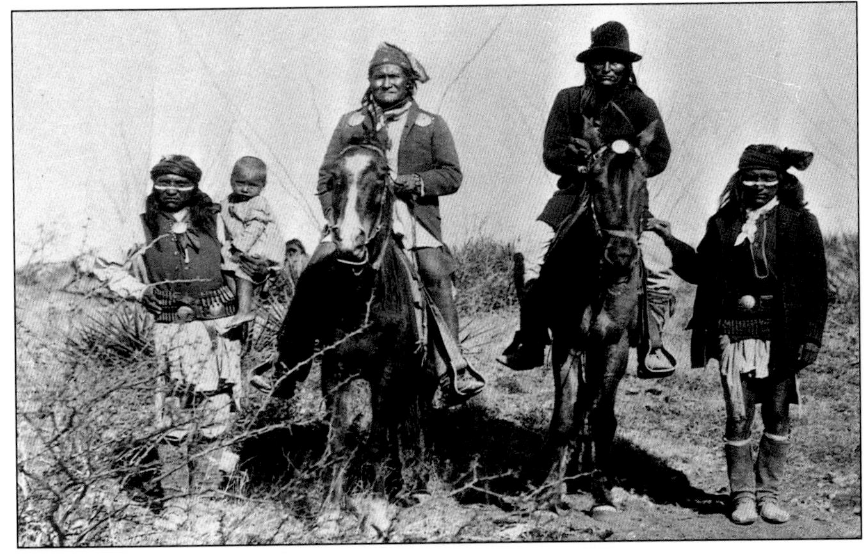

(ABOVE) *Geronimo (mounted at left) and Natches (with hat) pose for an 1886 portrait at Geronimo's request. The warrior at Geronimo's side is his son.* C. S. FLY (ARIZONA DEPARTMENT OF LIBRARY AND ARCHIVES)

beloved native state through his camera. Eventually several books of his photographs were published. He has been acclaimed, and rightly, for his gracious and sympathetic photos of Arizona's Native Americans. A simple caption he wrote for a photo in *The Face of Arizona* reveals much about how he approached the work: "A young Navajo girl. The sweetness and charm reflected in the eyes and features of young Navajos is irresistible and indicates at an early age the qualities of goodness and kindness that mark these people in their later years."

Photography in modern Arizona has developed so many productive shoots and branches that a book could be devoted to each. Much of the diversification (and the opportunities for photographers) owes to the state's continuing boom. Growth means change, and the photographer is as vital to documenting and explaining it as are the journalist and historian. The Arizona nature photographer inevitably becomes an advocate for the beautiful things he sees through his lens, and will use those pictures to remind the rest of us how fragile they are in the face of careless development. A photographer who sets out today to document modern Indian culture will likely be drawn into the struggle over that culture's erosion. Endangered traditions cry out to be preserved, if nowhere else, on film.

All these concerns, along with the lure of endlessly dramatic light, sky, and landscape, keep bringing photographers to Arizona. What follows is a sampling of thinking from several of them, along with a gallery of their best work. ■

Monty Roessel

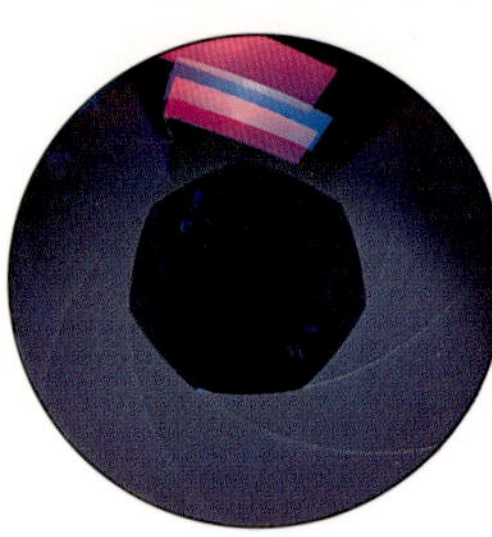

Monty Roessel has a single project that may consume his entire life. He outlined it in a grant proposal he wrote in 1983, calling it simply "A Navajo's View of Navajo Life."

Navajo life has been well documented by outsiders, but that is not the same as the view from within — where the photographer is a part of the culture he is photographing. Roessel's proposal, written when he was a journalism major at the University of Northern Colorado, attracted the attention first of the Schumann Foundation of New Jersey, and then of *National Geographic*.

The magazine gave Roessel a first right of refusal contract for his Navajo photos and he began work on the project — at the age of 22. He is candid today about what happened. "I didn't have much of an idea of what I wanted to do except just photograph life on the reservation. It was too unfocused, and that was what ultimately did me in." Reviewing his slides, *Geographic* couldn't find a story line, and terminated the project. Roessel, however, continues the work as a freelance photographer majoring in Navajo life. He has contributed to *Arizona Highways* and *Native Peoples*, among others, and in 1991 *Sports Illustrated* spread his picture of Navajo children playing baseball in the sands of Monument Valley across two full pages.

"I'm 30 years old now, and I still want to do the project," Roessel says. "I have a publisher who's interested, but I'm in no hurry. I want to take my time and fill in the holes. This is something I'm only going to do once in my life."

Many an outside photojournalist

goes onto the Navajo reservation predisposed to document the sad reality of eroding traditions. Roessel has a different point of view, which is part of what makes his photography important. "The line I grew up hearing from my parents was, 'only a dead culture doesn't change.' So part of my work is to show the positive aspects of that change. I don't see it so much as erosion. I think more than any other tribe, we pick and choose. We're not so proud that we're never going to change."

Roessel lives in Kayenta, just south of Monument Valley, and until recently, worked as managing editor of the now-defunct *Navajo Times*, an independent weekly newspaper. ■

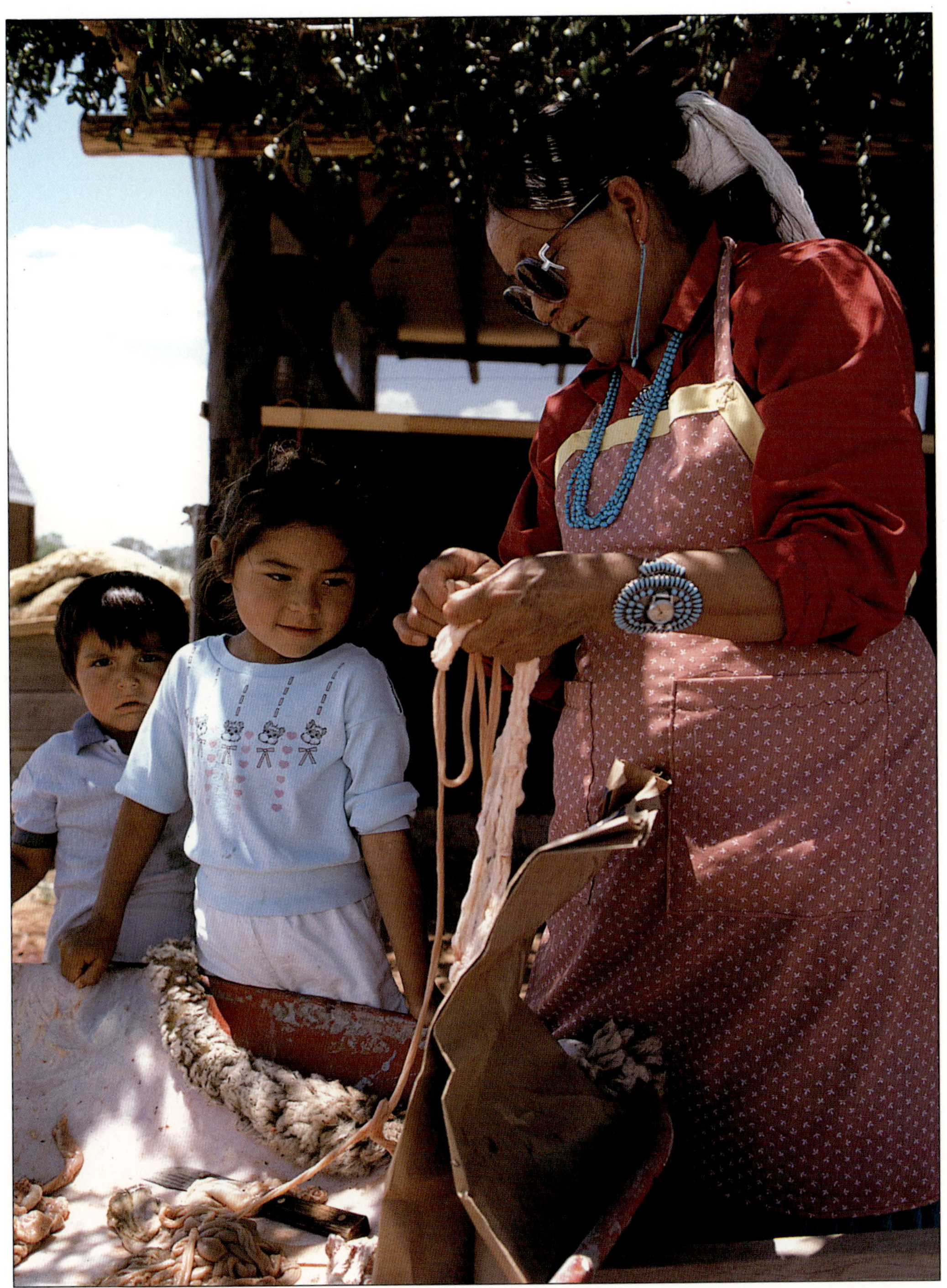

Portraits can be more than faces of people. They can tell something about their lives and lifestyle. A young child watches intently as a Navajo woman prepares food for a wedding feast.
MONTY ROESSEL

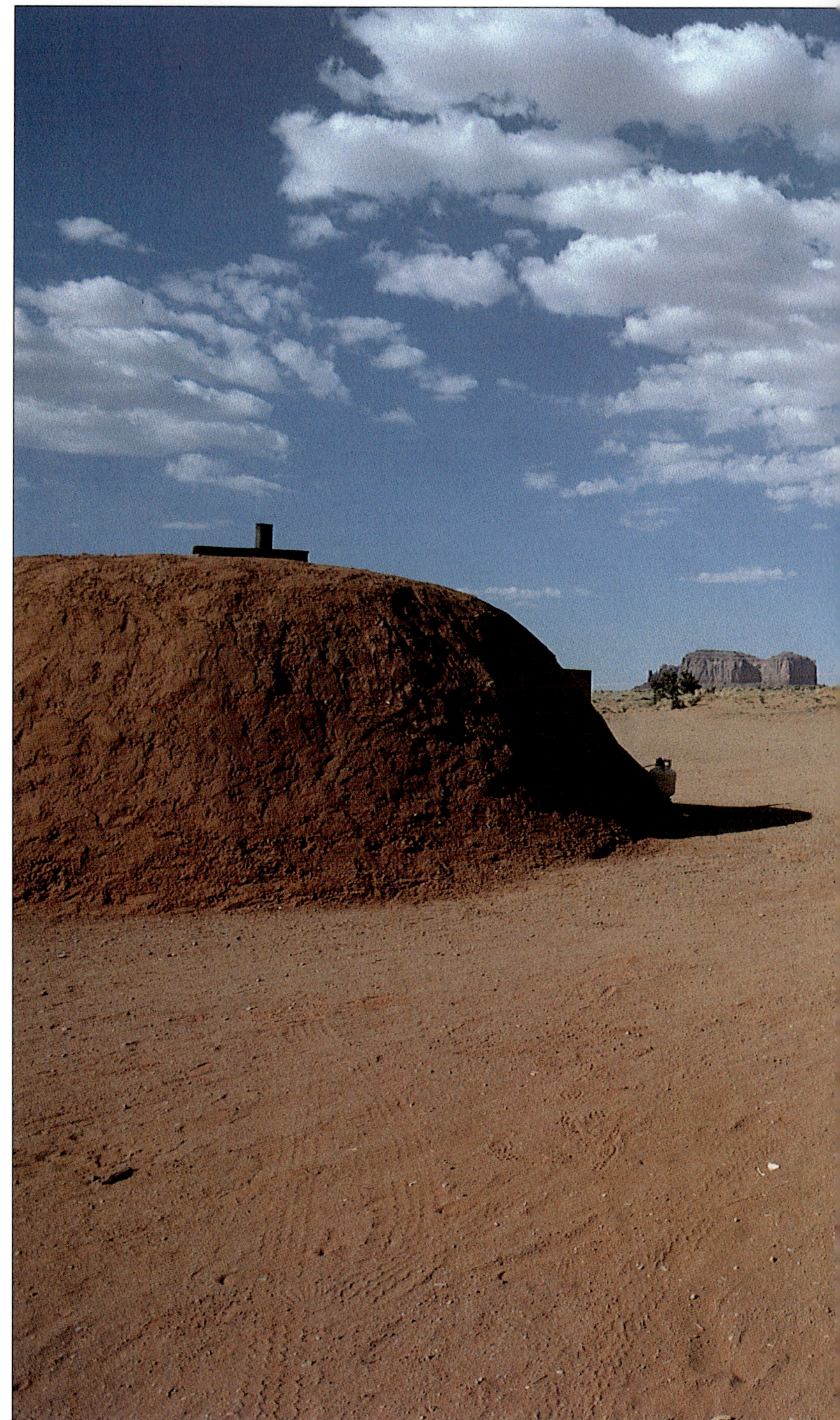

The national sport has taken hold even in the sands of Monument Valley on the Navajo Reservation. The vast, empty spaces included in this picture tell more about Navajo life and their environment than would a tight picture of the young players.
MONTY ROESSEL

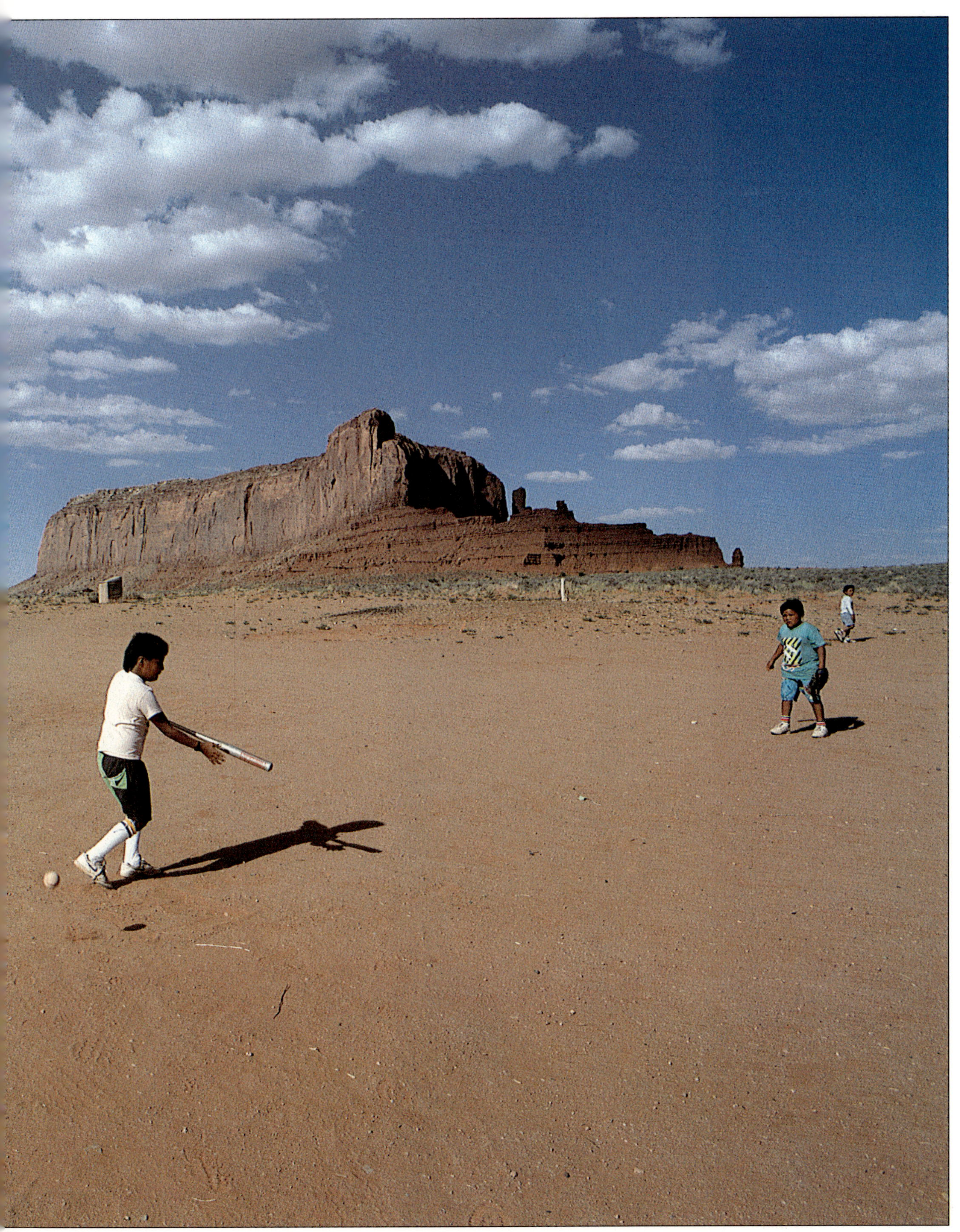

Frank Zullo

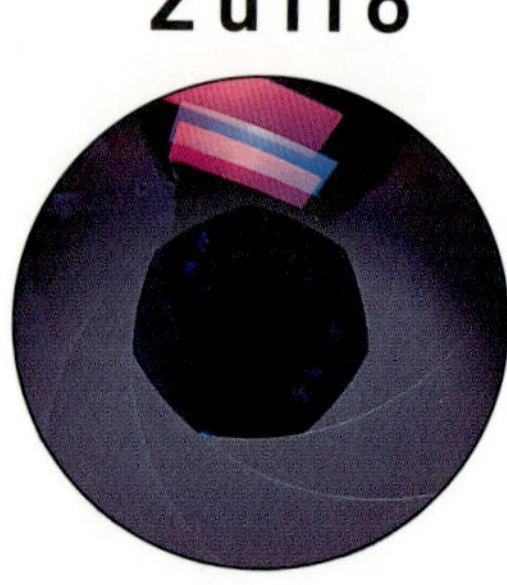

All good photographers put indirect sunlight to creative employment, softened and tinted in its reflection from bare ground, water, or a wall. Frank Zullo's Arizona landscapes, however, are lit with sunlight reflected from something most of us never think of using: the moon.

"Things have a different character at night," Zullo says, and his photo of the Chapel of the Holy Cross in Sedona dramatically illustrates the point. In daylight the famous chapel wedged in the red rocks has an authoritative and heroic mood, but in Zullo's photo it seems hauntingly lonely, as if it were the last citadel of man standing against the universe. The colors are different, too — the moonlight lends it a faint golden glow — but its altered mood is the lesson of the photograph.

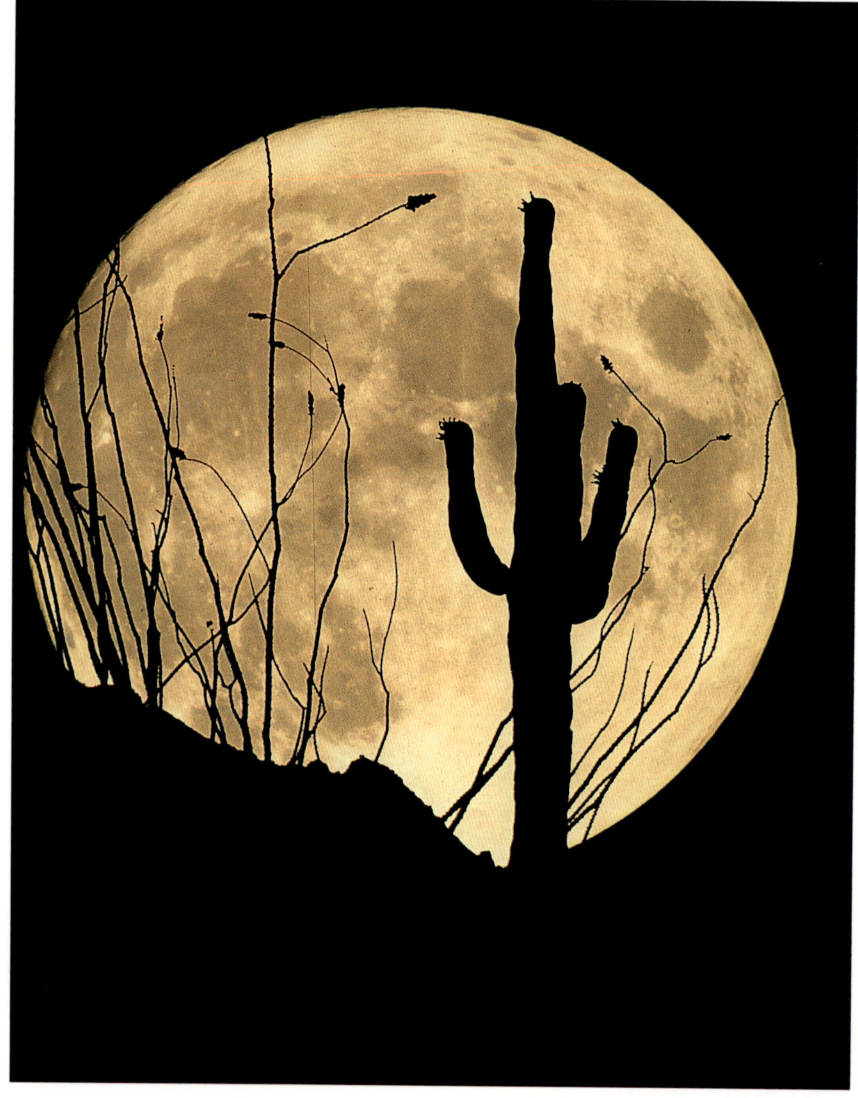

Zullo has always loved both nature photography and the night sky, so it was inevitable that he would eventually put the two together, forming a unique specialty. He doesn't want to be typecast as a night photographer — he's just as skilled in the light of day — but he has spent the bulk of his time over the last several years working at night. In 1991 *Arizona Highways* published a book, *Discover Arizona's Night Sky*, exclusively featuring Zullo's photography.

Blazing with stars and planets, the night sky often takes up most of Zullo's frames, but what he does isn't astronomical photography any more than a landscape with wildflowers is botanical photography. He tries to portray the heavens and the earth as two parts of the same experience.

"I like to bring the sky down to earth. The landscape gives it a scale that's lacking in pure photos of celestial objects. The other thing is that the universe is not this unimaginably distant subject; the stars are part of human experience. And our views of them include landscape, because we are people who live on the earth."

Zullo's night photography takes several forms. Occasionally he'll use exposures of several minutes, which turns the stars into trails appearing to rotate around Polaris. Sometimes he'll do tricky composites, sandwiching a dusk photo of a landscape or cityscape with another of brilliant stars in an ink-black sky. The technique for his moonlit landscapes, however, can easily be mastered by the amateur photographer.

You need a moon that is within

three days of full, Zullo says. It should be fairly high in the sky (45 degrees or more) for maximum light output. Most in-camera meters will not read light this low, but that's not a problem since the unobstructed full moon's illumination is always the same. With ISO 400 film and a 50 mm lens, says Zullo, set exposure for f/2 at 12 seconds, "and you'll always get something." With the 50mm lens, 12 seconds is the longest exposure possible before the stars begin to turn into trails due to the earth's rotation; with a 24mm lens it is 25 seconds. Simply divide the focal length of the lens into 600 for the longest shutter speed that will preserve jewel-like stars.

If you are using print film, Zullo advises, warn the lab that these are *night* photos. Otherwise the automated equipment will print the sky as daylight, washing out the stars.

Zullo says he loves photographing all kinds of celestial happenings — meteors, eclipses, lunar halos, crepuscular rays — out of an enduring sense of wonder. "Sometimes I think I was born 400 years too late," he says. "I would have liked being an amateur scientist in the 1500s, when science had not yet explained all these things, and there was still wonder and magic about them." There would not, alas, have been any cameras. ■

(LEFT) *Two images photographed separately are sandwiched together in this dramatic portrait of cactus and a gigantic rising moon. The frame-filling moon was shot with a 35mm camera attached to a telescope that acted as a 2,000mm lens.*

(BELOW) *In full moonlight, the Chapel of the Holy Cross in Sedona appears hauntingly lonely. The 12 second exposure is captured on 400 speed film.*

BOTH BY FRANK ZULLO

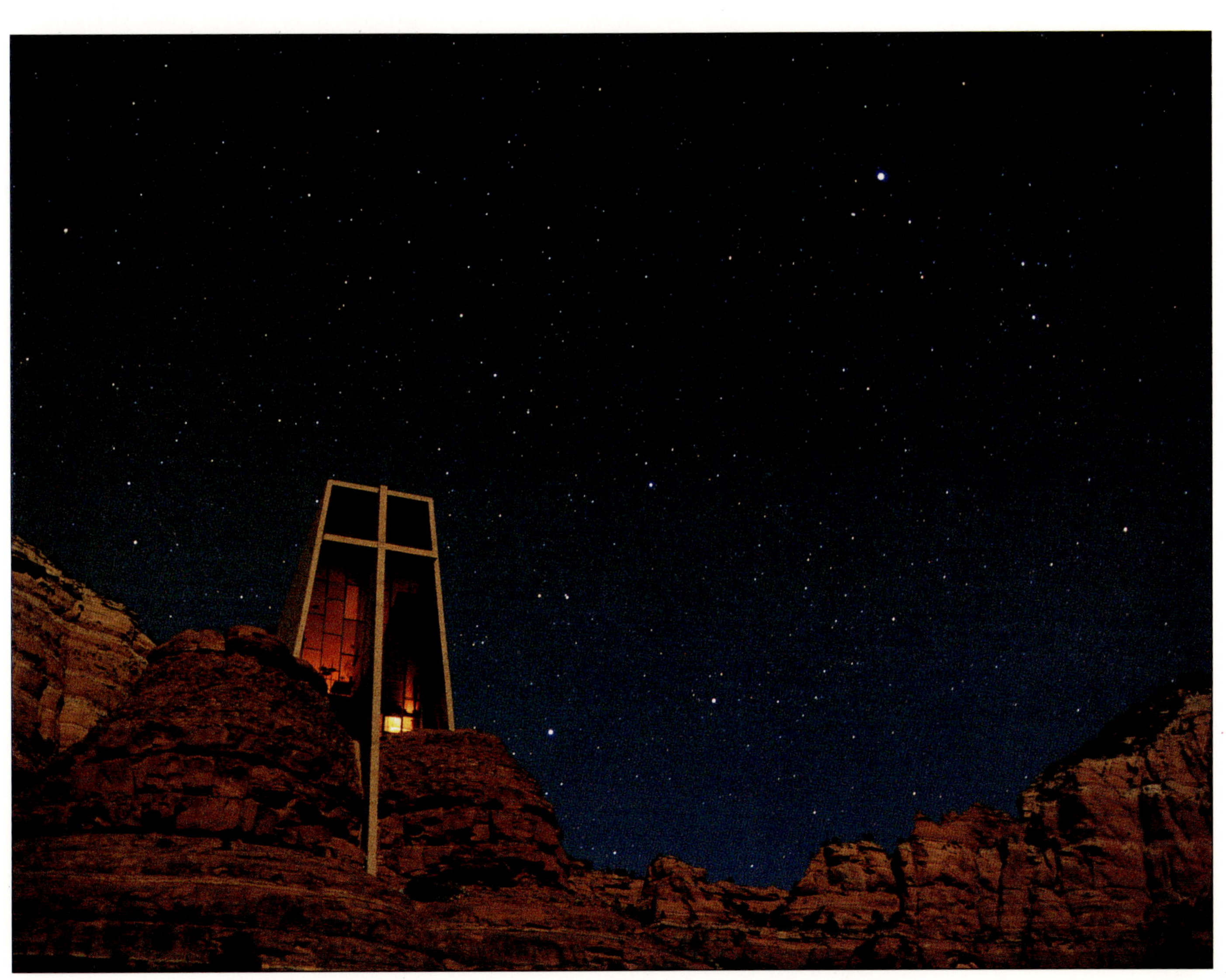

Jack Dykinga

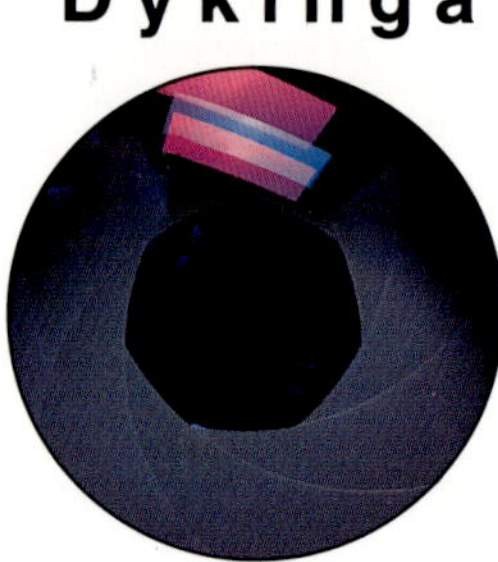

"The more strongly you get involved in issues," says Jack Dykinga, "the stronger your photography's going to be."

Dykinga is one of Arizona's most respected landscape photographers, and he is an unyielding environmentalist. His photography exudes passionate advocacy for nature, and it isn't always pretty: His illustrations for Charles Bowden's *Frog Mountain Blues*, a book about the Santa Catalina Mountains, near Tucson, ranged from pristine scenes of ferns and flowers to landscapes vacant of life and scarred with bulldozer tracks. The photographs paralleled the polemic of Bowden's text: leave the mountain alone.

This advocacy rose out of his background as a photojournalist. For the first 16 years of his career he was a newspaper photographer and then a photo editor, working at the *Chicago Sun-Times* and *Chicago Tribune*, and then *The Arizona Daily Star* in Tucson. He won a Pulitzer Prize in 1971 for a series on an institution for the retarded. A few years later he took a mountaineering course as part of a photo assignment. "That led to more and more contact with the outdoors, and the more I did that, the more I started questioning my own values. And then I picked up a book by Ed Abbey."

Dykinga left the newspaper business in 1981, not so much burned out as suspecting there was a more important world for him to photograph. "When I worked at the *Trib*, unless a picture had a person in it, we never ran it. What I believe now is that a picture can be bio-centered rather than just human-centered, and be equally important — maybe more so. You can go to the Grand Canyon and see how important human beings are."

For Dykinga, scenic photography is a two-edged sword of advocacy. The pictures of ineffable beauty, he believes, will help people understand the value of preserving it. The pictures of destruction and devastation may shock people into demanding action.

"Sometimes I really have to push myself to shoot the bad stuff," he admits. "One time I found these beheaded rattlesnakes being sold for souvenirs in a truck stop, and I had to drive back three times before I could stop and go in and ask to take a picture.

"I do photography because I believe it matters. Inadvertently, through its publication of scenic photography, I think *Arizona Highways* has created an ethic toward the land that's found in almost no other state. There's more public land, it's better protected, there's less off-road activity, less development. It's a consciousness that's almost subliminal, and I think it's because of the power of photography." ■

Intimate landscapes can be as powerful as sweeping vistas: witness this photograph of big tooth maple leaves in the Chiricahua Mountains. Notice how the photographer has followed the Rule of Thirds in his vertical composition but aggressively violated it horizontally — to fine effect — with the prominent tree trunk dividing the golden forest in half.
JACK DYKINGA

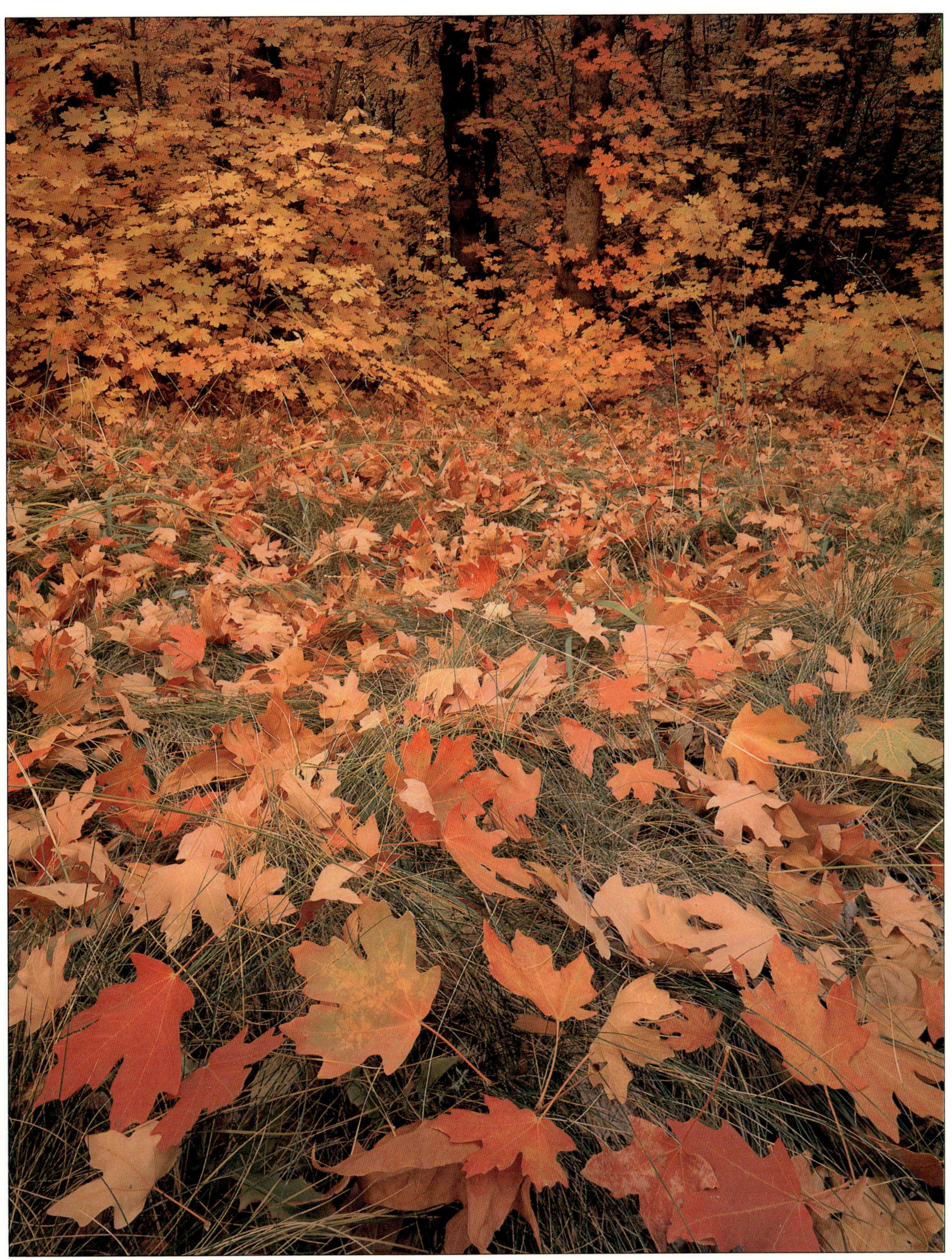

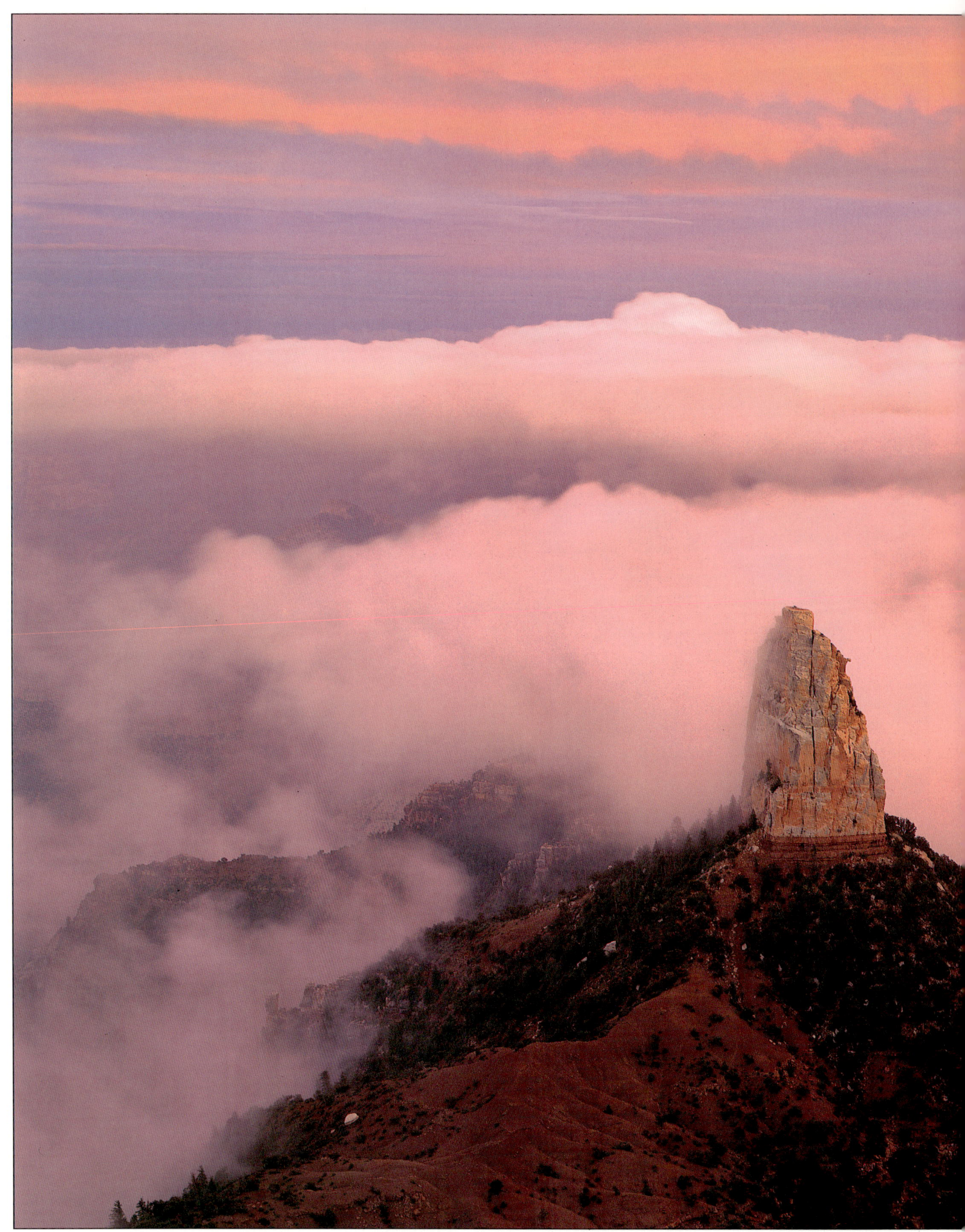

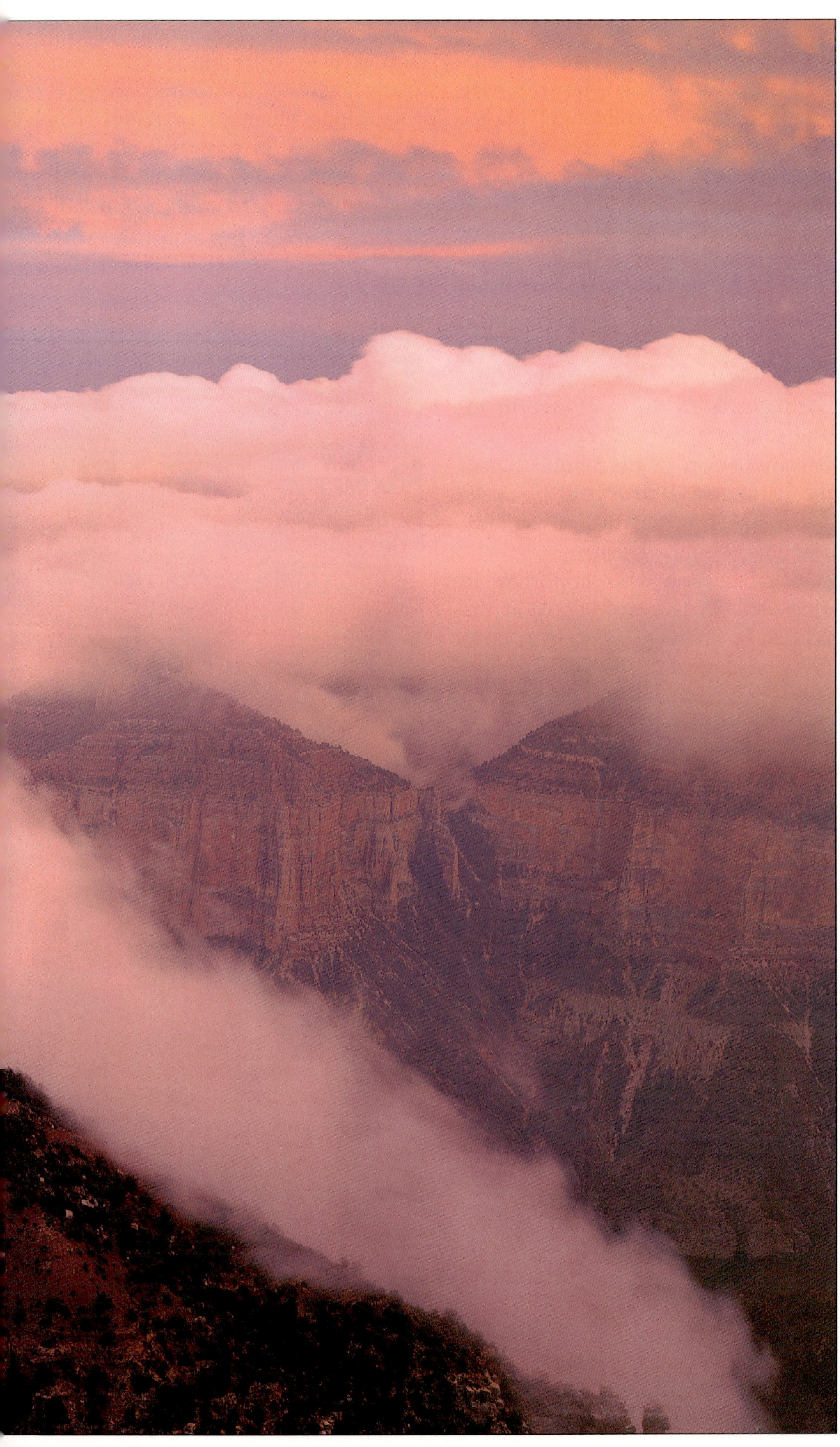

Clouds pose only for those who wait. Patience at the Grand Canyon's North Rim yielded this delicate lavender-tinted evening photo of Mt. Hayden from Point Imperial. A layer of clouds high above the Canyon reflects the lavender light of the sun that has already set.
JACK DYKINGA

Jay Dusard

Jay Dusard's original training as an architect is constantly slipping into his pictures. He doesn't do architectural photography, but his environmental portraits of people — Arizona cowboys, in particular — have an amazingly powerful sense of design about them.

For example, study the photo of Meño Orozco on this spread. The rhythm of the saddle blankets behind him is a wave motion that echoes the corrugation in the roof overhead. The stripes across Orozco's vest also become a part of the undulation of the pattern of saddles and blankets. This photo is posed, frozen, yet alive with graceful movement.

Visual tension is as important to architects as is grace. Look at the portrait of Rosamel and Ramón de la Ossa on page 72. The precise position of Ramón relative to the skull on the wall is no accident. As Dusard says, the space from Ramón's hat brim to the skull's jaw is a virtual "spark gap." The lightning-like crack in the plaster adds to the subliminal electricity. On the surface, this is a perfectly calm, peaceful photo, but its design gives it a great deal of inner tension crackling inside.

Dusard's unique philosophy: "A good photograph is an illusory environment that the viewer can have an adventure in."

Dusard is an anomaly among Arizona photographers. He grew up on a farm, worked on a ranch, earned a degree in architecture and taught himself photography, beginning in 1965 with the Ansel Adams books. Now living in Prescott, he works almost exclusively in black-and-white, both for his acclaimed cowboy portraits and his landscapes.

Why black-and-white landscapes, given today's extraordinarily vibrant and accurate color films? "I'm particularly interested in abstraction, photographing elements or patterns in the landscape in ways that eliminate some of the usual reference points, and cause you to think about the

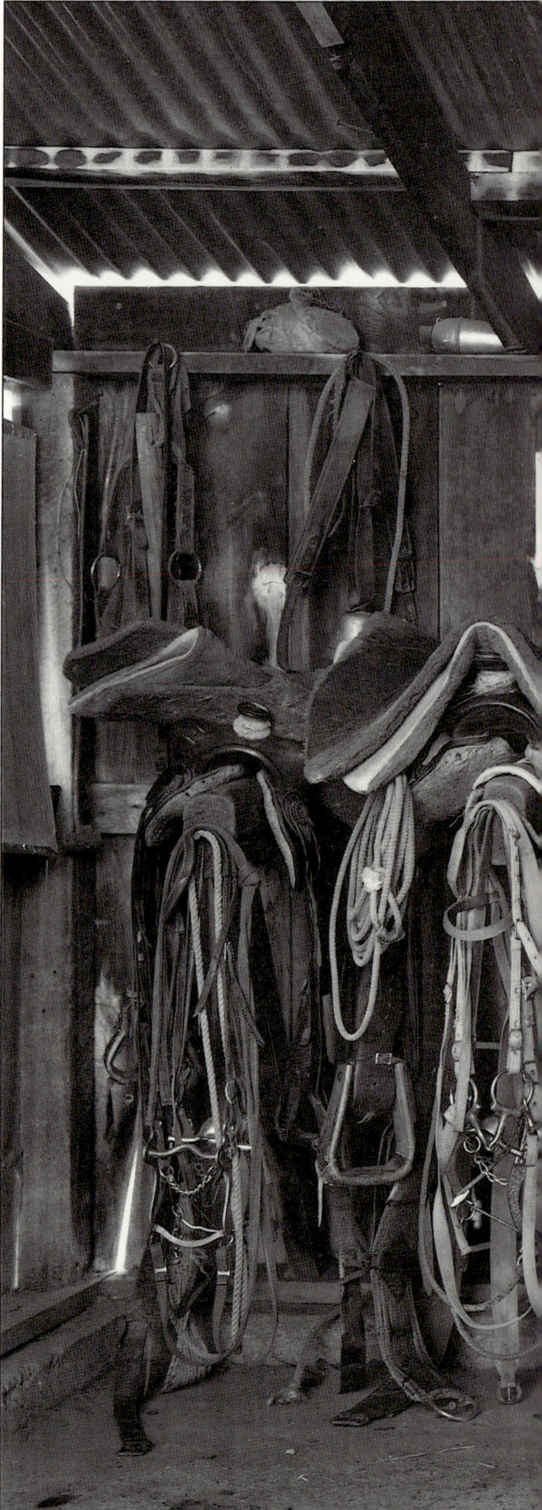

"Expressive power," the photographer's trademark, abounds in this portrait of Meño Orozco. Notice how the undulating pattern of the saddle blankets continues through the cowboy's vest. This isn't an accident.
JAY DUSARD

landscape in fresh ways. The minute you load black-and-white film into your camera, you've removed one of the major reference points. And also, in the darkroom, I've got a lot more control over the print. I may want to really depart from reality in the tonal scale. The reason is that I'm mainly interested in the expressive power of the photograph, rather than a literal rendering." ■

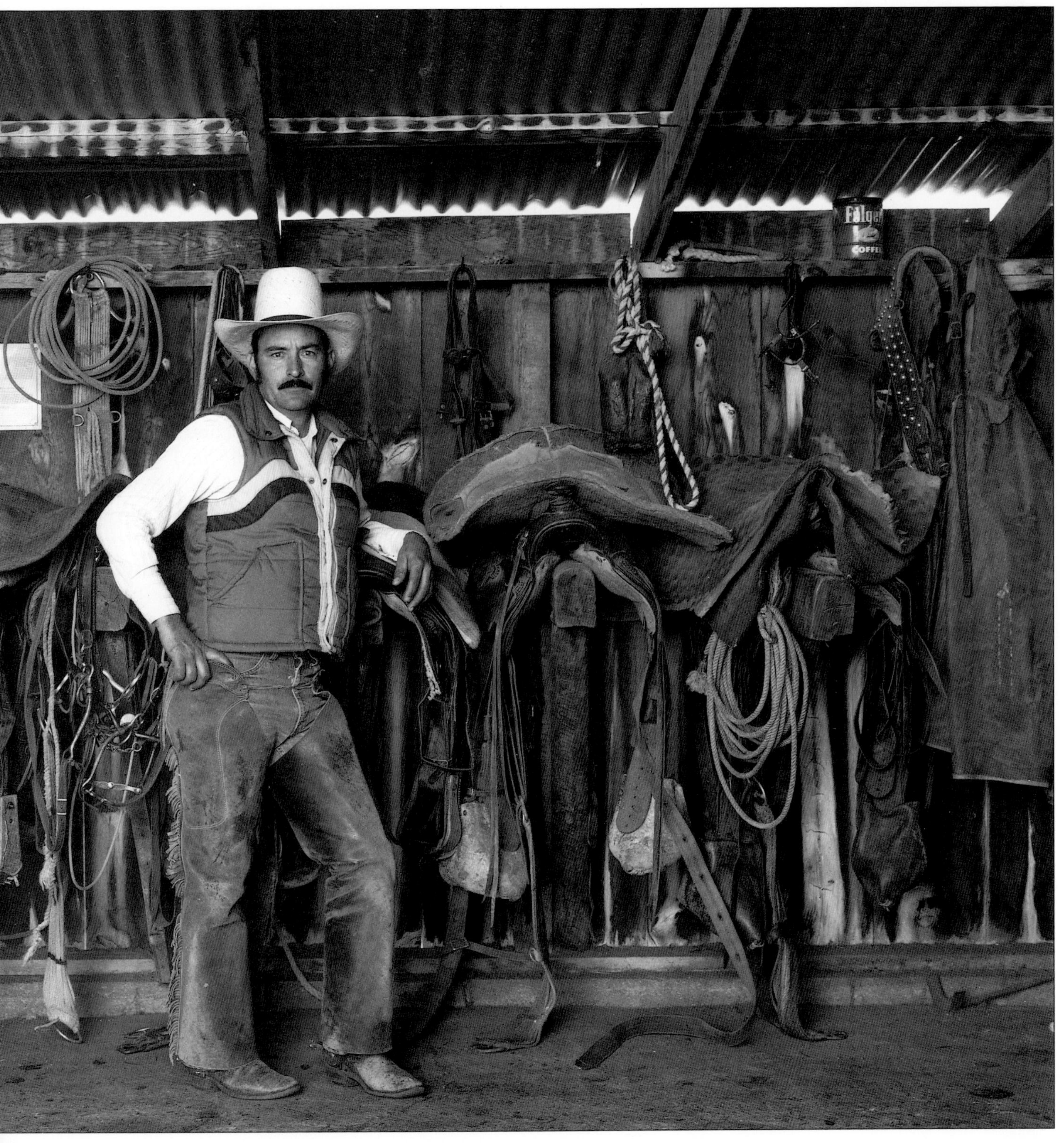

Kathleen Norris Cook

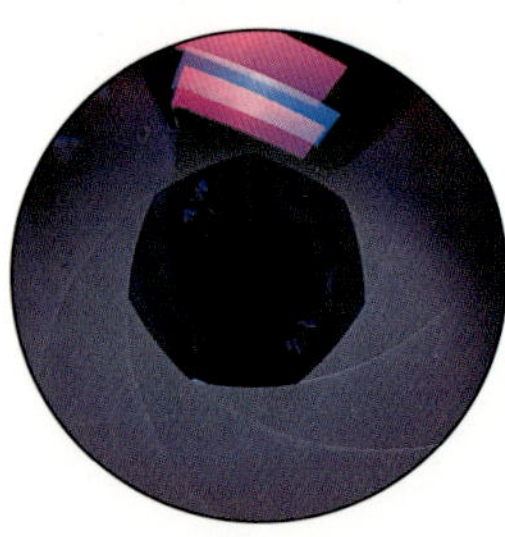

Anyone who aspires to become a professional photographer can learn from the way Kathleen Norris Cook did it. It wasn't the easy way — but there is no easy way. It was, however, quick.

In 1977, Cook moved to Arizona from Texas, and instantly found herself bewitched by the desert. She had a college degree in art, and had been a commercial artist. But she was thinking about a career change, and the transition to photography seemed a natural one.

She dug out the medium-format 6x7 Pentax she had bought a couple of years earlier — and never used — and began photographing landscapes. She had an ambitious goal firmly in mind: to hit *Arizona Highways* first. Before long, she made an appointment with the then-managing editor Wesley Holden to show him her transparencies. She remembers exactly the dozen words with which he appraised her work.

"You have a good eye, but you don't know beans about light."

Chastened, but not discouraged, Cook went back into the desert to learn about light. "I would jump in the Jeep every morning, go out to the desert, shoot until it got too hot, process it and study it 'till evening. Whenever I saw a storm coming, I'd throw a camera into the Jeep and chase it. I did this for three or four months.

In November of 1978 Cook realized her *Arizona Highways* ambition: a full-page photo of Toroweap, that awesome Grand Canyon overlook that drops 5,000 feet from the North Rim straight down to the Colorado River. Clearly she had learned something about light. White-to-gold morning sun nudged its way into the canyon from the upper right corner of the frame, while on the left, the face of Toroweap was beginning to glow ruddy amber. The photo previewed what later became Cook's signature: several different qualities, or moods, of light on exhibit in the same picture.

A few months later, Cook attacked her first major assignment for *Arizona Highways*, a full issue on Prescott, with the same determination she had shown pursuing an understanding of light. She spent six months exploring Prescott and its environs, sometimes scouting, sometimes shooting — when the light was right. The April 1980 issue used 22 of her photos, including front and back covers, but it had taken so much time, travel, and film she probably didn't clear $2.00 an hour on the job. But it served as a calling card to convince other magazines and agencies that she not only had a good eye, but also knew light — extraordinarily well — and could carry through an assignment.

Cook now has a successful career as a highly respected landscape and commercial photographer. She is an anomaly in several ways. First, she is entirely self-taught. Second, she still uses a 6x7 camera, which operates like a 35mm single-lens reflex, but records a larger 60-by-70mm image. Most landscape photographers use 4x5 (inch) field cameras. "I tried one, but it was way too slow and heavy," she says. "I like to run and gun. If I had to deal with a 4x5, I wouldn't be a photographer."

And finally, she is a woman in a branch of photography that is still mainly a men's club. Theories as to why it is that way abound: that little girls, until recently, weren't encouraged to tackle technical hobbies like photography; that the long treks and heavy equipment for landscape photography discourage some females; that a woman working alone in remote areas might be exposed to harassment or even danger. Cook believes it is because male landscape photographers traditionally have been able to draft their wives as assistants in the field, but it doesn't happen the other way around. She works alone, she says, and it's hard.

Her advice to the aspiring landscape photographer — of either gender: "Above all, patience. You have to spend a great deal of time learning how to discern the differences in light, and then you have to wait for it to happen. A lot of the good photographs I've taken were simply because I was there. It's like gambling: If you spend long enough at it, you're eventually going to come away with something." ■

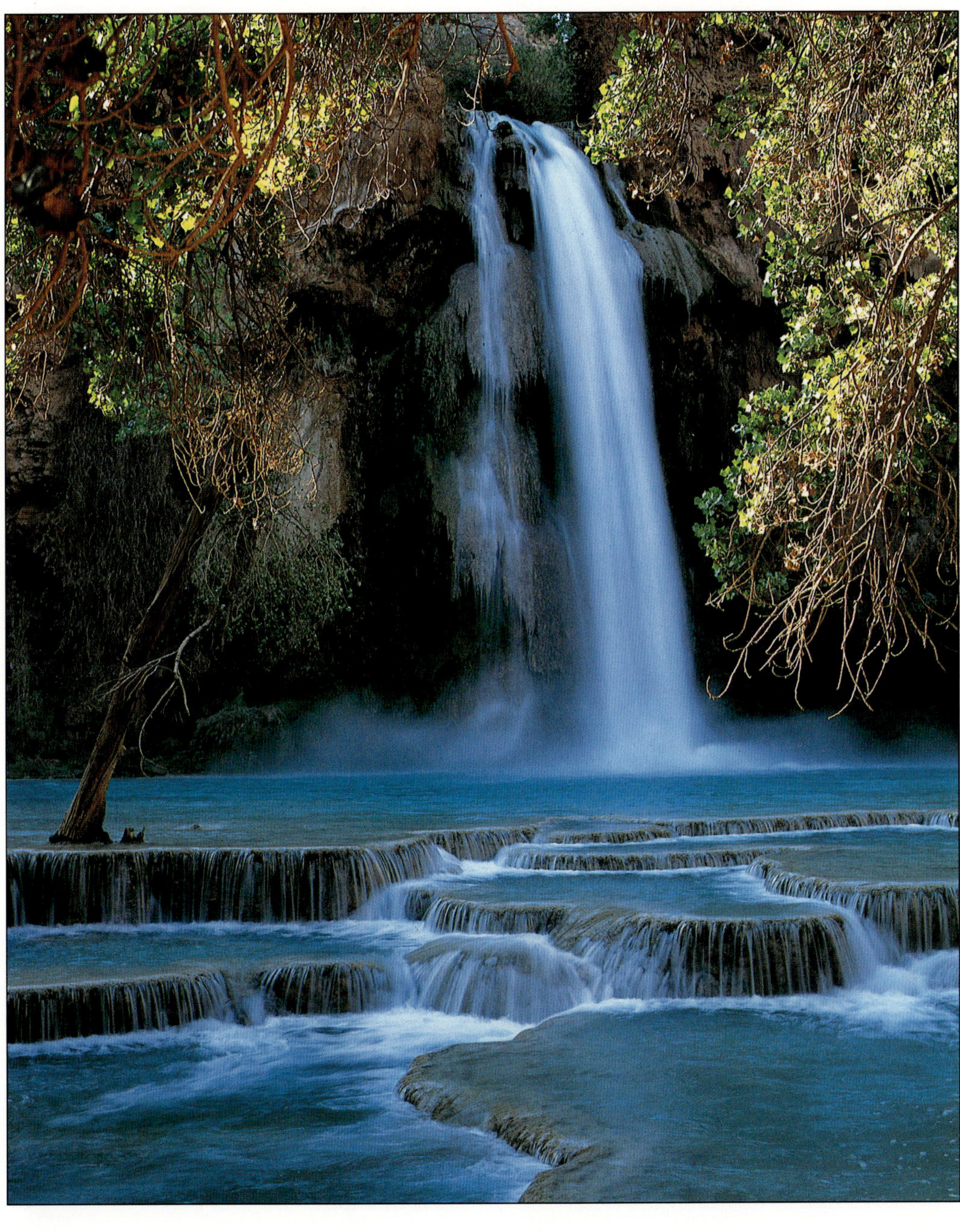

Seldom can a landscape photographer draw so many evocative elements into a single frame: power (the waterfall), rhythm (the foreground cascades), light (the backlit leaves) and dramatic color (the turquoise creek). Havasu Falls, west end of the Grand Canyon.
KATHLEEN NORRIS COOK

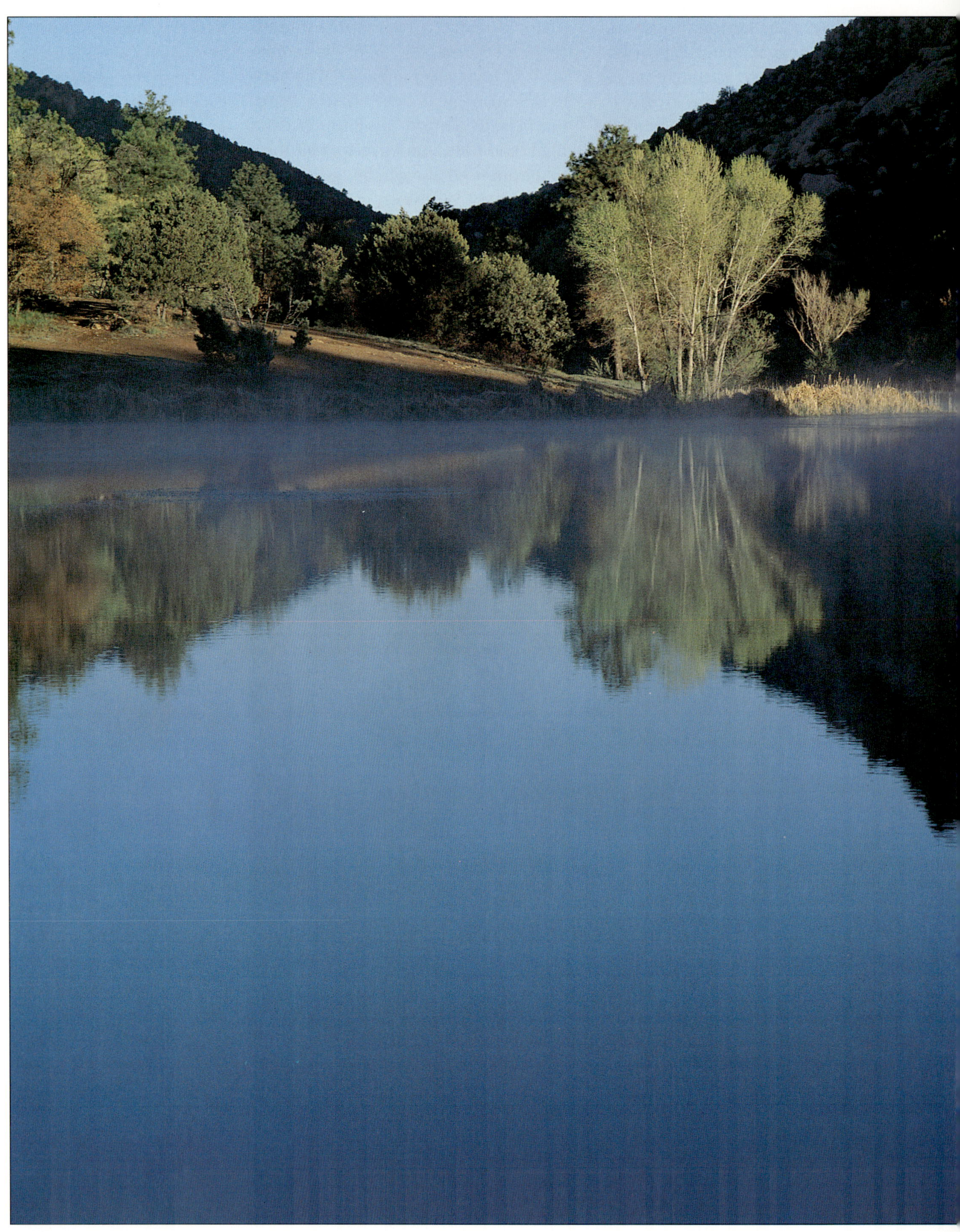

Illustrating the use of several qualities of light — direct, diffuse, and reflected — this photo of Granite Basin Lake is also compositionally, a classic example of the Rule of Thirds.
KATHLEEN NORRIS COOK

David Muench

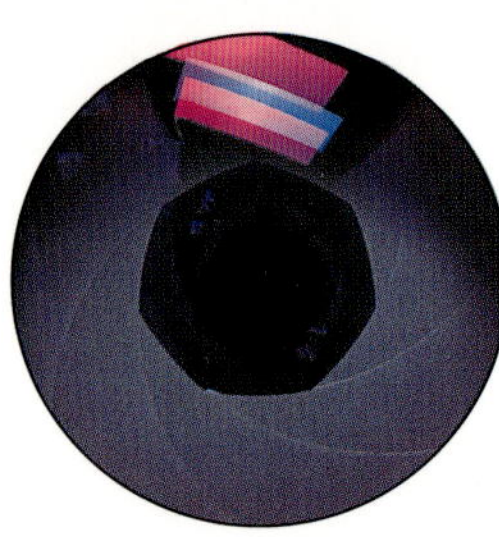

In a long conversation with David Muench, the word "urgency" appears again and again. An urgency to spend every possible minute of his allotted time on earth to understand the power and beauty of its landscapes. An urgency to commit those landscapes to film while they still exist in primal form. "I don't like to admit that," he says, "but there probably is an urgency, subconsciously, to show these things to people before they change. I hate to see things in nature slowly disappear, or a place become crowded, or a fee needed here, a fence there, a gate over there. I feel protective of the things I photograph."

Muench, who has lived all his life in Santa Barbara, California, is probably the best-known landscape photographer in America today. He has completed some 20 large-format photographic books and has had many one-man shows sprinkled across the country. In 1991 *Photographic* magazine named him one of the 10 best photographers in the world.

His scenic photography is both distinctive and profound: mountains seized by golden light; Monument Valley transformed from its usual orange-red spectrum to a monochromatic blue, not by filters but by snow and clouds; scenic vistas that sweep from brilliantly illuminated rocks and flowers at the photographer's feet to heroic mountains dozens of miles away. The latter is his signature device. Although many landscape photographers do this today, nobody is identified with the technique so closely as Muench.

He began photographing Arizona as a high school student in the 1950s, at first under the tutelage of his father, Josef. "It's essentially the first place I worked," he says. "It was like my back yard. It was a very special place. Four or five times a year I'd be in Arizona working on some project or another."

Muench's present style evolved gradually. Throughout the '60s and '70s, he admits, he was into scenic sensationalism — furious contrast, dramatic color, tense juxtaposition of elements. "I wanted to bowl you over; I wanted to just shout." In every measure, he says, his photography is now quieter. The subject has become his overriding concern, not the pyrotechnics of light and color.

Some connoisseurs may miss the razzle-dazzle. It wasn't shallow or pointless. Hanging on the wall of Muench's Santa Barbara dining room, for example, is an early (1968) black and white print of the White House ruin in Canyon de Chelly. The ruin appears minuscule, inconsequential, at the foot of the immense cliff looming over it. Somehow, a lonely sunbeam has slashed into the canyon to light up a tiny section of the ruin. The picture tells a story: Civilization at this stage is vulnerable and insignificant in the scheme of nature, yet the architecture, lit so dramatically and selectively, suggests the prescient fire of human ambition.

Muench describes his photographic style today as "softer." There tends to be less contrast, sometimes less drama, and more careful detailing of the subject. It draws more attention to the subject and less to the photographer. More and more, Muench finds himself making photographs in ambient light — pre-dawn, post-sunset, overcast or fog — rather than in direct sunlight. These landscapes seem to exist in a mood of profound peace, harmony, and silence.

"Silence" is also the word that

describes the Muench photography in *Eternal Desert*, published in 1990 by *Arizona Highways*. Leaf through it, and you feel as though you are utterly alone in viewing the desert — there is no sound, no interruption, no human intervention. Muench says this is exactly the feeling he experienced. "I get the most profound sense when I'm working in the desert. I don't want to talk to anybody. I feel intruded upon if there are people around. It really is a mysterious, magical place. How to capture this in a photo is the challenge, and I really can't put it into words."

But this is Muench's particular gift, the ability to somehow make photographs that record not only the objective features of the landscape, but also the way he feels about them. In all the art of photography, there is no more powerful achievement, and no more compelling goal to which every photographer, professional or amateur, can aspire. ■

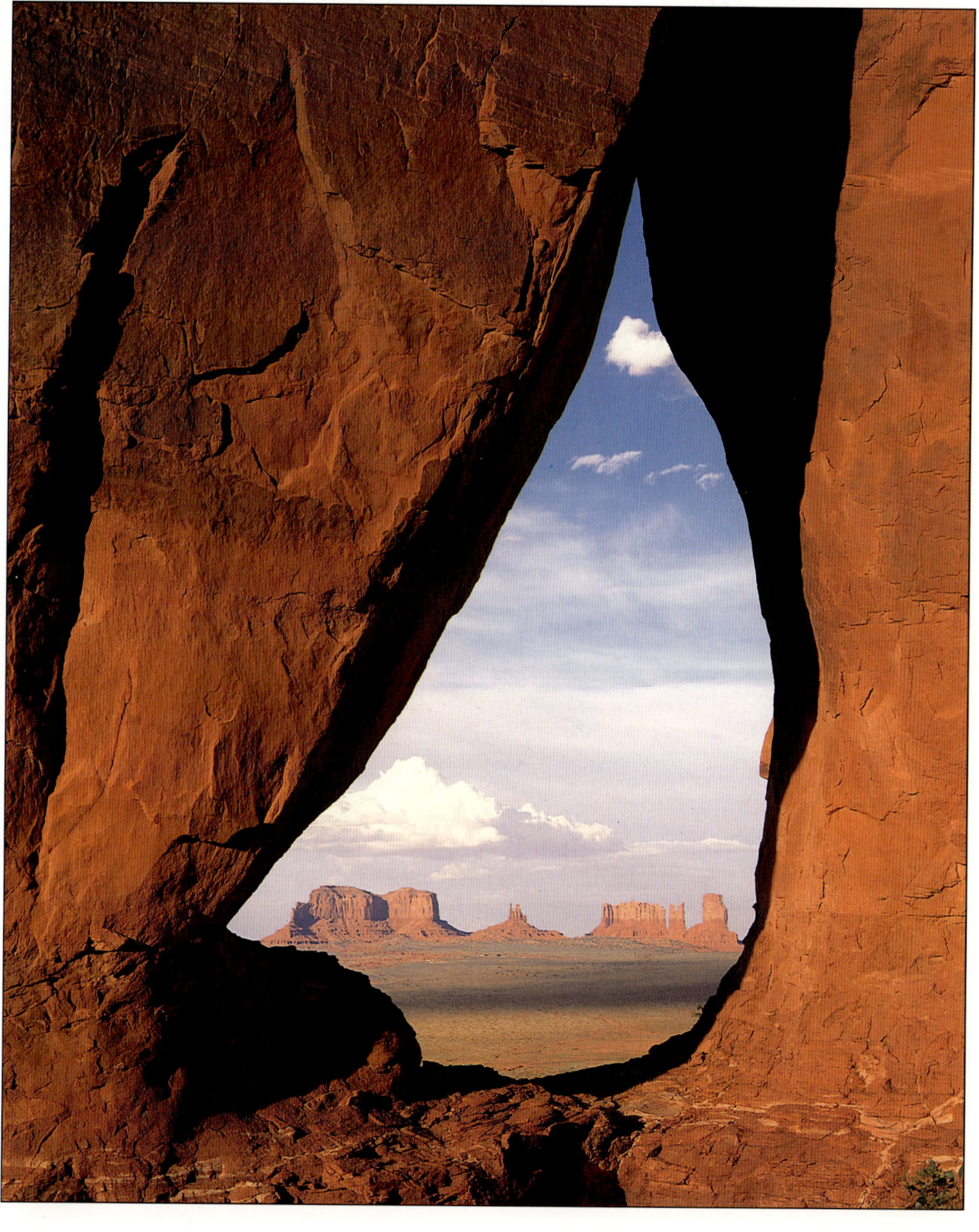

A distant Monument Valley is framed in a natural sandstone window. Both the "frame" and the monuments have to be in sharp focus for a photo such as this to work.
DAVID MUENCH

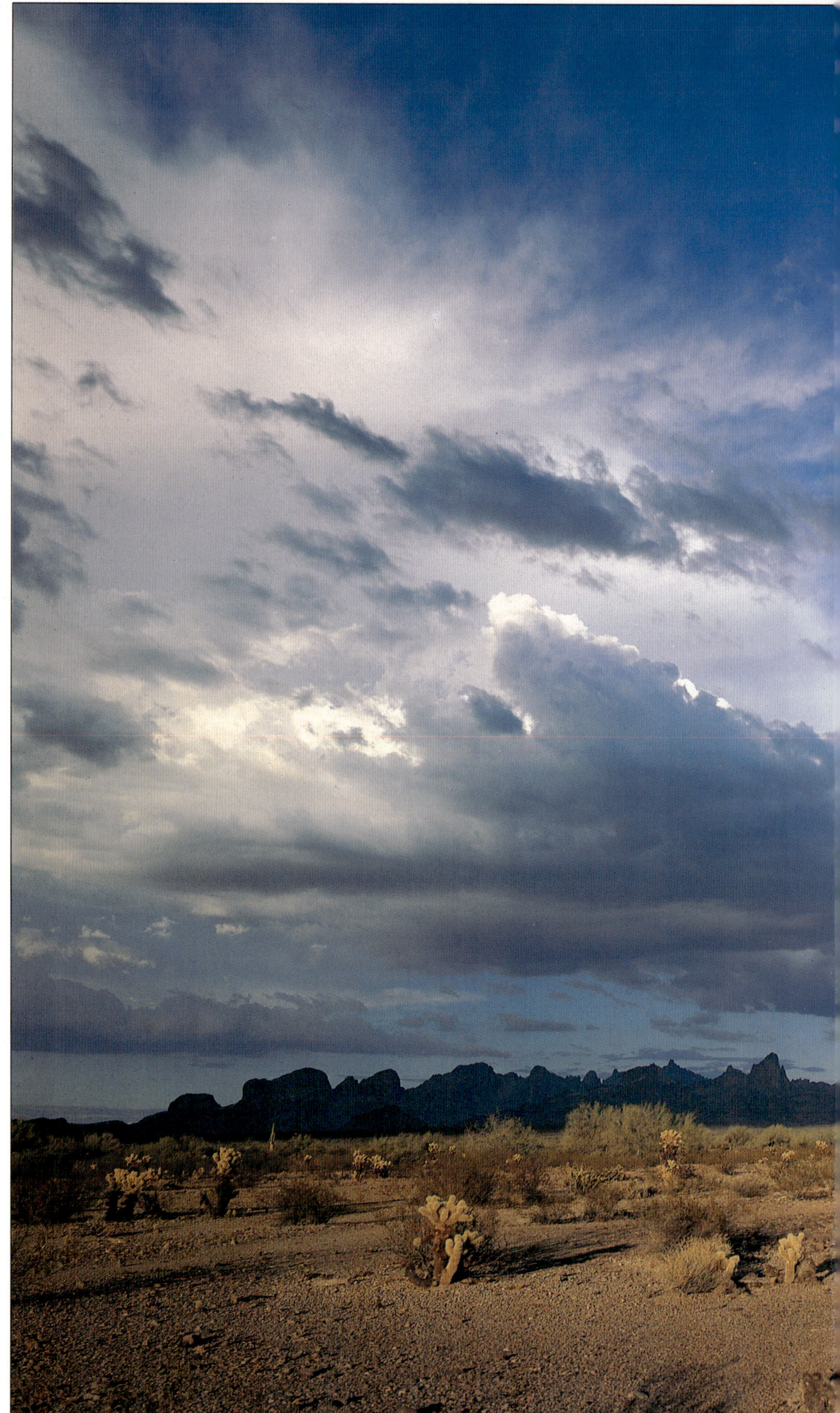

In landscape photography, light is at least four-fifths of the struggle — as this shot of the Kofa Mountains of southwestern Arizona proves. The converging lines created by a wide-angle lens lead the eye to the horizon of this skyscape.
DAVID MUENCH

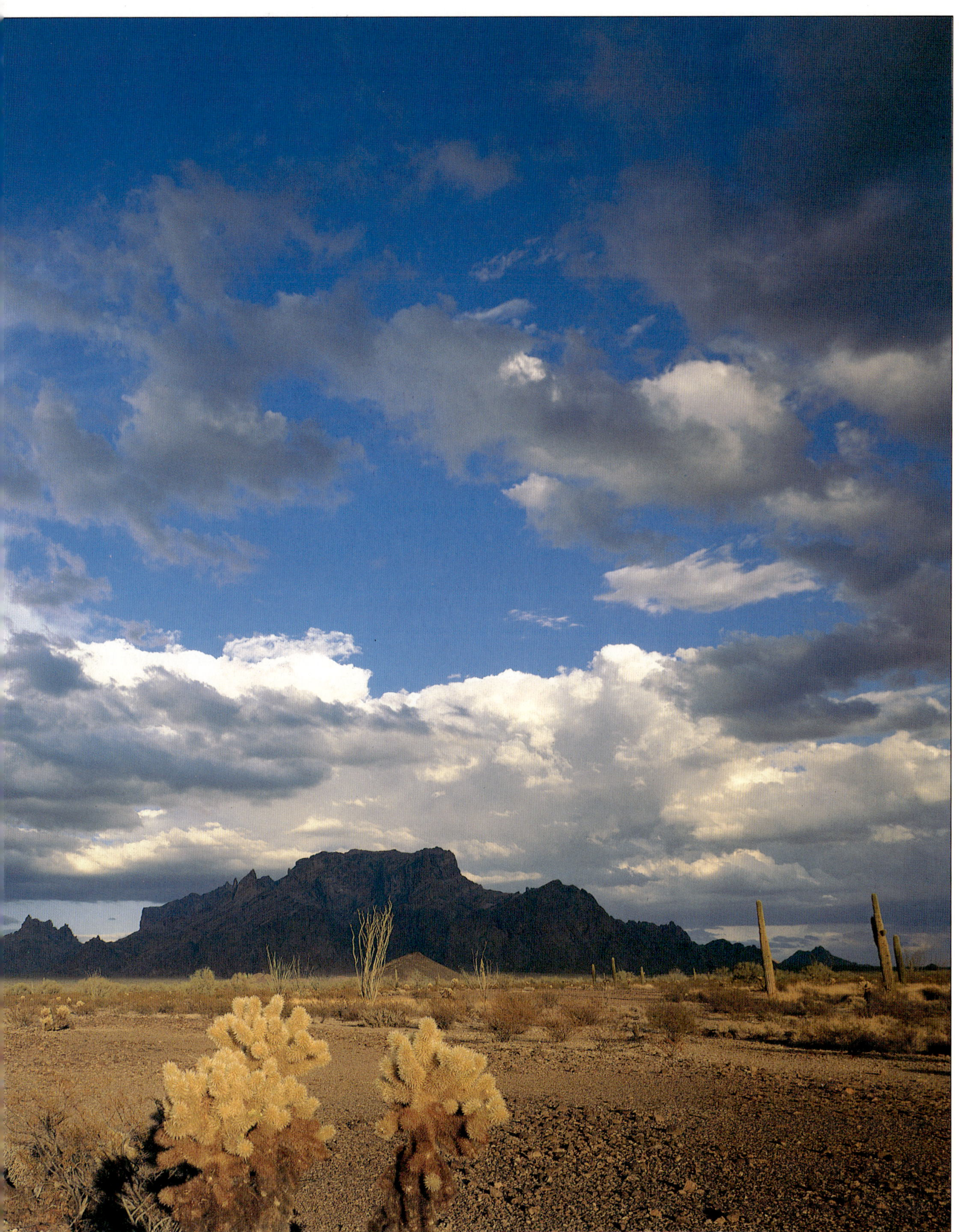

Glossary

Aperture The opening in the lens that regulates the amount of light reaching the film. Manually or automatically variable on most cameras (see f/stop).

Automatic exposure An on-board electronic program in a camera that reads the light coming through the lens and sets the aperture, shutter speed, or both.

Backlit A scene in which the light source, usually the sun, is behind the subject.

Bracketing Shooting a picture at the metered exposure, then one-half or a full f/stop over and under for insurance. Recommended with slide film in tricky lighting situations, usually unnecessary with print film.

Cable release A mechanical or electrical cable to release the shutter while the camera is on a tripod. Prevents camera movement that may occur and affect sharpness of the image when doing time exposures or when using slow shutter speeds.

Contrast The difference between bright and dark areas in a subject.

Dedicated flash A strobe made for a specific model of camera. Light output can be set by the camera's automatic exposure program.

Depth of field The zone of sharp focus extending in front of and behind a subject. Influenced by the lens' aperture: the smaller the aperture, the greater the depth of field.

Exposure The amount of light that strikes the film, controlled by aperture and shutter speed.

Fill flash Using strobe light outdoors, usually to highlight a backlit or shadowed subject.

Film speed Numerical rating that indicates a film's sensitivity to light, usually expressed as an ISO (International Standardization Organization) number: ISO 50, 64, etc. A low ISO number indicates less sensitivity to light and finer grain structure.

Filter A glass, plastic or gelatin disk or sheet mounted in front of a camera lens that alters the composition of the light coming through it.

Fixed focal length lens A lens in which the distance from the optical center of the lens to the film is always the same when the lens is focused to infinity. Expressed in millimeters, as in 50mm, 180mm, etc. The other type of lens is a zoom (see zoom lens).

Format The size and shape of the image recorded on a camera's film, expressed in millimeters, centimeters or inches. The most common formats, from smallest to largest, are 35mm, 2 1/4 inches, 6x7cm, 4x5 inches and 8x10 inches.

f/stop The size of the aperture, adjusted on most cameras by a numbered ring on the lens barrel. The greater the number, the smaller the aperture. A setting of f/8 admits half the light of f/5.6, f/11 half the light of f/8, etc.

Grain Specks of silver halide that become visible on a photographic print as grainy, textured surfaces. In general, the slower the film speed, the less visible grain.

Infinity In photography, a focus on the most distant subject possible — in practice, generally, the horizon.

Iris flare Usually undesirable polygons of reflected light caused by sunlight entering the lens.

Lens hood A plastic or rubber cylinder that shades the front of the lens, helping avoid iris flare (see iris flare).

Light meter A photoelectric meter that reads the light falling on a subject and gives the appropriate f/stop for correct exposure. Most modern 35mm cameras have a built-in meter that measures light through the lens, although professionals sometimes use more sophisticated hand-held meters.

Macro lens A lens that can focus on subjects very close to it, usually as little as two to three inches. Macro lenses also can be used for normal photography, but are more expensive than normal lenses.

Monopod A single-legged support used to help steady a hand-held camera.

Motor drive Electrically powered film advance.

Normal lens A lens with a focal length of 50 or 55mm on a 35mm camera, creating an image similar in size and scale to what the naked eye sees.

Panning Following a moving subject with the camera, blurring the stationary background to suggest speed.

Perspective control lens A lens whose elements can tilt or shift with respect to the film plane. Used mainly in photographing architecture to avoid converging parallels.

Point-and-shoot A completely automated camera in which aperture, shutter speed, and flash output are all selected by an on-board electronic program.

Polarizing filter A filter that in certain conditions will deepen the sky's color and eliminate unwanted reflections from glossy surfaces and glass.

Rule of Thirds A principle of artistic composition in which the picture is divided into thirds, both horizontally and vertically, and the main subject is placed at one of the intersections.

Sandwiching Combining two or more negatives or slides to create a composite image.

Shutter The camera mechanism that admits light onto the film. Controlled electronically on most modern 35mm cameras.

Shutter speed The duration of time that the shutter remains open to expose the film, expressed as a fraction of a second (e.g., 1/500) or in seconds.

Split Screen neutral density filter Half transparent and half color-neutral gray, this filter helps equalize the light entering the lens from scenes with a bright sky and shadowy ground.

Telephoto lens A lens with a long focal length (85mm or more on a 35mm camera) which makes distant subjects appear closer. Also called "long lens."

Time exposure An exposure longer than 1 second in which the shutter is kept open manually and timed by the photographer.

Transparency A positive color image on transparent film; e.g., a 35mm slide.

Tripod A collapsible three-legged camera support.

Ultraviolet (UV) filter Appears transparent to the human eye, but will absorb invisible ultraviolet light that records on film. Useful in reducing the effects of haze. May be left permanently on lens unless hazy shots are desired.

Wide-angle lens A lens with a short focal length (35mm or less on a 35mm camera) that takes in a wide field of view and makes subjects appear more distant.

Yellow/orange/red filters For use with black-and-white film, these lighten the appearance of objects their own color and darken those of complementary colors. Generally used to darken blue sky against clouds.

Zoom lens A lens with a continuously variable range of focal lengths, commonly 28-70mm or 70-210mm.

81A and 81B filters Also known as "warming" filters, these reduce the intrinsic blueness of subjects in shadow or under overcast skies. Effect of 81B is more extreme.

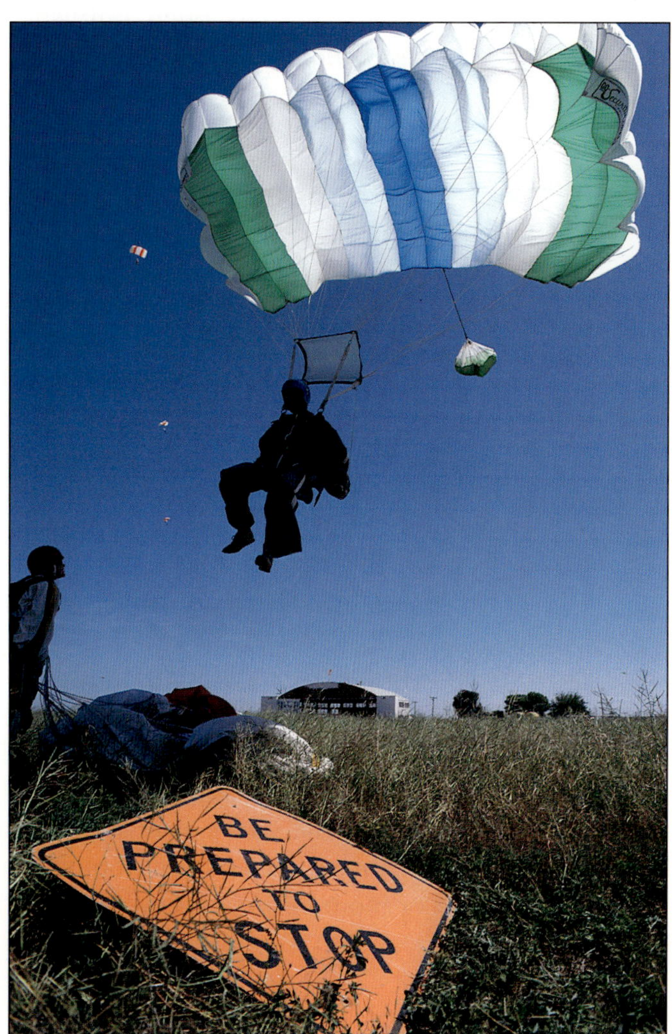

FRED GRIFFIN

Acknowledgements

Many photographers of Arizona have generously contributed their ideas and expertise to this book. They are: Robert Campbell, Michael Collier, Kathleen Norris Cook, Jay Dusard, Jack Dykinga, Peter Ensenberger, Hal Martin Fogel, Fred Griffin, Jerry Jacka, Jeff Kida, Gary Ladd, William Lesch, Inge Martin, Edward McCain, David Muench, Monty Roessel, Jerry Sieve, James Tallon, P.K. Weis, and Frank Zullo. Merry Jo Milner of Tucson's Jones Photo and Ernst Weegen of Phoenix Camera Repair provided expert technical advice.

My special gratitude goes to P.K. Weis, photo editor of the *Tucson Citizen*, who has patiently critiqued my slides and contact sheets for the last 20 years, gradually training a writer to become a photographer as well.

Lawrence W. Cheek

About the Author

Lawrence W. Cheek has lived and worked in Arizona for 20 years as a newspaper reporter, magazine editor, and freelance writer. His photography has been published in *Arizona Highways*, *Historic Preservation*, *Architecture*, and other national magazines.

Additional Books From *Arizona Highways*

Other books about Arizona and the Southwest are available through *Arizona Highways*. For a free catalog, call toll-free nationwide 1-800-543-5432 (in the Phoenix area, 258-1000), or write to *Arizona Highways* at 2039 West Lewis Avenue, Phoenix, AZ 85009-2893.

Arizona Highways Photo Tours

Explore and photograph the dramatic natural beauty of Arizona with photo tours hosted by the Friends of *Arizona Highways* auxiliary. These workshops for aspiring photographers travel to some of the state's most spectacular locations. *Arizona Highways* contributing photographers are the faculty. For more information, write the Friends of *Arizona Highways* Travel Desk, P.O. Box 6106, Phoenix, AZ 85005-6106; or telephone 602-271-5904.